Threescore and Ten

OTHER BOOKS OF BARRY BLACKSTONE

Though None Go With Me
Rendezvous in Paris
Though One Go With Me
Scotland Journey
The Region Beyond
Enlarge My Coast
From Dan to Beersheba and Beyond
The Uttermost Part
Homestead Homilies
Rover: A Boy's Best Friend
North to Alaska and Back
Another Day in Nazareth
Sermonettes from the Seashore
Earth's Farthest Bounds
Angling Admonitions
Beyond the Bend
Expendable
Meows from the Manse
At a Moment's Notice
Reaching the Unreached
Satan's Super Soldiers

Threescore and Ten

by
BARRY BLACKSTONE

RESOURCE *Publications* · Eugene, Oregon

THREESCORE AND TEN

Copyright © 2024 Barry Blackstone. All rights reserved. Except for brief quotations in critical publications or reviews, no part of this book may be reproduced in any manner without prior written permission from the publisher. Write: Permissions, Wipf and Stock Publishers, 199 W. 8th Ave., Suite 3, Eugene, OR 97401.

Resource Publications
An Imprint of Wipf and Stock Publishers
199 W. 8th Ave., Suite 3
Eugene, OR 97401

www.wipfandstock.com

PAPERBACK ISBN: 979-8-3852-2929-1
HARDCOVER ISBN: 979-8-3852-2930-7
EBOOK ISBN: 979-8-3852-2931-4

I dedicate this book to all those who during my life have helped, encouraged, and been an example of the believer in Jesus Christ to me. I wouldn't have gotten this far if not for the grace and mercy of the Good Lord and your wonderful support.

Table of Contents

Acknowledgement | xi
Prelude: Threescore and Ten | xiii

1. Somewhere in the Middle of Nowhere | 1
2. Proverbs for Seventy Years of Living | 5
3. An Unchanging Message for All These Years | 9
4. Just a Simple Country Pastor | 13
5. Starts and Stops and Stays | 17
6. Greatness is Not Geographical | 24
7. "Purpose-Driven" or Divine-Purpose Living | 28
8. The Emerging Church of the 21st Century | 32
9. Nicolaitans: Alive and Well Today | 36
10. The Ministry to the Few | 40
11. Costly Grace | 47
12. More Proverbs for Seventy Years of Living | 51
13. A Stress-Free Church in a Stressful Time | 56
14. Just Another Member? | 60
15. What I Have Learned About Money in Seventy Years | 64
16. The Dandelion Doctrine | 71
17. A Religion or The Religion | 75
18. The Cow Path I Never Followed | 79
19. Climbing the Wrong Wall | 83
20. Is the Church a Business? | 87
21. Shifting and Drifting | 93
22. My Personal Proverbs Continue | 97
23. Trendism and Trendists | 101
24. What Time is it? | 105
25. Elitist and Entitlements in the Faith | 109

26. Some Disciples Just Stay Home | 115
27. Eagles Do Not Fly in Flocks | 119
28. God's Highway Program | 123
29. In Times Like These | 127
30. Whatever Happened to Christianity in My Lifetime? | 131
31. A Causality of the Coronavirus Who Never had Covid-19 | 138
32. Adding to My Personal Proverbs | 142
33. Ministry | 146
34. Not an Ideal but a Divine Reality | 150
35. What Do You Do When God Takes Away Your Health? | 154
36. Of and To and Through Jesus Christ | 161
37. The Emmanuel Community | 165
38. Ignoring the Past | 169
39. Embarrassed By Its Implications | 173
40. Transparency in Christianity | 177
41. What a Preacher Should Be | 184
42. A Lifetime of Proverbs | 188
43. The Stub of the Sword | 192
44. The Master's Minority versus the Moral Majority | 196
45. The Scourge of Legalism | 200
46. One of Those Days | 206
47. Instead of India | 210
48. Disturbers and Disrupters | 214
49. Who is Qualified | 218
50. Separation of Church and State? | 222
51. Bowing out Gloriously | 229
52. More Personal Proverbs | 233
53. Get Your Head Up | 237
54. Walking the Waves | 241
55. Is America a Christian Nation? | 245
56. Give Me Liberty or Give Me Death | 251
57. The Internet Generation | 255
58. A Home Run to Win the Game | 259
59. How Will the Lord Find You? | 263
60. Perilous Times Are Here | 267
61. The Dangers of …isms | 273
62. The Last of the Proverbs | 277
63. It is Time | 281
64. If My People… | 285

65. Unity in Diversity | 289
66. A Falling Away First, A Departing from the Faith | 295
67. The Neon Gods | 299
68. Consumerism and Christianity | 303
69. When Did Academics Replace Faith? | 307
70. The Final Major Crossroad | 311

Postlude-Fourscore | 318

Acknowledgement

I WOULD NOT HAVE gotten this book project finished if not for the editing and compiling by my friend and sister-in-Christ, Rosemary Campbell. I would like to thank her for the numerous hours and many days she spent reading and correcting the errors in the original script. Thanks again Rosemary for all your work; may you share in the eternal rewards of this book.

PRELUDE

Threescore and Ten

PSALM 90:9–10
"*...we spend our years as a tale that is told.
The days of our years are* threescore years and ten."

Wow! I MADE IT. Who believes they will make this magical and meaningful time slot in their lives? Today I begin my seventieth year (because today 69 years of my life will have past, and I have 365 days to get to threescore and ten officially). I will never forget the surprising start of this crossroad year for me because I am not in India on my sixth short-term missionary trip to the subcontinent where I had planned to start this book and begin a compilation of my experiences turned to beliefs, but instead I am in the church office of the Emmanuel Baptist Church of Ellsworth, Maine. It is a fine, early spring day. I have been the pastor of this my "church of a lifetime" for nearly 29 years. (I will start my thirtieth year here in July, Lord willing.) The Good Lord has shown me that my best laid plans can be changed according to His will and my circumstances, and, when I plan to be in India to start my seventieth year, He can just as easily keep me on the coast of Maine. If I have learned anything in 70 years it is to trust the will of my Father!

Today is graduation day (March 6, 2020) at Kerala Baptist Bible College and Seminary in India where I was asked in the spring of 2019 to be the graduation speaker to the eighteen graduates of the class of 2020. This was planned to be the fourth time in the six times I would have been privileged to visit that fabled land to be there for graduation, and it would have also been the third time I would have been in India on my birthday. But because of my wife Coleen's liver disease (NASH) complication (my wife's right lung was filling up with fluid), I had to delay and eventually cancel this long-awaited spiritual experience on Valentine's Day, 2020. On the very day I was supposed to fly out from Bangor, Maine, for Philadelphia, Pennsylvania, then on to Doha, Qatar, and then Cochin, India, I was at the Northern Lights medical enter (Maine Coast Memorial Hospital) in Ellsworth waiting to see if the lung that the fluid was drained from on Tuesday could be re-inflated on Thursday after the top of it had collapsed. It did, but within a few days the lung started to refill so the message from the Lord was clear. There would be no trip to India this year. Also, this entire event took place with the shadow of the Coronavirus pandemic hanging over the world, so in the end my Heavenly Father said, "Stay." And if I have learned anything in 70 years it is to trust the Lord's timing!

I should have already been in Edayappara a month before leading up to the beginning of my seventieth year, teaching the book of II Thessalonians to seven wonderful students at the college; speaking at my first ever mission's conference; sharing at my fourth Bible conference; exhorting at an evangelistic crusade in Edayappara; instructing at the chapel services on campus, and preaching at a number of churches in the area on the four weekends I was supposed to be there; including a weekend side trip with a pastor friend (Johnson Matthews) of mine who was reaching an unreached people group in the hills of Eastern Kerala. For a pastor (I am in my 47th year) like me, this would have been the best of the best, the greatest of spiritual opportunities, the best of times doing a solid month of daily meetings (sometimes two or three meetings a day) expounding and exhorting and explaining the Word of God to an eager audience. In my lifetime I have not found a people more eager to listen to the Word of God than the people of India.

Anyone having reached their seventieth year and over a half century of preaching would naturally have reached a few conclusions about the life, the lifestyle, and the living of the Christian faith. Of my 69 years I have been in the Faith 62 of them. I believed early in the teachings and instructions of the Teacher from Galilee. Over the years I have come to believe in not only the theology of Jesus, but the philosophy of the Christ. The closed door to India hasn't changed my desire to share my observations and interpretations of the Bible over these seventy years, so as Vance Havner wrote in the introduction to his book entitled *Threescore and Ten*, "Anyone who is nearing threescore and ten and has well over half a century of preaching behind him is entitled to make a few observations. At any rate, I am going to make a few whether entitled or not!"

What you have before you is not an autobiography because I will share little about me, but a collection of articles on my Christian philosophy on a variety of topics that have become important to me over these seven decades. My life spans from the early 1950s (I was born the day the United Nation's forces liberated Seoul, Korea) to the third decade of the 21st century, and during that time I have been a student of my period of history, in particular Church History, and what has been happening to the institution I have dedicated my life to. You might not agree with my impressions and reflections on the matters I will address, but I hope you will at least consider them in the light of Scripture and will find them trustworthy and truth-worthy. I have watched in my lifetime the amazing progress of mankind (I was fascinated through the 1960s of man's ultimate conquest of walking on the moon) and the equally impressive advancement in technology (the computer age has taken me by storm and I still can't quite understand it). I have watched a world go from the horse (the last horse on the Blackstone Homestead left just a few years before I was born) to the computer-controlled car. I have experienced a time without the television to a time where the internet and the cellphone and FaceTime have brought everybody closer from my corner of Maine to far off India. (As I put this book to bed I am now sharing a weekly lesson with a group of Bible students in central India from FaceBook Chat, and it was just a simple cellphone call to my friend Shibu Simon in Kerala over 9000 miles away to tell him I couldn't come for graduation.) I came from a day by day labor intense living to a life that is easier by comparison with all the modern advancements that have made life on this planet the easiest it has ever been for most.

This is the bright side of my threescore and ten years, but as with life there is a dark side. I have experienced the death of a 39-year-old son to lung and liver cancer. I have watched my youthful bride lose her health at 67 (Coleen would leave for heaven on April 17, 2021, just five weeks into my 70th year). I have experienced the death of numerous family members that were dear and near to me, not counting the countless church members I have had to bury. I have watched as the morals of our land have changed from virtuosos to alley cat in nature. I have watched the standards of decency and civility in politics decline to childish bickering and backbiting. Granted, our land has become the sole superpower in the world (I am afraid China will soon be our equal) with the greatest economy in the world, but we are far poorer than we ever were. And as my country has slipped into apostasy, apathy, and anarchy so the Church has defiled itself with wickedness, worldliness, and wantonness.

    I was raised in a Norman Rockwell America. I was brought up in a rural country church and on a family farm. I was taught the "faith of my fathers" early, and, though most of the Church has moved on, I am stuck in the "old-fashion way." I have never become a citizen of this world (why saving the planet means nothing to me), but am just a pilgrim passing through to a better world (Hebrews 11:14–16). It is my prayer that these remembrances and reminiscences of my philosophical Faith that has sustained me to this seventieth year will help another pilgrim making his or her way through these final days, to the end of the age. I have lived in Vance Havner's motto: **"What matters, of course, is not how long we have been on the road, but how far we have traveled."** Amen and Amen.

Barry Blackstone
March 6, 2020

1.

SOMEWHERE IN THE MIDDLE OF NOWHERE

I HAD STRUGGLED INTO my seventieth year with my own personal understanding and definition of my place (where I lived and worked) in God's huge world and how to explain it to others and myself. That is, until I found the title printed above in a sectional division in a book about one of the greatest meetings of world history, when the newspaperman Henry Morton Stanley met the world-famous explorer David Livingstone in the village of Ujiji on the shore of Lake Tanganyika in Africa on November 10, 1871, and those, now famous words, were uttered from Stanley's lips, "Mr. Livingstone, I presume!"

"Somewhere in the Middle of Nowhere" is a perfect description of where I have lived all my life, even though I thought for most of my life that I was actually from somewhere, always lived and ministered somewhere, only to discover I have spent the bulk of my life in the middle of nowhere. I was born in the northern Maine city of Caribou, just a few miles from the Canadian Border, in the most northeast corner of these United States and raised through most of my boyhood in a small, isolated village thirteen miles west of Caribou in a town they call Perham (an unknown place to most). It was only as I began to travel around this big planet that I realized that "the uttermost part" places I have journeyed to, the people there thought the place I had come from was an uttermost part place. It shocked me the first time I mentioned my State of Maine to somebody in India that they had never heard of it. The closest I could come to getting them to understand where I had come from was to mention the city of Boston.

In the summer of 1972 I travelled with my cousin Bob to a remote Aboriginal village in the heart of the Gibson Desert of Western Australia. I thought then I had reached "the uttermost part" of Jesus' Great Commission Acts 1:8, (*"But ye shall receive power, after that the Holy Ghost is come upon you: and ye shall be witnesses unto me both in Jerusalem, and in all Judaea, and in Samaria, and unto **the uttermost part** of the earth."*) only to discover in that "somewhere in the middle of nowhere" place that the missionaries we stayed with for six weeks thought that it was Bob and me who had come from "the uttermost part" of the earth! In actuality Bob and I had come from an exact- opposite spot on the planet. In my early presentations of that trip I would take one of those old, round globe maps to show my audience the extent of that summer's missionary journey. I would put my right index finger on Maine and my left index finger on Warbunton Range (a remote outpost of the United Aboriginal Mission of Australia, a settlement of a dozen missionaries and 600 primitive natives located 300 miles north, south, east, and west from any other town or village of people), our final destination, and the two fingers were exactly on opposite sides of the globe--my right finger on the farthest reaches of the northern hemisphere and my left finger on the farthest reaches of the southern hemisphere. Were we somewhere in the middle of nowhere? After a journey across the continental United States and the Pacific Ocean and across three quarters of Australia and then another 600 miles northeast into the Gibson Desert, I thought we were. When we started to share where we had come from with our new Australian and Aboriginal friends, it was they who thought that we had come from somewhere in the middle of nowhere!

During three mission's trips to different parts of India (Andrah Pardesh, Orissa, and Punjab), I was confronted again with the reality of one man's nowhere is another man's somewhere. When I am in Maine, I feel that I am somewhere, but when I get to earth's farthest bounds (Acts 13:47: *"For so hath the Lord commanded us, saying, I have set thee to be a light of the Gentiles, that thou shouldest be for salvation unto **the ends of the earth** [earth's farthest bounds].").* I find that I have come from earth's farthest bounds! I have now spent 186 days in the subcontinent of India, and during those days I have travelled thousands of miles in-country to some pretty remote places like Dangel, Orissa; Kanekel, Andrah Pardesh; Khasa, Punjab; Hosur, Tamil Nadu; Anchuruly, Kerala; Corramore, Assam, and Rohini, West Bengal. Each of these places was thousands of miles from Maine, and in each place I found brothers and sisters in Christ that were happy to see me, but once again the distance was measured by the phrase "somewhere in the middle of nowhere." Each of these places are at the end of the line for that particular mission's trip because from those destinations I would retrace my steps back to my somewhere having reached the end of nowhere. Granted, there were lands beyond my last stop, like in the case of Khasa which is located on the heavily guarded India/ Pakistan border, but for me I had reached another no man's land in a nowhere place, but two nations think this place is someplace because of the value they put on it by stationing thousands of troops along its edge. Such is the reality of this simple explanation of where one spends his or her life on this earth.

So now I see that even the last place (I have stayed in Ellsworth, Maine, longer than in any other place in my life including my hometown-33 years at this writing) the Lord has led me is a somewhere place in the middle of a nowhere place. Granted, Ellsworth is a thriving coastal community of nearly 6,000 people, but in the scheme of things it is really a nowhere place. Granted, many people come to this place because of Acadia National Park and the spectacular coastal scenery, but compared to New York, Philadelphia, Paris, London, San Francisco, Delhi, Los Angles, Edinburgh, Chicago, Boston, Sydney, Dallas, and Tel Aviv, places I have been, these places would say they were somewhere while a place like Ellsworth was in the middle of nowhere. And yet these are the places I have been at home for nearly seventy years now, places much like my Lord and Saviour spent the bulk of His time in while here on earth. A few years ago I wrote a book (<u>Another Day in Nazareth</u>) that was published by Wipf and Stock Publishers in Eugene, Oregon, about the concept of Jesus' "silent years" in a place a future disciple would ask, "**Can any good thing come out of Nazareth?**" (John 1:46) I have come to believe what Nathanael was saying is that Jesus had come from "somewhere in the middle of nowhere."

I like this from an unknown poet:

> "Father, where shall I work today, and my love flow warm and free?
> He pointed out a tiny spot and said, tend that place for me.
> I answered him quickly, Oh, no! Not that!
> Why no one would ever see, no matter how well my work was done; not that little place for me!
> The word he spoke then wasn't stern; he answered me tenderly.
> Nazareth was a little place [a nowhere place], and so was Galilee."

Nazareth was the extent of Jesus' life for the bulk of His life. Just three short years were given to ministries among the "multitudes," and thirty years were given to the "few" in a nowhere place, but was somewhere to Jesus. I, too, have spent my life among individuals, small groups, and tiny congregations in nowhere places. For years I thought I was somehow losing out, wasting my time, and accomplishing little. Then it came to me like a revelation--what of Jesus' time in Nazareth? It was then I began to ponder just how blessed a life I have had, a life much like Jesus' life, somewhere in the middle of nowhere life. It was in one of these places I was raised to know Jesus, found my beloved wife, raised my cherished children, and found my "church of a lifetime."

2.

PROVERBS FOR SEVENTY YEARS OF LIVING

IN OVER FIFTY YEARS of preaching (1966–2024) and over thirty years of writing (1988–2024) I have been inspired to say and write certain phrases, sacred precepts, and spiritual proverbs. I will not lay claim to their original thought because I believe these "personal proverbs" all come from the Holy Spirit that dwells within my heart and soul. I have also been inspired by the men and women that I have read over the years that have provoked a "certain catchy concept" in my mind. Then there is the Holy Word itself that has inspired many of these "personal proverbs." (At the time I put this book project to bed and submitted it to my publisher I have complied over 2000 proverbs!)

Years ago I began to write my thoughts down, and, at the writing of this chapter in my "threescore and ten" book, I have completed over 250 sacred and secular book projects. I have had 1777 chapters published, forming twenty-one books. It is my goal in this chapter to share with you sayings, insights, and precepts in proverb form that have come from my lips, my devotional projects, and those inspired by others, and this will be just one of a number of these chapters in this book.

One of my favorite books of the Bible is the Book of Proverbs, Solomon's classic work on basic, fundamental, godly wisdom. I will only take the format of those that put Solomon's proverbs together (verses), but unlike him I will never attain to 3000 proverbs (or will I) (I Kings 4:32), and, as for the 1005 songs, I have only written just under 200 to date. Inspired by the Spirit of God, Solomon developed and delivered to his people, and, now to us, some wonderful couplets of Hebrew poetry. I will never seek rhyme or rhythm in these proverbs, just simple sayings and Biblically sound bywords. It is my prayer that as you read them they will provoke in you a desire to study the verses from God's Word that either inspired the proverb or contains some truth straight from Holy Writ. No writing project is worth its weight in gold unless it points you back to the Scriptures or the Savior. My words, my proverbs, will return void, but we are promised from the pen of Isaiah, *"So shall My Word be that goeth forth out of My mouth: it shall not return unto Me void, but it shall accomplish that which I please, and it shall prosper in the thing whereto I sent it."* (Isaiah 55:11) The verdict is still out for what purpose I have been writing all these years. I still wait for "the thing" to "prosper," but in the meantime I write on and record on the thoughts and insights on God's Word in proverb form in the nearly threescore and ten years I have lived on this planet.

One final instruction. Read these "personal proverbs" with your heart and not your head. I write for the hearts and souls of people, not their intellect. My final prayer is that the Good Lord will use something that I write to draw you closer to Him in these very 'unwise' kinds of days. We need more Godly wisdom to direct our ways and guide our paths through the ungodly minefield that is found in most writings and instruction today. I like what Vance Havner wrote about Solomon: "He lived a full life and is considered to be the wisest man of all, but no man ever made a bigger fool of himself. His career premiered in wisdom, peaked in wealth and perished with women." A warning to us all is to start with wisdom. Anything else can be very dangerous!

Here are a few proverbs:

1- A Christian lives in such a way that he is always ready to die.

2- Decisions determine destinies.

3- The greatest hindrance in Christianity today is Christians.

4- All you have for all He is.

5- The Word of God is fixed, it is final, and it is filed in Heaven.

6- Make the Holy Spirit the teacher of your Bible study.

7- To do as much as you can with as little as you've got.

8- A good deed done for the wrong reason is a bad idea.

9-Man writes history after it happens, but God writes history before it happens.

10-Make me a servant of Thine, not a servant of "mine."

11-Think things through.

12-Forgive all everything.

13-A life is a lot of 24-hour days so live each day as a life.

14-Every sin denies Christ.

15-I just quote it, the Lord wrote it.

16-Prayer prevails when all else fails.

17-People love to follow the sensation instead of the Savior.

18-Seize every opportunity to work for Christ.

19-Reward will come when no earthly reward is received.

20-Lord, give me the grace to face tomorrow, tomorrow, and the grace to face today, today!

21-Anytime is time for prayer.

22-Choosing Christ costs.

23-Waiting without worrying.

24-Master the Scriptures and you will master Satan.

25-All Old Testament stories have some New Testament applications.

26-Christ died for sin so that we might die to sin because He doesn't want us to die in sin.

27-You can be a Christian in the heart and a sinner in your thoughts.

28-Sound service for the saint is serving the Saviour who saved him.

29-More often than not, when the Church becomes popular and is not persecuted, it becomes polluted and no longer productive.

30-God can do anything without us, but He has chosen to do everything through us.

31-You can be theologically sound, but at the same time be practically dead.

32- The sooner we get the Church out of the church and into the home, the sooner we will get the home into the Church and the world out of both.

33- Often lonely, but never alone.

34- God will honor our best when we can only do our best.

35- We must learn to pray to the Father, through the Son, and in the Spirit.

36- All things will be ultimately for God's glory and our good.

37- A man of God can always do more for God in the doorway than he can, drinking with a buddy in the byway.

38- Courage is contained in encouragement.

39- God loves a child that asks largely, that seeks continually, and knocks uninterruptedly.

40- If God is only your co-pilot, than you had better swap seats.

41- The best way to be defeated by temptation is to sleep through it; the best way to defeat temptation is to pray through it.

42- Do not follow where others lead; go instead where there is no path and leave a trail for someone to follow you.

43- We are to be sufficiently equipped and prepared at a moment's notice to do any good deed.

44- We are never outnumbered, we are never outmatched, and we are never out classed when God is on our side.

45- Christ did not bear His Cross so that you and I could escape it, but so that we could learn to endure it.

46- Heaven will be the great equalizer.

47- Love and loyalty cannot be separated.

48- Fear is a spiritual arthritis that paralyzes faith.

49- Whenever possessions take priority over godly principles, good people will suffer.

50- "Wait" is a four-letter word that brings a chill to our body, goose bumps to our skin, and shivers to our spine.

3.

AN UNCHANGING MESSAGE FOR ALL THESE YEARS

I HAVE ARRIVED AT Vance Havner's time (70) when he wrote, "When a preacher reaches my age, he either retires [like my Cousin Clayton did last Sunday] or finds that there are not many calls for his service. Such, however, has not been my experience [mine neither]. I have kept as busy as ever to old age. I owe it first of all to the Lord who has opened doors I never could have entered by any strategy of my own [a church of a lifetime that still wants you as pastor after 33 years and blogs on the internet and sermons on 'live stream']." Each day I get up I thank the Good Lord that I have somewhere to go and someone to minister to each day. I received a few months ago an invitation to again be a summer pastor at a Christian horse camp in northern Maine (this will be my 52nd such camp, an average of over a camp a summer in the length of my ministry- that number now numbers 63). What amazes me isn't that I am going to camp, but I am still being asked to minister to my favorite youth group, 8 to 12-year-olds. They could be my grandchildren (my grandchildren are now 9 and 6), but God thinks I still can relate and help them. And though my message has never changed, I have tried to keep current, up to date, and abreast of the times. PowerPoint is my new favorite way of reaching kids for Christ and teaching kids already in Christ about Him. But though the methods change, the message has never change!

Whether 55 years preaching in nursing homes, 50 years in a local church, 51 years preaching at summer camp, or the countless other ways I have preached the Word of God over the years, I have been governed by this one truth: "*For all flesh is as grass, and all the glory of man as the flower of grass. The grass withereth, and the flower thereof falleth away: **but the word of the Lord endureth for ever**. And this is the word which by the gospel is preached unto you.*" (I Peter 1:24–25) Others have tried to modify it, while others adapt it, and still others rewrite it, but I have never changed my message or the content of that message. I learned very early the truth of Psalm 100:5: "for the LORD *is* good; his mercy *is* everlasting; and **his truth endureth to all generations**." Whether generation-X, or any other generation, God's Word is applicable and teachable and dependable, so why change? There are many of my colleagues that have given up on the basic truth that the Word of God is unchangeable, unalterable, and indisputable. They are rewriting it to their own liking or the liking of their hearers, republishing it (all the modern paraphrases of today) in so many forms one questions if the Word of God is any longer in the Word of God. I think part of the problem is the times in which we live. Paul wrote of these times in these words: "*For the time will come when they will not endure sound doctrine; but after their own lusts shall they heap to themselves teachers, having itching ears; and they shall turn away their ears from the truth, and shall be turned unto fables.*" (II Timothy 4:3–4) The Word of God should be unaffected by what people want to hear. The unchangeable message always proclaims what God wants the people to hear.

I feel this is the only thing that will keep the preacher from changing the message. If one believes the Bible is the Word of God, not just a container of the Word of God, it will keep him from trimming out the tough parts and slanting the meaning of the difficult parts. He will be a God-pleaser versus a man-pleaser, and instead of feeding on the fear of men he will be feeding on the fear of God which is the beginning of wisdom (Proverbs 1:7). If a preacher can get over whether or not his sermon will be accepted by man, for it often times isn't, and focus totally and completely on saying *"Thus saith the Lord,"* he will have no problem being tempted into changing the message. If the preacher can stroll into his pulpit without the slightest hesitation, caring not whether his message is praised or rebuked, then he has nothing to fret about. A preacher must have a blissful indifference to the outcome of the message as long as he knows he is speaking for God. I know of preachers who change the message depending on who is in the audience. The preacher should never alter the message whether or not the President of the United States is in the front row or the King of England is in the gallery. Some have and some do, but we must be like John the Baptist who preached: *"It is not lawful for thee to have her."* (Matthew 14:4) Granted, it cost John his head, but a headless preacher is better than the preacher who gets to dine at Herod's table. Just yesterday a group of preachers gathered at the White House to receive from our current president the support of a "faith-based" committee that will help to funnel federal funds into charitable works. Have we gotten so needy in the Church that we need the help of the world? There is no worse bondage in my opinion than to be fettered to the world while still in the pulpit.

I feel that there is no greater liberty in the pulpit than a free preacher that is able to say what the Lord wants him to say. I know some preachers are told what to preach and, yes, what not to preach. The pulpit is being censured by "political correctness" today. His hands are being tied as sure as Samson's hands were tied by the Philistines, and we all know where that ended up, working for the Philistines in the local mill. The man of God, the preacher of God, that gives up on the Word of God will soon lose the Spirit of God, just as Samson did. It is time we simply tell it like it is. Preachers are shying away from commenting on "the signs of the times" because the picture is bleak and black. I like what Vance Havner says on this topic: **"One need not be either an optimist or a pessimist but a 'truthist!'"** And there is only one place to find the real truth on any social issue, moral issue, Middle East issue, or any other issue there is. The current age is not just a new chapter into the progressive, evolutionary upward climb of mankind to a world brotherhood where all nations will treat each other with love and respect. Utopia will only come when the Prince of Peace returns, but so many preachers have changed this Biblical teaching. I believe the Bible is very clear that we are witnessing the birth pangs of a terrible age that will bring to an end the world as we know it.

I hate to burst the current bubble of many within the Church who have been falsely assured that civilization can be Christianized. Jesus never told us to Christianize, but to find Christians that will be taken away at the Rapture of the Church. Again, Vance Havner put it best when he wrote, **"Churchmen who whoop it up for socialism under religious auspices are on the wrong bandwagon and totally misunderstand the program of God!"** Of course, this has resulted in mass confusion because most of the famous religious leaders, spiritual celebrities, and Christian headliners have changed the message to suit their popularity, to sell more books, to get more speaking engagements, to get their own television show or radio program. This preacher knows and has known for years that he is on the wrong side of this issue, but has chosen to not change the message.

Could I say in conclusion that this should not make ours a bitter or harsh, unloving or uncaring pulpit, but the true Biblical New Testament preaching that simply proclaims the message without regret, shares the message unjudgmentally, and preaches the message in love? We can't shy away from the tough issues like abortion and homosexuality, but we must warn the world and worldly people lest they miss the opportunity to repent. This unchanged message is about changing souls, not the sides of an issue. It is about changing hearts because until the heart is changed nobody will be changed by social improvement or legitimatizes decree; only the message can do that.

4.

JUST A SIMPLE COUNTRY PASTOR

WHEN I WAS YOUNG, I thought about being many things, a baseball player for the Boston Red Sox, a soldier in the United States Army, or a high school history teacher. I still remember the day a college professor challenged our class with these words, "If you can do or wanted to be anything other than being a pastor, go do it and don't waste my time!" At the time I thought this was a severe and harsh statement, but after 50 years as a pastor and watching man after man fall by the wayside, I think that pastoral instructor was right. Pastoring is not a job, it isn't a profession, and it isn't fun or financially rewarding. It is a calling, and, if God isn't in it, there will be no hope for success or happiness in it.

I do not call myself a preacher, though I preach. I do not call myself a teacher, though I am *"apt to teach"* (I Timothy 3:2). I do not call myself an evangelist, though I do the *"work of an evangelist"* (II Timothy 4:5). I am just a pastor (Ephesians 4:11). Despite the fact there are those who call themselves pastors on about every street corner in America, few are real pastors. They are CEOs and administrators and counselors and speakers and organizers and Heinz 57 variety of other things, but the last thing anyone wants to be is "just a simple country pastor." Ministers might exercise a pastoral ministry occasionally, but few spend much time shepherding, pastoring the flock of which they have been put in charge. Of course, one can hardly call himself a pastor today because the title conjures up the portrait of an old man with little hair, bent over, with a suit that doesn't fit, and a stride that doesn't quit. When I think of a pastor, I see only one man, my Uncle Read, my grandfather's brother. Despite being a farmer and a pastor, Uncle Read was a pastor first and a farmer second. He pastored a small congregation in an isolated community in northern Maine for 40 years (my desire-I have seven year to go to that goal), and he never did anything that wasn't for his flock, and in reality neither have I.

The true pastor has no regard for rites and rituals, forms or ceremony, and his actions are not dictated by some board or committee or convention or denomination. He seeks no favor from man and only seeks to please the Lord that called him into the work. He doesn't fit into the pattern described by a form or religion because his only focus is on the care and caring for his flock. He is never interested in being a part of the "in" group, the progressive factions of the church, and he never seeks a place at the table even though at times he might become an enemy of the established order. The true pastor is a rebel at heart. Now, for those who think that word can only be used in a negative way, consider this. Was not Amos a rebel in his day? Just a fruit picker called to be a prophet against the religious hypocrisy of Bethel. Was not Paul a rebel? A Pharisee that turned against everything he was brought up to be. Was not Jesus a rebel? Did He not stand up against everything that was lifeless and Pharisaical? Was His own heart focused on being the Shepherd to those without one? (*"But when He saw the multitudes, He was moved with compassion on them, because they fainted, and were scattered abroad, as sheep having no shepherd."* Matthew 9:36) Everybody needs a shepherd (pastor) whether they believe it or not, and Jesus came to be ours. Those of us who are called, we are under-shepherds at best: "T*he elders which are among you I exhort, who am also an elder, and a witness of the sufferings of Christ, and also a partaker of the glory that shall be revealed: feed the flock of God which is among you, taking the oversight thereof, not by constraint, but willingly; not for filthy lucre, but of a ready mind; neither as being lords over God's heritage, but being ensamples to the flock. And when the chief Shepherd shall appear, ye shall receive a crown of glory that fadeth not away."* (I Peter 5:1-4)

Vance Havner once wrote: <u>"When religion becomes a performance (II Timothy 3:5) instead of an experience, when the living faith of the dead becomes the dead faith of the living, prophets [pastors] are needed!"</u> Israel needed a pastor when God sent Moses to Egypt. Israel needed a pastor when God called David from the sheepfold (Psalm 78:70-72). Both had been shepherds before they became deliverers and kings. What is special to me in this consideration of "just a simple country pastor" is the reality of Psalm 23 and the truth that "the Lord is my pastor." I have been called to the job by God. Consider the divinely highlighted ministries of the pastor:

1) **Leading the flock** to *"green pastures"* and by *"still waters"* (Psalm 23:2), thus *"restoring the soul"* (Psalm 23:3). For me, that is talking about the pastor's responsibility of "feeding" and "watering" the flock with the Word of God (II Timothy 4:2).

2) **Leading the flock** *"in paths of righteousness for His name's sake"* (Psalm 23:3). For me, that is talking about the pastor's responsibility to exalt Christ, not himself, and to be an example of righteous living (I Peter 5:3 and I Timothy 4:12).

3) **Walking through death** with the flock (Psalm 23:4). The promise is the Lord will be there, but the pastor ought to be there as well. I have come back from vacation to walk with a member of my flock through *"the valley of the shadow of death."* Nothing has ever gotten in my way to be there when I must be there to help a parishioner through the worst experiences of life, the passing of a loved one.

It is also important that if we are to be a true pastor, to not get so focused on one food or one doctrine, that we forget or neglect to give the flock a complete variety of foods. Today we have so many preachers/pastors who are only fixing meals of "love." They are making a part of God's Word more important than the whole of God's Word. When we feed a flock only what they like, we do them a disservice. We have so many malnourished Christians today, dehydrated saints today. It is important that we prepare a balanced diet of God's Word lest the sheep fall into theological errors that will harm their spiritual health. Remember what Paul told the brethren of Ephesus: "F*or I have not shunned to declare unto you all the counsel of God."* (Acts 20:27) This ought to be the goal of every pastor because there is always a danger of making one's own preferences the norm and force that so-called norm on others. The pastor's job is to take the flock to the grass and the water, but to force feed anyone is wrong. Ultimately our goal is to bring our flock to this final decision: *"Let every man be fully persuaded in his own mind."* (Romans 14:5) Ours is to guide and lead and provide, but only when the sheep learn to eat on their own and drink on their own will we have a healthy flock. It is not our job to create people in our own image as the Pharisees did (Matthew 23:15), but to help the flock to eventually be *"conformed to the image of Christ."* (Romans 8:29) Amen!

My goal, if the Good Lord chooses to allow it, is to be a pastor for at least fifty years. I have two more years to reach that goal (I did it in 2023). The reality of the urgency of time came to a head a couple of years ago when a cousin of mine retired from the pastorate. Clayton and I started out the same year (1973) in our first pastorates. Like me, he had four pastorates in 45 years with the last one lasting 21 years. He was ready and felt the Lord calling him away, but I can't because I don't feel my pastoring days are over. I still feel I have a lot to offer the flock and in particular the flock I have been leading for 29 years now (my hope is to pastor them for 40 years). I want to retire from this flock, this church of a lifetime. I am just a pastor. I don't know what a retired pastor does. I only know what a pastor does. Oh, I have other interests, but they are hobbies at best. I was called to be a pastor, and it is my hope that I can continue in this place until the Lord calls me home or comes and takes me home as "just a simple country pastor."

5.

STARTS AND STOPS AND STAYS

This year (my 70th year) I was reminded again of a "divine" precept from God's Word that has happened a number of times throughout my life, and sometimes in a very dramatic way. I am talking about those times when God says "start or stop or stay" to my plans and changes my schedule to His. Sometimes, God simply puts us on hold for a while, then allows us to go forward in His timing, and at other times He simply stops us cold and the well-planned event never happens. I learned very early that God has the right to alter or change our plans according to His will, not ours. Solomon perhaps wrote of this divine right in this simple proverb: *"There are many devices in a man's heart; nevertheless the counsel of the Lord that shall stand."* (Proverbs 19:21) In the end God's plan and purpose will ultimately prevail over our schemes and themes. I still remember the first time God tried to teach me this precept.

It was the spring of 1972 and, after a year of careful planning, my Cousin Bob and I were off to Australia for a 70-day mission's trip into the Gibson Desert of western Australia to minister among an unreached tribe of Aboriginal people. The team was set, the plane tickets were purchased, and the schedule was in place. All we had to do was wait the date of departure and our visas from the Australian Embassy in Washington D.C. We had made application to the embassy months before; surely, they would get there on time? Yet on the morning of June 5, 1972, the time of our planned departure, there were no visas. We had to call our travel agent and cancel our tickets because there was no reason to go until we had the important documents. The Australian government wouldn't let two farm boys from northern Maine into their country without them. My very first mission trip had been delayed, put on hold, but why?

Our natural reaction was disappointment and even a bit of doubt. Was this the Lord telling us at the last minute that we shouldn't go? There were plenty of people that thought that, but Bob and I were sure that this was just another test of our faith, so despite the setback we simply "waited on the Lord" and reclaimed our trip promise: *"Faithful is He that calleth you, who also will do it."* (I Thessalonians 5:24) And interestingly, the visas showed up in the afternoon mail of the day of our leaving, but it was too late to catch up with our flights. Because flights from America to Australia were not a daily event back in those days, we had to wait 48-hours for our great spiritual adventure to begin, but God had taught Bob and I a very valuable lesson. Again, Solomon says it best in this proverb from his grand book of wisdom: *"A man's heart deviseth his way: but the Lord directeth his steps."* (Proverbs 16:9) For me, the Lord was teaching us that He was in charge of our journey, the timing of it, and the events involved in it. Granted, God only slightly changed the timing, instead of 70-days we would spend 68-days on this trip, but from the very start we realized that despite our planning and scheduling God would *"direct our steps."* To this day I don't know any other reason for the 48-hour delay other than the fact it was an explanation point to Whose trip it really was. Bob and I were just along for the ride on God's trip to Warburton Range and beyond!

Forty years after this time delay I wrote a final conclusion to this divine "hold" in a book that was published under the title of <u>The Region Beyond</u>. "Today I am reminded of the great chorus that goes, 'I just keep trusting my Lord as I walk along; I just keep trusting my Lord and He gives a song. Though the storm clouds darken the sky over the heavenly trail; I just keep trusting my Lord, He will never fail! He's a faithful Friend, such a faithful Friend. I can count on Him to the very end. Though the storm clouds darken the sky over the heavenly trail; I just keep trusting my Lord He will never fail!' I can see now that my trip to Australia was over a 'heavenly trail,' and the Good Lord was leading all the way even during the 48 hours He forced us to 'delay.'"

The second time the Lord reminded me of this concept of "start and stop and stay" to my plans was on another mission's trip in 2007 when my daughter and I were heading to India. I had been asked to be the graduation speaker at Kerala Baptist Bible College that year. Marnie had just gotten back from a three-year mission ministry in Slovakia and was looking for her next mission assignment. (Marnie would return in 2008 to teach three months at Kerala Baptist Bible College.) I had been to India the year before to teach at the college, and I thought it would give Marnie a new perspective about missions in a third-world country. This time, instead of a two-day delay, Marnie and I experienced a four-day delay. This is how I wrote about it in a book I got published under the title of <u>Though One Go With Me</u>. "Because of a huge east coast snowstorm two days before we were supposed to depart and the confusion that followed, our Delta flight out of Portland, Maine, to New York had been cancelled. Despite clear weather on the day of our departure, the JetBlue meltdown at JFK airport had messed up everybody's schedule from Maine to New York City. Therefore, our Friday takeoff had to be moved ahead to Tuesday, four days to ponder one of life's most frustrating circumstances--divine delay!

Both Marnie and I took the delay in stride as we traveled back to our home on the coast of Maine to await our new departure date. We had learned long before that all 'starts and stops and stays' of God's people are a part of God's perfect will. It might be frustrating, but our faith still taught us that God is in control of all such delays: *'When the cloud tarried long upon the tabernacle . . . then the children of Israel . . . journeyed not.'* (Numbers 9:19) As the Good Lord guided the children of Israel though their wilderness journey, He delayed them at times. These divine 'pauses' were for rest, reflection, and recreation. So why were we delayed? What divine purpose could God have had for us? One of the most famous 'delays' of the Bible is the time that Jesus *'stayed two days longer'* (John 11:6) before going to visit His sick friend Lazarus. The only reason given for the procrastination was that the power of God could more vigorously be demonstrated (certainly a resurrection shows greater power than a recovery). Was that the reason for Marnie's and my delay to India? What was it that the Lord had to show us? That He was in charge of our itinerary, not the Simon brothers; that He would make the final plans for this trip, not Marnie nor me? We love promptness and things done pronto, whether answers to prayer or travel plans. What I have learned is that God does have appropriate schedules and His delays are always within the boundaries of His greater purpose for our lives. From the very first moment of our India trip together, Marnie and I were reminded of who was in control of this endeavor. We would experience no other 'delays' on the trip, for God had made things perfectly clear in the first four days!"

In 2020, I was confronted again with "start and stop and stay," and I came across these verses in Isaiah 14:26–27: *"This is the purpose that is purposed upon the whole earth: and this is the hand that is stretched out upon all the nations. For the Lord of hosts hath purposed, and who shall disannul it? And his hand is stretched out, and who shall turn it back?"* Granted, these two verses are talking about God's plans for the nations, but for me the precept is clear, "who shall turn it back?" None of us can stop the perfect purpose of God, whether for the nations or us as individuals. Again, it was Solomon who wrote: *"Man's goings are of the Lord; how can a man then understand his own way?"* (Proverbs 20:24) I had felt called nearly a year before to once again go to India to teach at the Bible College and help in the ministry of the Independent Baptist Gospel Churches of India. Because of a liver issue with my wife Coleen, the fall trip for October 2019 was postponed until February 2020. Everything seemed to be in order until just a week before the trip Coleen began to develop a cough and a shortness of breath. After a catscan, it was revealed that she had fluid building up in her right lung. The fluid was removed two days before my scheduled departure for my sixth trip to India. Thinking I could still make the first flight on Thursday afternoon, all hopes were dashed when on Wednesday the top of Coleen's right lung collapsed, and it would have to be re-inflated on Thursday. It was clear that the Good Lord had once again put me on hold, or was this a "no?"

This was not the first time that Coleen and I had been involved in such a timing of the Lord's versus our timing. In 2003 Coleen and I took a dream vacation to England, Scotland, and Wales to celebrate our 30th wedding anniversary. We were so impressed with Scotland, five years later we planned a revisit to the fable land to witness the "heather" in full bloom. Once again, the tickets were purchased and the itinerary was made, including visiting the Lock, Sterling Castle, the Isle of Sky, as well as the Scottish Highlands with all that heather! On the very day we were to board the plane for our Scottish adventure, Coleen woke up very early, very sick. At first we thought it was just a bug, but within a few hours I had Coleen in the ER. Seeing we were not scheduled to leave until late that afternoon, we thought surely Coleen would be feeling better by then. But as the morning progressed, it was clear that there would be no trip to Scotland in 2008, and to this day, over a decade later, Coleen has still not danced in the "heather." So, as I sat before my computer waiting God's will about my trip to India in the winter of 2020, He began to highlight the Biblical stories of three great heroes of the faith and the experiences they had when God said, "start, then stop, and finally stay."

The first story deals with David and the death of his first son by Bathsheba (II Samuel 12:15-22). Most of us have heard the saying: "When God shuts a door, He opens a window." Does this saying contain Biblical truth? I believe it does in relationship to God's saying "no" to David's request to save his son. David clearly understood and believed that God had answered his petition with this statement: *"But now he is dead, wherefore should I fast? Can I bring him back again? I shall go to him, but he shall not return to me."* (II Samuel 12:23) God had certainly shut the door of death on the boy, but God had also opened a window of hope for David to believe that he would see his son again. God shut the door to Coleen and me going to Scotland and to me going to India in 2020, but He left us and me with a hope that sometime in the future we might still make the trip. (God's answer was a final 'no' as I would find out when Coleen died of a liver disease in 2020!) God might have said "no" to David, but David still believed and trusted that God knew best, and so must we no matter the situation or circumstance of God's "stay," for in the end Father Knows Best!

The second story deals with Paul and his desire to take the gospel of Christ east. *"Now when they had gone throughout Phrygia and the region of Galatia, and were forbidden of the Holy Ghost to preach the word in Asia."* (Acts 16:6) Even when Paul tried to readjust his mission, God said "no" again. *"After they were come to Mysia, they assayed to go into Bithynia: but the Spirit suffered them not."* (Acts 16:7) God said "no" to David once but twice to Paul on the same mission trip. Could I adapt the well known saying repeated in the last paragraph with, "When God shuts a door, He opens another door!" Sometimes a "no" or a shut door is only a redirecting of our lives as in the case of the Apostle Paul. Paul wanted to go east, but God wanted Paul to go west and in the famous Macedonian Call (Acts 16:8-12) Paul was redirected to Philippi and Lydia and the Philippian jailer. Is this what is happening in your life with the closed door? Can you believe that God is re-stationing you? Can you yield to the change of direction? An old church hymn, <u>Anywhere With Jesus</u>, Jessie Pounds writes two wonderful stanzas, but for me it is the third stanza written by Helen Dixon that speaks to me: "Anywhere with Jesus over land or sea, telling souls in darkness of salvation free; ready as He summons me **to go or stay**, anywhere with Jesus when He points the way." Like Paul, I simply want to go where God wants me to go, say what God wants me to say, and do what God wants me to do, whether here or there, wherever He points, I am willing "to go or stay."

The third story deals with Joseph and the plan the Good Lord had with his life. We start with the dream Joseph had as a teenager: *"And he dreamed yet another dream, and told it his brethren, and said, Behold, I have dreamed a dream more; and, behold, the sun and the moon and the eleven stars made obeisance to me."* (Genesis 37:9) And we end with Joseph remembering that dream nearly twenty years later: *"And Joseph remembered the dreams which he dreamed of them, and said unto them . . . "* (Genesis 42:9) Between those two events Joseph heard "no" at least three times. When he was in the waterless pit crying for mercy from his brother, they still sold him into slavery (Genesis 37:23-28). When he stood before his boss Potiphar innocent of the rape charge issued against him by Potiphar's wife, he was still thrown into prison (Genesis 39:17-20). When after Joseph had given a good prediction to Pharaoh's butler that he would be restored to his post and that he would remember Joseph, in the end the butler forgot Joseph for two years (Genesis 40:9-41:1). All these shut doors, yet in the end God's original door for Joseph was eventually opened. Could we adapt that familiar saying one more time, "When God shuts a door, he can also open the same door?" Sometimes, we forget that doors are for both shutting and opening, and just because God shuts a door it doesn't meaning He won't in His time reopen the door. Like Joseph, we have to learn to wait on the Lord and continue our trust of Him despite the times we hear "no," and the door is shut in our face. Sometimes it is nothing more than the perfect timing of God versus our flawed timing.

Though I have referenced this Biblical story before, I believe it is worth repeating so that we might recognize that all "starts and stops and stays" are of the Lord. In the famous journey from Egypt to Canaan known as the Exodus, we have underlined and highlighted this divine dealing with God's people, whether Old Testament saints or New Testament saint. Just before God led the children of Israel out of Egypt, His presence was ever before them in the Shekinah Glory (Exodus 13:21-22). And as they left Mount Sinai for the Promised Land we read by the pen of Moses: *"And when the cloud was taken up from over the tabernacle, the children of Israel went onward in all their journeys: but if the cloud were not taken up, then they journeyed not till the day that it was taken up. For the cloud of the Lord was upon the tabernacle by day, and fire was on it by night, in the sight of all the house of Israel, throughout all their journeys."*

(Exodus 40:36–38) How God led then God leads now; how God guided then is how God guides now, and how God directed then is how God directs now. Instead of the Shekinah we have the Spirit, but the method of God is still the same. He is in charge of all our "starts" and when He wants us to "stop," we will stop or He will cause us to stop. Sometimes we want to stop too soon or start too soon so God will exercise His "stays." God's stays are hard because they require much grace as was needed in my 2020 stay, as you will see!

6.

GREATNESS IS NOT GEOGRAPHICAL

I ONCE DREAMED OF pastoring a big church in a big place and making a big difference in this big, old world, but as I enter my seventieth year, my dreams and desires have changed because of a concept I finally came to understand.

I haven't and will never pastor a big church. I haven't and will not live in a big place. And as for making a big difference, the verdict is still out because it's in the hands of God. What has made this dramatic change in my basic church philosophy? It all happened quite suddenly when I came to the realization that my dear Lord and Saviour Jesus Christ had lived nearly ninety percent of His life on earth in Perham (my hometown and like every other town I have lived in, including Ellsworth), or in my Savior's case, Nazareth.

Remember what Nathanael said to Philip when hearing Philip's testimony about finding the Messiah? *"Can there any good thing come out of Nazareth?"* (John 1:46) How often have we thought that greatness is geographical? When a man is born in a big place where he finds great opportunities for advancement that is the reason he becomes important. Greatness, however, does not depend on location or largeness. When Alexander marched out of the insignificant Greek province of Macedonia, there were those who probably said, "Can any one great come out of Macedonia?" And yet before he was done, after he conquered his world, he would be known as Alexander the Great of Macedonia. Most would have thought he should have come from Athens or Sparta, but greatness is not geographical.

Greatness also doesn't take into consideration how long one stays in Nazareth, or Ellsworth (33 years now). I see now that I have spent most of my nearly seventy years in Nazareth or places like Nazareth. I was born in a small farming community in northern Maine. In the first century in Galilee Nazareth was a typical farming village where agriculture determined nearly every aspect of daily life—just like in Perham, Maine. Jesus' boyhood home was located in a sheltered basin nearly 1300 feet above sea level. Perham is also located in hill country just above the Aroostook River Valley. My four pastorates have taken me to rural hamlets in southern New Hampshire, back to northern Maine, to a small island off the downeast coast of Maine, and now to the riverside (Union River) and seaside (Gulf of Maine) town of Ellsworth. Even in His hometown Jesus was trying to demonstrate to the world that God looks at people, not places.

Nazareth was the extent of Jesus' life for the bulk of His life. Just three short years were given to ministries among the "multitudes," and thirty years were given to the "few." I, too, have spent my life among individuals, small groups, and tiny congregations. For years I thought I was somehow losing out, wasting my time, accomplishing little. Then it came to me like a revelation, what of Jesus' time in Nazareth? (The final event that convinced me that this would be my philosophy for life was the day I actually spent in Nazareth, Israel. I was on a Dallas Theological Seminary tour of the Holy Lands with my daughter Marnie. We were supposed to only drive through Nazareth on our way to explore Mount Tabor, but our bus got two flat tires in the middle of town [a good size city today]. Because it would take all afternoon to fix the blown tires, we were diverted to "Nazareth Village," a reproduction of Nazareth town as it would have been during the times of Jesus. They had individuals playing characters that might have lived in Jesus' day, a blacksmith, a carpenter, a shepherd, a candle maker, a farmer, etc. The houses, synagogue, vineyards, orchards, and olive press were surrounded by animals including sheep and donkeys and chickens which added to a genuine Nazareth atmosphere.) It was then I began to ponder just how blessed a life I have had, a life much like Jesus' life. Who better to know what "another day in Nazareth" (I was so impressed that day in Nazareth that I came home and wrote a book by the same title sharing my observations of the similarities between my boyhood in Perham and Jesus' boyhood in Nazareth; better known as the silent year of Jesus!) is like then one who has spent most of his days in small country towns. I have often speculated what the "silent" years in Nazareth were like for Jesus. Then it came to me--much like my days, both as a farm boy and a small town pastor.

Dr. J. H. Jowett writes:

> "Our Lord Jesus lived for thirty years amid the happenings of the little town of Nazareth. Little villages spell out their stories in small events. And He, the young Prince of Glory, was in the carpenter's shop. He moved amid humdrum tasks, petty cares, village gossip, trifling trade, and He was faithful in that which was least. If these smaller things in life afford such riches of opportunity for the finest royalty, all of our lives are wonderfully wealthy in possibility and promise. Even though our house is furnished with commonplace, it can be the house of the Lord all the days of our lives."

Once I realized that my Lord had called me to "His lifestyle," I became more content, more confident, more thankful, and more determined to be found faithful in my Nazareth place, like Ellsworth.

Nettie Rooker put it this way:

> "When I am tempted to repine that such a lowly lot is mine, there comes to a voice which saith 'Mine were the streets of Nazareth;' so mean, so common and confined, and He the monarch of mankind, yet patiently He traveleth those narrow streets of Nazareth. It may be I shall never rise to place of fame beneath the skies but walk in straitened ways till death narrow as the streets of Nazareth. But if through honor's arch I tread and there forget to bend my head, ah, let me hear the voice which saith "Mine were the streets of Nazareth."

It is with this message ringing in my ear and singing in my heart that I share with you a few thoughts along the way, my way through, in, and around my Nazareth. Most of us will never know the greatness of a great accomplishment, the creation of something totally new, or the success of changing the world like Christ did. But we all can experience "Another day in Nazareth." Let us come to the conclusion that our best days will probably be our Nazareth days, and that there is service to be done, there is duty to be performed, and there are people to be helped even in Nazareth. "Can any good thing come out of your little, insignificant, small life?" I will let you be the judge.

But as for me, where I once desired, sought, thought of fame, I do no longer. I seek only to be found faithful in my "tiny spot," my "streets of Nazareth," my "little town." Others sought to be recognized in Jerusalem, at Bethel, in Ephesus, but not Jesus. Could He have gone to Rome or Athens or Alexandria in His day? Certainly, yet He never did. We all know of preachers who can't preach their way out of a paper bag in the big cathedrals in a large metropolitan church, while the truly great preacher proclaims faithfully God's Word in a backwater place with few in attendance. God seems to dole out assignments in His "mysterious ways" where some get more than they deserve and others less than they deserve. Our place might not look like much, small and insignificant, but, if God has called us to it, we need to be found faithful in it, just like Jesus was in Nazareth.

7.

PURPOSE-DRIVEN OR DIVINE-PURPOSE LIFE

During my tenure as pastor in these final decades leading up to my seventieth year, I have watched as the Church has embraced a "purpose-driven" view of establishing a heaven on earth without the need of Jesus and a kingdom on earth without bringing back the King. A global utopia is now the plan and the purpose of the Church, all based on human reasoning, human power, and human talents. Jesus is no longer needed, and neither is the Holy Spirit. Churches and their pastors of this persuasion can be clearly identified by these simple characteristics: 1) spirituality (mysticism) is more important than doctrine; just be good and love everybody and don't point out sin; 2) prophecy, especially the Coming of Christ, is no longer necessary or applicable; 3) Israel and what is happening in the Middle East isn't important because the promises to the Jews are now our promises (this is called replacement theology); 4) Bible study is replaced by studying someone's book, watching videos of upbeat speakers; 5) the health of the church is based on numbers, the more, the healthier the Church; 6) the truth found in the Word of God is less and less important giving way to "political correctness;" 7) nobody need be offended because topics like sin, hell, homosexuality, abortion, and repentance are downplayed. These are the characteristics of a "purpose-driven" Christianity, a "purpose-driven" church, and a "purpose-driven" Christian. But my Bible speaks of another purpose, a "divine-purpose." *"To everything **there is** a season, and a time to every purpose under the heaven . . . I said in mine heart, God shall judge the righteous and the* wicked: for **there is** a time there for every purpose and for every work." (Ecclesiastes 3:1, 17)

When "purpose" is taken out of the hands of God and placed in the depraved hands of man, "purpose" gets twisted. I believe this is the depleting of the Faith to the rise of the apostasy of the last days. *"Let no man deceive you by any means: for **that day shall not come**, except there come a falling away first, and that man of sin be revealed, the son of perdition."* (II Thessalonians 2:3) The Greek for "a falling away" is our word "apostasy." Paul repeats this warning in I Timothy 4:1, and I have been watching this truth unfold my entire lifetime. What started as a simple slide is now an avalanche. The people I have witnessed who have walked away from the Faith is disheartening, and I believe part of the blame is the teaching of the "purpose-driven" pastors and preachers who have gotten away from warning of the pitfalls that will come to those who "fall away" or "depart." (II Peter 2:20-22) People who think they are saved aren't because who can really be saved and "depart" from the Faith, "fall away" from the Faith. I know the Lord knows those who are His (II Timothy 2:19), but, if they are His, He will keep them in the Faith (Philippians 1:6 and II Timothy 1:12). Man's purpose and God's purpose are often far apart. *"For my thoughts are not your thoughts, neither are your ways my ways, saith the LORD. For as the heavens are higher than the earth, so are my ways higher than your ways, and my thoughts than your thoughts."* (Isaiah 55:8-9)

The modern church is being overtaken by feeling, touching, smelling, and seeing God in the natural man. Anybody and everybody can find "the God within," and a relationship with Jesus Christ is not required or a prerequisite. This has been tried before in Church history with Gnosticism and the Roman Catholic mystics and monks. The theory was if you were in a sacred spot, isolated from the world, surely you could find God. How often has God been blamed, told it was His purpose (I think of the crusades). Today the church is turning to the Buddhists and the Hindus for instruction to find a deeper meaning of God. But we hear that all these things are just a new moving of the Holy Spirit, a fresh and a new moving of God, but I suggest to you they are neither new, nor of God. We are told clearly that when the Spirit comes, He will not speak of Himself (John 16:13). We have heard it before that "a new age of enlightenment" has come, but for what purpose, for whose purpose. A few years back a man made a lot of money writing a simple book called "the purpose-driven life." It was all the rage when in reality it was as old as the letters of Paul: *"And we know that all things work together for good to them that love God, to them who are the called according to his purpose."* (Romans 8:28) The same thing happened a few years before when another famous man wrote a simple book on "the prayer of Jabez" (I Chronicles 4:9–10) and made plenty of money; spirituality in "five minutes a day," an easy believism, a cheap salvation, and grace promoted by marketing and the making of money. NavPress and Zondervan have flooded the markets over the years with a flood of books promoting practices based on eastern mysticism, not Biblical doctrine, simply because it is what society wants to hear.

For me, the Bible makes it crystal-clear that "purpose" is only in God's hand, not man's hand: *"In whom also we have obtained an inheritance, being predestinated according to **the purpose of Him** who worketh all things after the counsel of his own will,"* (Ephesians 1:11) and *"According to **the eternal purpose** which He purposed in Christ Jesus our Lord."* (Ephesians 3:11) Any activity, any plan, any program that leaves Christ out of the mixture is not of God. The same is true with the Bible. Any doctrine, teaching, or program that denies the ultimate and absolute authority of the Scriptures is not part of the "purpose" of God. To promote church growth is a divine purpose, but if the Gospel is not at the center of that purpose, then it is not of God (I Corinthians 1:18–22). *"Who hath saved us, and called us with a holy calling, not according to our works, but according to **His own purpose** and grace, which was given us in Christ Jesus before the world began."* (II Timothy 1:9) The dangers of seeking a purpose outside the PURPOSE of God is to fall into the snare of those that would change the church from "the Body of Christ" to the social arm of an organization that seeks to solve all the world's ills by good works. As I have taught most of my life, Jesus never left an organization behind, but an organism, a living spiritual group of His followers who were instructed to go into all the world and share the Gospel with everybody. Is this the purpose of this emerging church?

If the purpose-driven philosophy continues to engulf the Church and the eternal purpose of God is ignored then it won't be long before the Gospel that I have preached for over a half-century will be too narrow (isn't that what it is supposed to be? Matthew 7:13–14) and too restrictive. Eventually, the narrow way to Heaven, the only way to Heaven, will be abandoned to a broader way. We know where the broad way leads, but will those who embrace this new Christianity know? Reinventing and re-imagining the Faith has been attempted by many before me, and to this point the Word of God and the Church of God has prevailed in time (just remember the great revivals of Church history when the Church seemed almost lost but there was revival). My fear is the church has no more revivals in it! Didn't Jesus Himself warn: *"Nevertheless when the Son of man cometh, shall he find faith on the earth?"* (Luke 18:8) I must admit I am convinced that we are seeing the beginning of the apostasy: *"and that they may recover themselves out of the snare of the devil who are taken captive by him at his will."* (II Timothy 2:26) The devil is raising havoc because his days are numbered, and his focus is on the Church. "Purpose-driven" is just another one of his devices (II Corinthians 2:11), and we should know it!

8.

THE EMERGING CHURCH OF THE 21ST CENTURY

To say the world is changing would be a gross understatement, and to say the Church isn't changing would be a lie. I have come to believe as I pastor into my seventieth year that mainstream Christianity and traditional churchianity has moved into what the church historians are calling a **"post-modern, post-Christian"** era. For many of us the change came, and we never noticed it because, like me, we were more concerned with the trends and tendencies happening in our local assembly. Yet, even in the midst of our busy lives there were enough signs that told us something was wrong in the universal church, something was happening to the church of our fathers, and someone had to say something or do something, but we ignored our spiritual feeling that the Church was sick and simply pressed on hoping to raise up a healthy, vibrant local church.

This dangerous movement to "reinvent" Christianity to be more acceptable to the world and to "reinvent" the Church so that it would be more appealing to the masses is here whether we like it or not. Some, early on, thought this was just a passing fancy of a few, but while most of us took our eye off the Church in general, "the emerging church" has fully emerged from the shadows and now appears to be the new established Church. Only God knows if it is too late to reverse the trend, but I have the feeling that what has happened to our beloved Church is the transition from the True Church (Revelation 1–3) to the Apostate Church (Revelation 13–18) talked about in the Revelation. The "signs of the times" seem clear to me that we are in the last days (II Timothy 3:1–5), and, if the world is in the end times, then so is the Church. The rapture (I Thessalonians 4:13–18) is at hand and the "lukewarm" Church (Revelation 3:14–22) is here. The only difference is the modern Church historian is calling it "the emerging church."

As for me, as long as I am a pastor, I am determined to speak up against these modern changes and to the best of my ability direct the church I have under my charge to stand firm, stay grounded: *". . . stedfast, unmoveable, always abounding in the work of the Lord, forasmuch as ye know that your labour is not in vain in the Lord."* (I Corinthians 15:58) Throughout church history, the Church has faced times like this before, when culture changes, fads, and trends alter the way things are done, but for some Biblical Christianity doesn't need to change with the times. There are those fundamental truths that must remain constant if the Gospel is to be preached and received with the hope of eternal life. Recently, my statement of faith has been summarized into these five phrases: **By grace alone, through faith alone, in Christ alone, according to the Scriptures alone, for the Glory of God alone!** We can't compromise on one of these items no matter what the reward. Many are compromising so they can get bigger congregations, get more recognition by the mass media, get approval by the political establishment, or just make more money. But, if we realize, it is how we respond to these truths that really makes the difference between heaven and hell because without a clear teaching of the Gospel salvation is impossible. I have come to believe that there is a large amount of deception in "the emerging church" because this modern church movement seems to have all the hallmarks of the "lion's paw" (I Peter 5:8), and the leaders of this church seem to be classic "ministers of righteousness" (II Corinthians 11:13–15).

If Jesus never changes (Hebrews 13:8), then why should His Church? Just because we are living in the twenty-first century, why do His teachings and doctrines concerning His Church need to change? There are the preachers and prophets of this movement that say that the rational and factual aspects of the Faith must be changed to the experiential and mystical to reach the modern, sophisticated individual of the day. The people of the first century were uneducated and ignorant so the Gospel took hold, but the highly educated, cultured citizen of the world needs something more? We forget that Paul wrote: *"For Christ sent me not to baptize, but to preach the gospel: not with wisdom of words, lest the cross of Christ should be made of none effect. For the preaching of the cross is to them that perish foolishness; but unto us which are saved it is the power of*

God. For it is written, I will destroy the wisdom of the wise, and will bring to nothing the understanding of the prudent. Where is the wise? Where is the scribe? Where is the disputer of this world? Hath not God made foolish the wisdom of this world? For after that in the wisdom of God the world by wisdom knew not God, it pleased God by the foolishness of preaching to save them that believe. For the Jews require a sign, and the Greeks seek after wisdom: but we preach Christ crucified unto the Jews a stumbling block, and unto the Greeks foolishness; but unto them which are called, both Jews and Greeks, Christ the power of God, and the wisdom of God." (I Corinthians 1:17–24) If the Gospel be changed, it is changed to the loss of salvation and eternal life to all.

"The emerging church" has come to believe that no faith can preach absolutes, just generalities that will point people to a particular brand of "faith." We forget that **"Faith has no value in itself; it is the object of faith that is the difference."** All world religions believe in something or someone, but the Bible is clear: *"Neither is there salvation in any other: for there is none other name under heaven given among men, whereby we must be saved."* (Acts 4:12) To change the message is to change the truth, and to change the truth people will not have the information necessary for salvation. For years the Church has been trying to come up with methods to reach the masses without changing the message, but in time they changed the message to reach the masses. As I write this article, the evangelist Billy Graham has died in his 100th year. Though I didn't like some of his methods and hobnobbing with other world religious leaders and political leaders, I never heard his message change, but I am afraid the post-Graham evangelist won't have the same convictions. Remember, Paul warned: *"For if he that cometh preacheth another Jesus, whom we have not preached, or if ye receive another spirit, which ye have not received, or another gospel, which ye have not accepted, ye might well bear with him."* (II Corinthians 11:4) And what is true of the Gospel is certainly true about the doctrine of the Second Coming of Christ. Most messages today are about how to live better here rather than "This world is not my home, I'm just passing through. My treasures are laid up somewhere beyond the blue." The prosperity preachers have redirected the Christian from heavenly treasure to earthly treasure. Oh, the message is popular and these preachers are drawing great crowds, but is it the right message?

"The emerging church" has also embraced the "social gospel" pioneered in the 19th century, refined in the 20th century, and has now emerged in the 21st century as the primary outreach of the church. I like what Vance Havner once said: "We are not here to save the ship, but to rescue the passengers." Instead of preaching an urgent message, we are deceiving people in believing we can create a heaven on earth or that we can bring in the Kingdom without the King. The concepts sound wonderful, "good works" and all that, but they are not Biblical works, and they are not Scriptural. That for me is the major difficulty I have with the new "emerging church" philosophy. There is more and more about the goodwill of man to man and less and less about the Will of God and our will.

9.

NICOLAITANS: ALIVE AND WELL TODAY

CHRIST ONLY PREACHED ONE form of Christianity. He never offered a bargain to anyone, He never cut the cost to anybody, and He never put His teachings on sale. Christianity isn't cheap, it's costly. As I continued my reading of Dietrich Bonhoeffer's classic challenge to the church under the title of <u>The Cost of Discipleship</u>, I realized that there was much more about discipleship I had to comment on. There are plenty of fancy recipes of religion and delectable tidbits of doctrine abounding today, but the only thing that will satisfy in this life and the next is the Bread of Life. Jesus said, *"I am that Bread of Life."* (John 6:48) Christ is looking for disciples that are 100% committed to Him, content to eat one bread and drink one drink (John 4:10–15), and half-hearted followers need not apply (Luke 9:57–62). In my opinion this is the message that Christ gives to would-be disciples, even to this day.

Religious activity is not synonymous with spirituality and to recruit more Ephesians for simply more works and more labor without returning to our "first love" (Revelation 2:4) only makes matters worse and the Church more of a laughingstock in the world. So, what happened between the early recruitment of believers to a generation later when the Church had a body, but no heart; had a body, but no Head? When did action overtake affection; when did man supersede Jesus? Why this matters is that the Church today is still struggling with these problems. The twenty-first century Church is a beehive of activities. Has it ever done more in the area of charitable works, world-wide outreaches, and worship services and yet at the same time done less of what Christ asked? Something must have happened in between the gospels and the Revelation to change God's view of His own Church, some historical or psychological event that changed the Church so dramatically that God warned: *"Remember therefore from whence thou art fallen, and repent, and do the first works; or else I will come unto thee quickly, and will remove thy candlestick out of his place, except thou repent."* (Revelation 2:5)

Wow! That is a serious exhortation, one that is still proclaimed from the Revelation to this very hour.

Are you a noun Christian or an adjective Christian? God never intended His followers simply to be statistics. I believe one of the mistakes that have happened in the Church, the early Church and the latter Church, is the fact that the Church has become an identity unto itself, and it has forgotten that we are called to follow Christ, not the Church or churchmen. The Church at best is the body of Christ (Ephesians 1:22–23), but Jesus hasn't always maintained the "Headship" of the Church. In the ancient church and the modern Church that position has been abducted. To answer our original question, I believe you only must continue the reading of the Revelation about the Church at Ephesus to get the answer: **"But this thou hast, that thou hatest the deeds of the Nicolaitans, which I also hate."** (Revelation 2:6) Who were these Nicolaitans? I have come to believe they were the first individuals in the Church that believed their role as leaders in the Church included activities and directions only Jesus should control. Some feel it started with one of the first "deacons" of the Church, Nicolas (Acts 6:5). From those early days of influence and teaching this concept, that eventually created the pope, grew into the monstrosity we today call ministry (the so-called professional Christians)! *"So hast thou also them that hold the doctrine of the Nicolaitans, which thing I hate."* (Revelation 2:15) In other words, the love of the Church had changed from the love of Christ to the love of the Church or the love of churchmen. Certain men and women (Revelation 2:20), then and now, have fallen into the trap of the self-righteous, self-exalting, self-important Pharisee, Pharisees like the one that went to the Temple to pray and saw the publican there: *"And he spake this parable unto certain which trusted in themselves that they were righteous, and despised others: two men went up into the temple to pray; the one a Pharisee, and the other a publican. The Pharisee stood and prayed thus with himself, God, I thank thee, that I am not as other men are, extortioners, unjust, adulterers, or even as this publican. I fast twice in the week; I give tithes of all that I possess. And* *the publican, standing afar off, would not lift up so much as his eyes unto heaven, but smote upon his breast, saying, God be merciful to me a sinner. I tell you, this man went down to his house justified rather than the other: for every one that exalteth himself shall be abased; and he that humbleth himself shall be exalted."* (Luke 18:9–14) Could I ask which sounds more like you?

It wasn't long into the history of the Church when men like Paul began to warn against those who held to **"the doctrine of the Nicolaitans."** *"Now this I say, that every one of you saith, I am of Paul; and I of Apollos; and I of Cephas; and I of Christ. Is Christ divided? Was Paul crucified for you? Or were ye baptized in the name of Paul?"* (I Corinthians 1:12–13) Man loves to glorify man, even in the Church. Over the years many men like Paul tried to redirect attention back to the Christ, but over time the Church has made "saints" of many, individuals that are put up on pedestals and thrones, bowed to, their rings kissed, and honored above the Lord Himself. This stumbling block has claimed many a man and many a woman who were all too ready to receive the applause and accolades of their fellowman, their fellow Church members, their fellow brother and sister in Christ. Like the Pharisee in the Temple who thought themselves better than others, more religious, more pious, more worthy of God's ear, and, as Jesus so fitly taught, it was the lowly sinner, the lowly publican that got his prayer answered. Jesus would rebuke the Pharisees by saying that publicans and prostitutes would go into the kingdom ahead of them. I believe the same is true today. Titles and honors, robes and rings, fancy positions and places are no guarantee for Heaven. I am still haunted by these words by Jesus: *"Not every one that saith unto me, Lord, Lord, shall enter into the kingdom of heaven; but he that doeth the will of my Father which is in heaven. Many will say to me in that day, Lord, Lord, have we not prophesied in thy name? And in thy name have cast out devils? And in thy name done many wonderful works? And then will I profess unto them, I never knew you: depart from me, ye that work iniquity."* (Matthew 7:21–23) The Nicolaitans might be a part of the church, but they have no part with Jesus. **Today many believe in Jesus, but He doesn't believe in them.**

One of the great tragedies of our age is that many people think they are getting to heaven by being religious instead of being righteous. The Nicolaitans were and are that kind of people. They have substituted the Christ for the Church; they have assumed the leadership of the Church from Christ and placed it upon their own shoulders; they have ignored the Holy Spirit for the spirit of man, and they are making a case that they can do it better than the early church. They are verifying their importance by statistics and souls saved, forgetting this admonition of the Pharisees by Jesus: *"Woe unto you, scribes and Pharisees, hypocrites! For ye compass sea and land to make one proselyte, and when he is made, ye make him twofold more the child of hell than yourselves."* (Matthew 23:15) Instead of compassing the world to make a Christian (a Christ-like individual), they travel the earth to make another Nicolaitan. Bonhoeffer wrote, "When we are called to follow Christ, we were summoned to an exclusive attachment to His Person."

10.

THE MINISTRY TO A FEW

I HAVE BEEN STRUGGLING for most of my spiritual life with the meaning and doctrine of the title of this chapter in my book of "threescore and ten." In my ongoing annual sermons for the church's annual report delivered to the congregation of my churches at their annual church meeting each January since 1980, I have used the time to write about topics that challenge me. Each year I debate what to write on, the theology that needs to be underlined and the message I want to highlight to the flock the Good Lord has called me to shepherd. I started this series of sermons while pastoring Calvary Baptist Church in Westfield, Maine, (8 years) and continued the practice at the Washington Street Baptist Church in Eastport, Maine, (5 years). In my longest series of these messages to Emmanuel Baptist in Ellsworth, Maine, my church of a lifetime (33 years), I tried to deal with a troubling issue that the flock was facing that particular year, but this year I would like to tackle God's view of the "few," and why most of us in His body will only "minister to a few," and how we need to be content and encouraged in this wonderful ministry to God's faithful few.

    I officially started my service for the King when 1970 rolled around. Granted, I had been saved since 1958, baptized since 1964, and had done a few things in God's service, like praying at prayer meeting, Bible reading at church services, some song leading during a singspiration, and, yes, a bit of preaching (1965), as well as serving in our BYF (Baptist Youth Fellowship) youth group at the Perham Baptist Church. Until I gave my life to Christ for full-time Christian service, I had not really begun my God-ordained, God-gifted ministry for and with Jesus. Jesus might see this differently (heaven will reveal that), but, as for me, I have always marked 1970 as my start time for affecting Church history, and at the writing of this chapter I have but to finish this year, and I will have been at it fifty years, a half-century ministering to a "few" and only the "few" because I have never had one big ministry, a large work with the many, the masses, or the multitudes at any time or anywhere, as is the case for most of us.

From the very start of my life-long service for the King of Kings, I did have great aspirations and even greater expectations that the Good Lord would eventually lead me into "a great work," and by a great work I mean among the many, the multitudes, the masses. I dreamed of a big foreign mission assignment to an out-of-the-way place, to the uttermost part (Acts 1:8). When that door was closed in 1972, I dreamed of a big church calling, maybe not to a big city, but to turn a small church into a mega-church. While still at college (Bob Jones University) I would hear from successful pastor after successful pastor that had grown a local assembly from a handful to thousands, reaching hundreds upon hundreds every week and seeing scores saved with every message. Surely, that would be me, but it never happened. I must be a slow learner because until recently I still dreamed of such a ministry to the many, touching and helping great numbers of people at the same time. Oh, granted, I had lost my desire for foreign service and a big church years ago, but what about a best-selling devotional author in whom my books would reach across the country and, maybe, around the world with book signings and opportunities to speaks to the multitudes on my thoughts?

It isn't that the all-knowing Lord didn't show me very early in my ministry that this wasn't to be my calling, yet, I overlooked for years such instructions as these lines from Ezekiel that I got while travelling on my very first short-term missions trip to Australia in 1972, only my third year in His eternal work. I had desires at first to be a foreign missionary among the masses of the world and, in particular, the Aboriginal people of Western Australia, yet, the Lord redirected me back to my own people of small New England with these words. Hidden in these verses were the issue of the "few," but I failed to recognize it at first. *"And He said unto me, Son of man* [Barry]*, go, get thee unto the house of Israel* [your own people]*, and speak with my words* [the Bible] *unto them. For thou art not sent to a people of a strange speech and of an hard language* [foreign missions]*, but to the house of Israel;* **not too many people** *of a strange speech and of an hard language, whose words thou canst not understand.* **Surely, had I sent thee to them, they would have hearkened unto thee***.* [Could have, would have but not God's will for me!] *But the house of Israel will not hearken unto thee* [and in most works they haven't]; *for they will not hearken unto me: for all the house of Israel are impudent and hardhearted* [sounds like some of the people I have pastored over the years]." (Ezekiel 3:4–7) I should have realized then and there that my Master was sending me to minister to a "few" here and a "few" there in my own backyard, and that I would never speak to swelling crowds as George Whitefield, or teach in large auditoriums as Chuck Swindoll, or my books would never be read by the thousands like Vance Havner. Only a few for me!

I can't remember when I first noticed this Scriptural precept taught to me by a childhood hero, Jonathan, the son of King Saul. In Jonathan's greatest military exploit he taught me this: *"And Jonathan said to the young man that bare his armour, Come, and let us go over unto the garrison of these uncircumcised: it may be that the LORD will work for us:* **for there is no restraint to the LORD to save by many or by few.**" (I Samuel 14:6) You see, God doesn't focus, as we do, on the many as being important, necessary, or a bench mark for success. Wasn't it the Lord that took away Gideon's "many" and left him with a "few?" (Judges 7) The Church has fallen into the trap set by the world that if you only make a few bucks, then you must be a failure. If you run a small business then you can't be successful. It is all about large numbers, and more numbers are better than few numbers. Remember David's brother's rebuke when he showed up at the battlefield of Elah: "*And Eliab his eldest brother heard when he spake unto the men; and Eliab's anger was kindled against David, and he said, Why camest thou down hither? And with whom hast thou left those* **few sheep** *in the wilderness? I know thy pride, and the naughtiness of thine heart; for thou art come down that thou mightest see the battle.*" (I Samuel 17:28) This is a big battle, and you're only good enough to take care of a few lambs. Who of us hasn't heard that before in some kind of fashion or form? But we know that our God doesn't look at the numbers, but at the faithfulness in relationship with the numbers, and a good look through the Bible will reveal that God would prefer to deal with the "few" and not the "many." "*For ye see your calling, brethren, how that* **not many** *wise men after the flesh,* **not many** *mighty,* **not many** *noble, are called: But God hath chosen the foolish things of the world to confound the wise; and God hath chosen the weak things of the world to confound the things which are mighty; And base things of the world, and things which are despised, hath God chosen, yea, and things which are not, to bring to nought things that* are: *That no flesh should glory in his presence."* (I Corinthians 1:26–29) How have we missed this concept after all these years?

It isn't that I didn't know or wasn't taught the theology of the "few" from an early age. It has been the application of that theology that has hampered and harassed me from my earliest days, *"So the last shall be first, and the first last: for **many** are called, but <u>few</u> chosen . . . For **many** are called, but <u>few</u> are chosen."* (Matthew 20:16; 22:14) Jesus told His earliest disciples that they would talk to the many, the multitudes, the masses, but of the many only a "few" would respond. What they found true I have found true. The ministry of the Church of God has always been among the "few" in comparison to the many of the world. Jesus might have died for them all (I John 2:2: *"And He is the propitiation for our sins: and not for ours only, but also for the sins of the whole world."*), but ultimately only a "few" would respond. (Recently, a dear friend of mine told me something that struck a chord, "Even God doesn't get His desires all the time!" And then he quoted II Peter 3:9: *"The Lord is not slack concerning his promise, as some men count slackness; but is longsuffering to us-ward, not willing that any should perish, but that **all should come to repentance**."*) So, in reflection I see that from the beginning it was only about the "few," but that didn't take away my expectation that eventually a gathering of a few would at least for me total many. I think even the disciples questioned this doctrine when Luke records this interaction with the Christ: *"Then said one unto him, **Lord, are there few that be saved**? And he said unto them, strive to enter in at the strait gate: **for many**, I say unto you, will seek to enter in, and shall not be able. When once the master of the house is risen up, and hath shut to the door, and ye begin to stand without, and to knock at the door, saying, Lord, Lord, open unto us; and he shall answer and say unto you, I know you not whence ye are: then shall ye begin to say, We have eaten and drunk in thy presence, and thou hast taught in our streets. But he shall say, I tell you, I know you not whence ye are; depart from me, all ye workers of iniquity."* (Luke 13:23–27) It has always been about the "few," not the many, and I believe it still is to this modern day, but most in the Church are failing to see, or believe it.

So if only a few will make it (Matthew 7:13,14: *"Enter ye in at the strait gate: for wide is the gate, and broad is the way, that leadeth to destruction, and many there be which go in thereat: because strait is the gate, and narrow is the way, which leadeth unto life, and **few** there be that find it."*) in the end, why was I troubled over a ministry to the very ones the Lord had called? I began to understand that not only would there never be the numbers, that we would always be in the minority (my problem with the Moral Majority movement of the 1980s was the false truth that deceived many into thinking we were many compared to being a few), but I also began to realize that even among the "few" there would be fewer still that actually wanted to minister or be ministered to. Remember what the Lord told the "few" (Luke 10:1) (rarely have my congregations numbered above 70) when He sent them forth to minister: *"Therefore said he unto them, the harvest truly is great, but the labourers are **few**: pray ye therefore the Lord of the harvest, that he would send forth labourers into his harvest."* (Luke 10:2) Jesus spoke of this prayer request earlier in his ministry (Matthew 9:37-38) when He confronted the multitudes (Matthew 9:36). This is a "few" among the "few." Many get saved, but few present their lives to God in His service (Romans 12:1-2). Like the first concept of only seeing a few saved from the many I have shared the Gospel with, I have also witnessed in my fifty years the few that have actually gotten involved in serving the Lord in some capacity after they got saved. Most believers in my era of service for the Lord Jesus have been pew-warmers, balcony people, and religious fans instead of involved participants. So why have I been so surprised with a ministry to a "few" and with the "few?"

But it wasn't until I came across this prophecy about the Church that I really began to realize that the Good Lord had never misdirected me (New England instead of Australia) or deceived me (the few instead of the many) about what He had called me into. *"And unto the angel of the church in Sardis write; these things saith he that hath the seven Spirits of God, and the seven stars; I know thy works, that thou hast a name that thou livest, and art dead. Be watchful, and strengthen the things which remain, that are ready to die: for I have not found thy works perfect before God. Remember therefore how thou hast received and heard, and hold fast, and repent. If therefore thou shalt not watch, I will come on thee as a thief, and thou shalt not know what hour I will come upon thee. Thou hast **a few names** even in Sardis which have not defiled their garments; and they shall walk with me in white: for they are worthy."* (Revelation 3:1-4) God knew in the end there would only be "a faithful few," just as there were in the days of Noah: *"Which sometime were disobedient, when once the longsuffering of God waited in the days of Noah, while the ark was a preparing, **wherein few**, that is, eight souls were saved by water."* (I Peter 3:20) And remember, Jesus told us that as the days of Noah so would the days be like when He came back (Matthew 24:37-39). Is one of the signs we have overlooked "the sign of the few?" Has there only been a ministry of the few for a few?

I have been living this sign my entire ministry life. A few here, a few there has been my lot. Where others speak of preaching to hundreds, thousands, I preach only to a few. If I get through this year, I will finish fifty-five years in my first ministry of nursing homes, boarding homes, and private homes within the sphere of my ministry area. In nearly 3300 services, the most I have ever preached to is a dozen or so at one time. I am into my 44th year of teaching my 51th Evening School class on Tuesday night pertaining to some Biblical topic, but only a handful ever show up. Some might ask why I haven't quit, or why spend so much time in study and preparation for so few. My church ministries have been to congregations of the few, compared to the mega-churches of my day. My summer camping ministries (sixty of them now) have been to a few kids at a time. The youth groups of my four churches have been to groups of only a few kids at a time. I have been writing spiritual devotionals for thirty years and have 21 books published, but even that ministry has been only to the few, a small handful who read my challenges. Yet, now I know these are who I have been called to minister to, "the few." May I be faithful reaching "the few" and may I be faithful to "the faithful" few until Christ comes and may we all be faithful to the "few" we have been called to minister to.

I am here to encourage you in the "few" you're ministering to. Dear Sunday School teacher with a class of two, your dream was twenty, but give them your best. Maybe you are a shut-in at a senior citizen's center, and you only have a few neighbors you interact with--minister to them. I have come to believe that while the mega-ministries get all the press and all the acknowledgments, the bulk of the ministry of Christ is happening among the "few," the ones that minister to a few here and a few there, but affective and necessary to the Body of Christ. How did Paul put it in I Corinthians 12:22–24? *"Nay, much more those members of the body, which seem to be more feeble, are necessary: and those members of the body, which we think to be less honourable, upon these we bestow more abundant honour; and our uncomely parts have more abundant comeliness. For our comely parts have no need: but God hath tempered the body together, having given more abundant honour to that part which lacked."* It has never been about the many or the few, but about the overall health of Christ's Body, and the few are just as important as the many whether in America or Australia. Whether Grace Thirsten at Birchwood Living

Center, or one Awana kid at the Bryant E. Morse Community Center, or the one that reads your book, the time we spend with the "few" among us is an honored ministry and worthy of your time, energy, prayers, and support. Remember Jesus was given only "a few small fish," (Mark 8:7) and He fed a multitude. It always starts with the "few."

11.

COSTLY GRACE

During a trip to visit my new granddaughter Elena Hope in Salinas, California, I took along a book I have wanted to read for years, Dietrich Bonhoeffer's classic work <u>The Cost of Discipleship</u>. I had gotten a copy from my friend Mark Honey, and I thought it was time for me to read the book I had heard about for nearly half of my life. Over my February 14–24, 2018, trip I read through the work. The first thing I noted about this book was that it was published the year of my conversion, 1958. I had waited nearly 60 years to read this classic written by a martyr of the Faith. If you are not familiar with Bonhoeffer, let me give you this short biography which will help you understand the purpose of this remembrance in my seventieth year.

Born on February 4, 1906, the son of a university professor, Dietrich was raised through the very turbulent times of the ending of Imperial Germany and Nazi Germany. By the time Bonhoeffer was in his college years Germany was embracing National Socialism. He was one of the first, despite his youth, to understand the philosophy behind the popular movement, history without God and the importance of the strength of man. By the time Hitler came to power in 1933, Dietrich was a leader in the Confessional Church. Leaving Berlin, Germany, for a pastorate in London, England, Bonhoeffer only stayed two years before he returned to face the challenges with his fellow believers in a world in which Nazism was in complete control, including the church. Bonhoeffer helped start illegal Bible schools and training centers which brought on a period of local persecution. In 1939 some American friends talked Dietrich into immigrating to the United States, but within a short time he wrote to a friend, "I shall have no right to participate in the reconstruction of Christian life in Germany after the war if I do not share the trials of this time with my people." Picking up pastoral responsibilities upon his return, Dietrich and a small group of others sought by peaceful means the overthrow of the Third Reich, but on April 5, 1943, Dietrich and his sister Christel and her husband Hans von Dohnanyi were arrested by the Gestapo. Moved from prisons to concentration camps, Bonhoeffer showed his indomitable courage and unselfish goodness, not only to other prisoners, but to the guards as well. Through his months of imprisonment, he smuggled out his writings and written poems. One of his most famous was a set of prose called Who Am I? By October 5, 1944, Dietrich was in the infamous Gestapo prison in Berlin. When that prison was bombed and destroyed, Bonhoeffer was moved to the Buchenwald Concentration Camp. The entire time Dietrich was behind bars he wrote and shared his faith in Christ. Eventually, upon the special order of Himmler himself, Dietrich Bonhoeffer was executed on April 9, 1945, at the Flossenburg Concentration Camp, just a month before the war would have ended.

After his death and the end of the Second World War, friends and companions who had received Bonhoeffer's writings decided to get his works and philosophy out to the world at large, to people who didn't even know anything about this 39-year-old church martyr. One of the first successful books was published under the title of Letters and Papers from Prison, but Dietrich's best-known book would be called The Cost of Discipleship. Bonhoeffer's grave has never been found, but his legacy of faith lives on through his written word from behind prison walls. For me, Dietrich's theme and challenge for the Christian's life can be summarized in the two-word title I have printed at the beginning of this chapter, "Costly Grace."

Long before I ever preached and taught on this topic, Bonhoeffer wrote, "Cheap grace is the deadly enemy of our Church. We are fighting today for costly grace. Cheap grace means grace sold on the market like cheapjack's wares. The sacraments, the forgiveness of sin, and the consolations of religion was thrown away at cut prices!" When theology becomes just another set of rules; when doctrine becomes just another system of thought; when devotion means nothing more than a rite or ritual performed to please man; when principle and precepts are only for the good times, but quickly discarded in bad times; when standards are only as good as long as they don't interfere with some code of political correctness; and when justification of sin happens without the justification of the sinner, this is cheap grace. The tragedy for me is that while Bonhoeffer was facing this "cheap grace" in the German Church of the 1930s, I have been dealing with this "cheap grace" in the later days of the twentieth century and the early years of the twenty-first century. Cheap grace is still alive and well. Nazism might have died with Hitler (but did it?), but cheap grace didn't die with Bonhoeffer. As he wrote, "Cheap grace is the preaching of forgiveness without requiring repentance, baptism without church discipline, communion without confession, absolution without personal confession. Cheap grace is grace without discipleship, grace without the cross, grace without Jesus Christ, living and incarnate."

I think what Dietrich Bonhoeffer was trying to tell his generation of Germans was the reality that I have been trying to teach my parishioners for over a third of my lifetime. Salvation costs us nothing, but that doesn't make it cheap because it cost the Son of Life His life, and to follow Christ will and should cost you everything including your life, for Dietrich Bonhoeffer was willing and yielding to that cost, a costly grace. *"So likewise, whosoever he be of you that forsaketh not all that he hath, he cannot be my disciple."* (Luke 14:33) Bonhoeffer's "cost of discipleship" is Jesus' teaching on discipleship, and it starts with "costly grace," not "cheap grace." The final tragedy of "cheap grace" is that it will keep you away from "costly grace." If there is anything that will cause you to give up and give in to the current political climate and forsake the traditions of the fathers in the Faith, it is cheap grace. Nazism is just one of the ages in Church history when the Church turned a blind eye to the truth. The Christian German Church (and many others around the world) was just as guilty for the loss of six million Jews in the holocaust as the Nazi Party was. Other than people like Bonhoeffer and others who stood up to Hitler and Himmler, the Church turned a blind eye to the atrocities of the Nazis. Other than a few of us who scream regularly about the atrocities of the abortion clinics and the abortion doctors, who is listening? The Church has yielded to the State just like the German people yielded to the Nazis in the area of life, prayer, and the Bible. In a society who has kicked God out of most public institutions, they are quick to blame God when an atrocity happens like the Florida school shooting of February 2018. I love the line coined by someone after the tragedy, "A man was blaming God for the shooting for which the Almighty said, 'You can't blame me. I haven't been welcomed in school for decades!'"

When will we realize whether in the 1930s and 1940s in Germany or the 2000s in America, grace isn't cheap? It never was cheap. It is the most valuable ingredient in all of time, and, if you are going to preach it, live it, and share it, it will cost you everything. In some cases, like with Dietrich Bonhoeffer and his young colleagues, it might cost you your life. The final thing I got from Dietrich's book was the thought that to be a disciple of Christ, Jesus taught the cost would be death. *"For whosoever will save his life shall lose it: and whosoever will lose his life for my sake will find it."* (Matthew 16:24–26)

12.

MORE PROVERBS FOR SEVENTY YEARS OF LIVING

In chapter two of my "threescore and ten" memoir I shared with you a few proverbs that have cemented my Christian philosophy into my seventieth year. Here are a few more:

1- For every Golgotha there must be a prayer warrior on his face in Gethsemane.
2- Merchandising not mediation, partying not praying, is the new norm in the house of God today.
3- Life's accomplishments and achievements are not based on how we end this life, but where we end up after we leave this life.
4- Better to face God's purifying flames now, than to feel hell's fire later.
5- This is the danger of Biblical illiteracy: a dull sword, a drooping spear, a dropped shield, none of them will defend you properly.
6- Some fighting fundamentalists have become ultra-fundamentalists, breaking fellowship over trivial truth.
7- Remember that legalism is just as dangerous as liberalism.
8- A right-handed God can use a left-handed man!
9- No matter what you do, if you do it in the name of the Son, for the glory of the Father, and in the power of the Spirit, it will be well-pleasing to God.
10- Form and fashion have replaced faith today.

11- As a moth to the flame, as iron to the magnet, as a compass to the north, so is the soul drawn towards God.

12- Salvation often begins with a curious inquisitiveness.

13- Several years ago an American president spoke of "a thousand points of light;" he was off by 999!

14- We once again live in a "builder of bigger barns" generation.

15- Many today trust in the security of their "hoard" and not in their Lord.

16- There are those that might try to get into the Church in "some other way," but they are only theological thieves and religious robbers.

17- Burdens steal our strength, attack our resolve, and cloud our minds.

18- A good leader, the best leader, is the one that leads in prayer.

19- Harmony at home brings recognition abroad.

20- When we cannot do what we would, we must do what we should in the service of our God.

21- The Almighty loves to take the least likely and the most uncommon to bring forth His amazing purpose. (Think of a shepherd boy named David.)

22- Some say to us Christians today, "pipe down, tone it down, keep it down," but we need to keep it up and speak up for Christ.

23- Pray now or pay later.

24- Mistakes in a past battle will always haunt us in a present battle.

25- Our God is a soul-seeking Lord and a sheep-seeking Shepherd.

26- Theology has changed so that respect and reverence for God no longer counts. God is someone we pat on the back, shake His hand, and say, "How's it going God?"

27- The best heart surgeon in the world can only give you a few more years of life at best, but Christ can give you a new heart that will go on beating throughout eternity.

28- Each person of the Bible will either warn us or warm us.

29- Imagine a murdering robber chosen over the spotless Son of God, and yet if a vote was taken today, I fear the result would be the same.

30-God has a purpose for each life, including the blind baby, the unwanted child, and the unintended kid. (Jeremiah 1:5)

31-The success of one man is so intertwined with another that life would not be the same without God's pairs.

32-The first Church meeting was a prayer meeting.

34-Whatever happened to the days when the first date ended up on the back porch instead of the back bedroom or the back seat? Whatever happened to the days when the first date ended up with a good night instead of a good morning? Whatever happened to the days when the first date ended up with a kiss instead of a kid?

35-The wiles of a woman ought to be feared more than the weapons of the warrior.

36-It takes women of God and men of God to make a man or woman of God.

37-No man will ever become greater than what he thinks of Christ.

38-Turn your eyes upon Jesus. It will be the best view you ever saw!

39-The larger books of the Bible may contain more of God's inspired Word, but the little books of the Bible do not contain any less of God's inspired Word.

40-God moved the world to get His Son to Bethlehem, and, while Augustus thought he was making a political decision, in reality he was making a divine decree.

41-Covetousness always begins with a look and ends with "I took."

42-When the day comes that the Good Lord picks His all-star team for my generation, I will be very content if he thinks me worthy of an honorable mention.

43-If God knows all the stars in the heavens by name, don't you think He knows your name?

44-Just because we are not listening doesn't mean the Lord isn't speaking.

45-Character is the root of the tree of life, and conduct is the fruit of the tree of life.

46-Health issues have never been an issue with God for His service.

47-One of the greatest hindrances to discipleship with Christ is a family relationship without Christ.

48-God is not limited by the experience or profession of His servants.

49-The devil is content with our "good." If that "good" keeps us away from God's best, every one of us is in danger of sacrificing God's best on the altar of "good" intentions.

50-The Devil has an inexhaustible expense account when it comes to paying any price for your disobedience. Have no price!

51-Instead of resisting we run; instead of standing we slip away; instead of trusting we turn tail, and instead of fighting we take flight.

52-God's answer for a tired, tested saint is not a good lecture, but a good lunch. (Elijah)

53-There is a time to fight, but there is also a time to flee; there is a time to resist, but there is also a time to retreat; there is a time to withstand, but there is also a time to go out the window; there is a time to war, but there is also a time to go over the wall.

54-Like Jonah, instead of an evangelistic crusade in our Nineveh, the average Christian prefers a Mediterranean cruise to another Tarshish called Florida.

55-How often the Christian decides to take a vacation, when God would have them involved with their vocation.

56-Jesus' silence before Pilate taught His Church more about selflessness, self-abasement, and self-abandonment than He did in all His sermons combined.

57-What's popular isn't always right, and what is right isn't always popular.

58-If we are to know the God of the universe, we must first come to an understanding of "the man from Galilee."

59-If you are trainable and teachable, an amazing transformation can take place in Christ.

60-Greatness, godliness, and goodness are not geographical.

61-Let us never forget that Jesus began His earthly ministry as a little boy in a small town.

62- The same water that destroyed Noah's world, delivered Noah's family. The same water that leveled Noah's earth, lifted Noah's loved ones above the destruction. The same water that slaughtered the inhabitants of Noah's time, saved Noah's wife and children and their wives from death.

63- A mortal is immortal until his work on earth is done.

64- The average Church congregation today sounds more like a crowd at an auction with the song leader as the auctioneer than a group gathered to pay homage to the Living God.

13.

A STRESS-FREE CHURCH IN A STRESSFUL TIME

I have argued for years that I know nothing of "stress" because I have never been stressed out over anything. I even bragged and boasted that I would never experience what Chuck Swindoll once called a "stress" fracture of the soul. There are those in the medical profession that claim that 70% of all illness is stress related. I laughed at such things until 2017. That year my father died in February, then my only son of 39 died in April from a very aggressive lung and liver cancer. My wife and I took care of Scott the last six months of his life, the final five in our home, the parsonage of the Emmanuel Baptist Church of Ellsworth, Maine. By August of 2017, I was diagnosed with Type 2 diabetes and a hernia. My doctor thinks the hernia was from lifting and tugging on my son for the last three months of his life, and the diabetes was from the stress of the whole affair. On top of the two departures there was also my mother-in-law's failing health and her constant needs being supplied by my wife and me. She passed in November. I was tired and exhausted, as was my wife, and for the first time in my 67 years I began to think maybe I was feeling the effects of stress.

The so-called experts tell me that the average human desires to be in control, but when they run into uncontrollable situations or circumstances, sometimes there is an emotional fracture, one's physical health will suffer, and they get tired mentally, resulting in stress. Being a pastor for 47 years, I have also seen a spiritual tiredness develop in others, and by the time 2017 ended I saw that same tiredness in my wife and me. The constant state of alert caring for my father, my son, and my mother-in-law had broken down my immune system. My body and mind were reacting to the external and internal pressures that were building, and, for a time one can cope, can cope with anything, but eventually fatigue and exhaustion take over. The modern word is "burnout," a symptom caused by prolonged stress with no appreciative time to relax, revive, or renew, exactly what happened to my wife and me for nearly a year. Periodically, I would lay claim to the promise that my God wouldn't give me more than I could handle (I Corinthians 10:13), and that with each day the Lord would provide the strength for me to get through (Deuteronomy 33:25). He did, but little did I know what the stress of the situations was doing to me physically.

I have also learned in my search for the answer for stress, that often expectations are responsible for "stress" fractures in one's life. From the first day (October 1, 2016) to the last day of our son's life (April 1, 2017), we prayed, believed, hoped that Scott would get a medical cure. In the end he got a heavenly cure. I had for years been able to visit people like Scott, pray for them, and revisit them another day, but was always able to walk away for a period between visits. We were warned from the first month of our ordeal that a 24/7 involvement would affect everything in our lives if we were determined to care for our son ourselves (which we did). Not knowing the effect, we pressed on and would do it again, but little did we realize the toll it would take on my wife and my life to this day in my seventieth year. I learned for the first time what an In-your-face trial was like. One of the reasons I have given for living a stress-free ministry is the ability to walk away from the church, from the problems of the church, from the lives of my parishioners, and go home. My dear wife has made a sanctuary for me in the houses we have lived in, and with that constant source of refreshment I have been able to survive 47 years in the work. With Scott's 24/7 care, there was no relief, no break, no reprieve from the anguish and agony of watching our son slowly die a painful and debilitating death. Can you spell "s-t-r-e-s-s?"

As the minutes, hours, days, weeks, and months passed, I ignored the signs of stress, shortness between my wife and I, anxiety, indecision, doubt, and fear. Coleen and I experienced periods of insomnia, depression, and despair. The first three weeks were the worse for me because I didn't know what I could do, and I am a doer. We drove to North Carolina to be with Scott, and it took us three weeks to get him home to Maine. Once we got back to familiar surroundings, I was a lot better, but each day brought its own set of challenges and difficulties which would raise the stress level in our lives. In some ways Scott was the least stressed out. My boy had a wonderful accepting spirit, and his days as a combat driver in Iraqi and Afghanistan for three years groomed him to face death and dying on a daily basis, but for his mother and I the situation was different as we maneuvered through the "mine fields" of doctor's appointments, emergency room visits, chemotherapy, and terrible pain that no manmade medicine could touch. We wanted Scott to be pain free, but his cancer wouldn't allow that, so there was not a moment that was stress free for us, that is, except for the one area in our lives that remained the same.

It was during that six-month walk "through the valley of the shadow of death" (Psalm 23:4) that we had a stress-free experience with our "church of a lifetime." What happened between October 2016 and April 2017 had happened before. From January 2005 to September of that year I shared my wife's battle with breast cancer with the Emmanuel Baptist Church. They were exceptional then, and they were exceptional throughout Scott's tribulation. Not once after we shared with them about our son's cancer, did they add one moment of "stress" on the situation. They were helpful, caring, and supportive. From beginning to the end, and even after the end, they only uplifted and encouraged. After Scott's death they allowed Coleen and I to go on a three-week sabbatical to the Jersey Shore and California to rest and recover. They never hurried us back into the reins of responsibility; their "joy of the Lord" became our "strength!" (Nehemiah 8:9) They believed in the *"thou shalt rest"* of Exodus 34:21, especially when they realized that after we got back we would have to start dealing with Opal, Coleen's mother, another seven-month ordeal. They also believed in the philosophy of "man is like a bow, the stronger by being unbent!" No bow can stay strung all the time, and no life can either. Periodically, we all need to be "unbent" for a while. Even Jesus instructed His disciples to *"Come . . . apart"* (Mark 6:31) before they came apart! That is good advice anytime.

I myself had believed for years that I could spend all my emotional, mental, and physical resources, and God would somehow fill my resource bucket miraculously. There was a purpose behind Him setting one day a week aside "to rest." The Almighty even rested Himself to set the example when in reality He doesn't need rest. To be stress-free you must get your rest. You must have a change of pace (getting away from monotony and routine) every once in a while. You must seek leisure when you can, and, as I have learned through this first trauma with "stress," the older you get the more often you must get away, go away, and be away from the things that cause stress. The good news for me is that isn't my primary occupation. I know and have known pastors who live and work in a stressful church, but not me. Granted, there were churches in my past in which I did, but I didn't know it at the time. I was a machine when I started in the pastorate, but the older I get I realize this machine needs a break or it will break. Many years ago I did a series of messages on Elijah's "stress in distress" over the refusal of the children of Israel (I Kings 18–19) to accept Jehovah over Baal despite the miracle on Mount Carmel. I now realize Elijah's biggest problem was he didn't have a flock like the Emmanuel Baptist Church!

14.

JUST ANOTHER MEMBER?

When did the Christian Church come up with the idea that one church member was more important than another? Yet, this is the prevailing belief of many in the Church as I pastor through my seventieth year of life. Surely, the pastor is more important than the janitor or the Sunday school teacher more important than the lady that prays at home because her health is too frail to allow her to go to the Wednesday Night Prayer Meeting. And isn't the missionary in China more important, holding a higher position, than the postman that witnesses as he delivers the mail? For my 47 years in the pastorate, I have never thought of myself as other than another church member. Granted, I teach and preach the Word of God, but I believe the ladies that cook for a church supper are just as important. Recently, I read an article written by Vance Havner for a book he called <u>Rest for the Weary</u> in 1956 (I was five) in which he brings up this topic in a very unique way, and I quote:

> I had been typing away at an article and now it was completed. Exultingly I went into the kitchen and announced to my lady there, "I've finished my piece." Just as triumphantly she replied, "I've finished my pie!" Now pieces in the study and pies in the kitchen go together. Creative folk who write manuscripts are sometimes wont to look down upon culinary artists who do up meals. And cooks sometimes poke fun at long-haired dreamers who frame essays but cannot fry an egg. But whether poems or pies, whichever our specialty, the Cult of Study and the Cult of the Stove need each other. Pieces would soon languish if there were no pies. And life is more than the meat-man, for man does not live by bread alone!

This is exactly what I am getting at in this "threescore and ten" challenge. This concept is Biblical as seen in Paul's instruction to the Church: *"Nay, much more those members of the body, which seem to be more feeble, are necessary: and those members of the body, which we think to be less honourable, upon these we bestow more abundant honor; and the uncomely parts have more abundant comeliness."* (I Corinthians 12:22–23) When did these competitions and comparisons begin in the Church, and why?

I would like to call this trend in Christianity "the Mary and Martha syndrome." You must remember the classic visit of the Lord to the home of Martha. If not, let me remind you of it: *"Now it came to pass, as they went, that He entered into a certain village: and a certain woman named Martha received Him into her house. And she had a sister called Mary, which also sat at Jesus' feet, and heard His Word. But Martha was cumbered about much serving, and came to Him, and said, Lord, doest thou not care that my sister hath left me to serve alone? Bid her therefore that she help me. And Jesus answered and said unto her, Martha, Martha, thou art careful and troubled about many things: but one thing is needful: and Mary hath chosen that good part, which shall not be taken away from her."* (Luke 10:38–42) I believe many misunderstand this story and the lesson Jesus would teach us. First, we must put this into historical context and be reminded that in Jesus' day a woman's place was in the kitchen, and that fixing a meal for a guest like Jesus was the best job, a honored task. It really was Mary who chose the lesser duty (a duty we see today as just the opposite), the best of the best, sitting at the feet of Jesus. I would have you note Mary's life for all three times (Luke 10:39, John 11:32, and John 12:3) she is found in the Gospel text, she is found at the feet of Jesus. Martha wasn't reprimanded for working, but gently rebuked for worrying.

I believe what Jesus was saying was "don't look down on your sister because she has chosen another way of serving." Martha was meticulous; Mary was meditative. Martha prepared a feast; Mary prepared Jesus' feet for burial (John 12:7). Mary could have written on her talks with Jesus, while Martha could have written on the meals she fixed for Jesus. There are those that minister in the kitchen and those that minister in the living room, and neither is more important than the other. We are not to judge which is more important. That is the lesson from Jesus' encounter with Martha to me, and I believe we as a Church must recognize that whoever or whenever they do anything for the Lord, it is a worthy deed and worth honoring. So why do we honor the soul winner, but not the seamstress? Why do we recognize the evangelist, but not the electrician? As I write this article in my church office, there are two men downstairs working on remodeling the Sunday School rooms and fellowship hall. Hidden away, watched by none, they are laboring so we might have a better facility to carry on the ministries of the Emmanuel Baptist Church. Bob and Bud are doing something for the Lord I can't do, and, to me, more important than this very article. Yet, they are the point of this chapter, a church in which each member does what they do, no better than another, no more important than another, just members working together for the honor and glory of God, whether using a computer or a carpenter's saw!

I have tried throughout my ministry to just be another member of a local church (five of them now for me). Granted, my job requires me to be more out front than most, more visible, and sometimes more recognizable, but none of those things makes me more important. I believe I have mentioned this before, but I feel it fits here as well and that being the story of Dorcas the seamstress (Acts 9:36–39). The church at Joppa needed her back because her ministry was vital to the health of the local assembly. Each side can overdo it, whether the eating or drinking, or the super spiritual that has their heads in heaven while their bodies are still on earth. Jesus always taught a balance. He even took time to eat. He thought eating was important enough that twice He finished preaching and fed the multitudes. I am convinced that sometimes Jesus is more honored at the dinner table when a father says grace than sometimes in the church when the preacher messes up the sermon. Jesus wasn't all about people sitting at His feet. Did He not eat with publicans and sinner, too? Did He not eat with his two discouraged disciples on the Road to Emmaus before He revealed Himself? After Matthew was called to be a disciple, wasn't the first thing that happened a supper? This idea that Mary was right and Martha was wrong is wrong, or Martha right and Mary wrong is wrong!

I believe that we will have to wait until the Great Bema Seat Judgment (II Corinthians 5:10) to have this matter fully settled, but as for here and now I believe what the Lord taught, and Paul confirmed, is that one member of the Church is no greater than another member of the Church. There should be no positions like popes and presidents and cardinals and potentates; people who need their rings kissed and their names honored; who need to be bowed to and recognized as "the most reverent doctor." But I am convinced that along with the janitor (our janitor Steve was also in this building as I wrote this article on a late Friday afternoon) and the usher and all the humble folks that go about their ministries while the celebrity pastor and the recognized missionary and the honored evangelist get the spotlight. The cooks and the seamstresses and the carpenters are in line for honors when we get over there. I am also convinced that in that day "they" and not "me" will get the greater honor. I will be on the back row and they on the front row!!!

15.

WHAT I HAVE LEARNED ABOUT MONEY IN SEVENTY YEARS

To say I am an expert on **"money"** affairs in the church would be an overstatement, but I have for 47 years, like most preachers before me and many pastors after me, had to deal with the reality and necessity of "money." God knew long before **"money"** was created in the economics of man that this would be the norm and normal dealings of mankind because He does give us a load of lessons about **"money"** in the best money management book ever written, the Bible. Surprised I didn't read Dave Ramsey or one of a host of so-called Christian "moneymen?" And no, " *... the love of money is the root of all evil...* " (I Timothy 6:10) is not the only verse in the Holy Writ that deals with **"money"** issues. Add to that my nearly 70 years of experience with money matters.

As soon as the ancient people groups after the flood stopped their lives of wandering (Genesis 11:9) and began to settle in agricultural communities, a system of barter and trade resulted in the creation of forms of currency that would eventually be called **"money."** In the Old Testament this kind of currency was usually in exchanges of livestock as in the case of Abraham in Egypt (Genesis 12:16). In the days of the kings King Mesha of Moab paid his taxes (called tribute in those days) to the king of Judah in the form of 100,000 sheep and 100,000 rams (II Kings 3:4). Grain, oil, and wine were also used in this way as King Solomon traded these items to the king of Tyre for lumber to build the Temple and his palace (I Kings 5:11). Perhaps, the earliest form of money mentioned in the Scriptures was Jacob's sons going down into Egypt with "*... bundles of money...*"

(Genesis 42:35) to buy grain. Most scholars believe this was probably a set of metal rings (copper or bronze or silver or gold) tied together with strings. Silver was such a common instrument for trading that the Hebrew word for silver came to mean "**money**." (Genesis 17:13) A history of "**money**" in the Bible can be clearly examined through a Bible dictionary, but our purpose is not a historical exercise, but a practical exercise into the proper Biblical concept of what is our responsibility in relationship with "**money**." Check the Bible before you check Dave Ramsey!

In a world that revolves around "**money**," where "**money**" is the end all for many, it is important that we as Christians learn the Scriptural precepts that will help us deal properly with the "**money**" the Lord gives us to live on and give. In this article I will not be speaking on refinancing, mortgages, loans, payment strategies, retirement funds, or a myriad of other topics most in the so-called Christian Money Advisors deal with. In my personal opinion "**money**" already gets enough press, and we actually spend too much time debating, discussing, and deliberating the topic of "**money**." Does "**money**" touch every aspect of our lives? Yes, but it shouldn't be the dictator of our lives, but, sadly, for too many people, including Christians, it does. "**Money**" is just another category in which we must recognize that God is the owner of all that we have because it is God that gives all blessings (Ephesians 1:3), including "**money**" blessings. I remember when I came across this amazing concept in Deuteronomy: "*And thou say in thine heart, My power and the might of mine hand hath gotten me this wealth.* **But thou shalt remember the Lord thy God: for it is He that giveth thee power to get wealth,** *that He may establish His covenant which He sware unto thy fathers, as it is this day.*" (Deuteronomy 8:17–18) Simple, but clear; it is God and God alone that gives any man or woman the ability to gain "**money**." I know this philosophy is not preached or proclaimed today in this self-made man environment, but I believe in this Biblical concept established long ago in the Book of Moses that all "**money**" comes from God and, therefore, it is all His in the end, not Bill Gates, the King of Saudi Arabia, or the Rockefellers.

As with Jesus famous parables, our "**money**" is simply given to us in trust: "*For the kingdom of heaven is as a man traveling into a far country, which called his own servants, and delivered unto them his goods. And unto one he gave five talents . . .* " (Matthew 25:14–30) We are those servants that have received that which the Good Lord would entrust us with, including "**money**." Our role is manager of the Lord's "**money**." We are to be "stewards" of the Lord silver! I hear it all the time when people don't want to give to the Lord's work that the Lord doesn't need our "**money**." We have it all wrong because it isn't our "**money**." This selfish, self-centered world has twisted the concept of cash into a belief that the "**money**" we possess is somehow ours to begin with. I made it, it's mine. It isn't because God still "owns the cattle on a thousand hills and the wealth in every mine!" (Psalms 50:10) When will we come to realize that we are just custodians of Christ's cash? (Matthew 25:18); that we are just caretakers of Christ's currency? That He is the source of all our silver deposits and God of all our gold reserves! Only when we recognize this simple statute can we then be instructed in the Biblical standards of spread sheets, "**money**" exchange, and proper scriptural giving. The world will never learn these lessons because they can't accept the truth clearly stated in Deuteronomy, but Christians should. Why is it we are going to the world with "**money**" questions instead to God? Dave Ramsey is a Christian and he at least consults the Bible!

I believe the first standard we must recognize in God's money management book is the highlighted and underlined truth, **Debt-free living is God's ultimate standard in "money" management:** *"Render therefore to all their dues: tribute to whom tribute is due; custom to whom custom is due; fear to whom fear; honour to whom honour. Owe no man anything . . . "* (Romans 13:7–8) We have too many believers living beyond their means. Remember, if we believe that it is God that gives us what we need (Matthew 6:25–34), then if He gives the means to have something or do something, then we are right to have and do it, but if He doesn't, then do we? Christians are in debt; churches are in debt. Why? Because they couldn't trust God to wait on God. We jump ahead of God believing He will pay for our debts after the fact. I will admit I swallowed this philosophy in my early years, both in relationship to my family and the churches I pastored. My problem, as with most, I was listening to the so-called experts in finance instead of reading my Bible. The old teaching of "pay as you go" got lost in the world as well as the church and the Christian community. We are too impatient to wait for God's window to open, so we kick down the door and rush into debt not realizing it is wrong and unscriptural; immoral and unrighteous in so many aspects.

No one that is financially bound to a bank, a neighbor, or another family member can truly be free. If you owe somebody or some institution something, you are their slave until you get out from under that debt. Financial bondage is the new norm today, and most people, including Christians, willfully and wants to get that "**money**" now, and there are always those willing and ready to enslave you. The effect of this slavery on marriages, families, churches, and individuals only eternity can and will tell. And the tragedy is that like with Judas we are willing to sell our financial freedom for something so cheap; a boat, a four-wheeler, a ten-day vacation in Mexico, a fancy house, an expensive car, a Super Bowl ticket. I believe that not only will every word we speak be judged someday (Matthew 12:36–37), but every dollar as well.

We waste our words, and we waste the Lord's **"money"** when we fail to account for what we buy. Paul told us: "*So then every one of us shall give account of himself to God.*" (Romans 14:12) When was the last time you thought of such an audit in relationship to **"money."** You see, if the **"money"** was yours, there would be no accounting, why would there be? My wife was the office manager of an engineering firm. She was accountable for all money that came in and out in that business. Why? Because it wasn't her money, it was the "capital" of the business. For her to spend the company money on personal items would have been a crime, so why can't we as believers believe that spending our Lord's **"money"** improperly wouldn't be a crime of the highest order. I was brought up in this simple truth. I remember my first dollar ever earned. My grandfather asked me to work in his field picking rocks before the spring planting of potatoes. My wages were a dollar a day. True to his word, at the end of my first day of work he got out his wallet and gave me a dollar, and with that dollar two wise words from my first financial adviser--tithing and saving. Give the Lord back a tenth and put the rest in the bank. "*Will a man rob God? Yet ye have robbed me. But ye say, wherein have we robbed thee? In tithes and offerings. Ye are cursed with a curse: for ye have robbed me, even this whole nation. Bring ye all the tithes into the storehouse, that there may be meat in mine house, and prove me now herewith, saith the Lord of host, if I will not open the windows of heaven, and pour you out a blessing, that there shall not be room enough to receive it.*" (Malachi 3:8–10) It starts with the tithe, the first fruits if you will, the first check you cut before you pay your other bills and spend the rest of the **"money."** I learned well from my grandfather. If you give God his tithe and offerings, you will always have enough to pay the rest. I am one that doesn't believe the only requirement for our giving is 10% because that is the tithe (Genesis 28:22), but an offering is above and beyond the tithe and that amount is between you and God as He leads. I still remember Mother breaking my dollar bill into change so I could put a dime in the offering plate at the First Baptist Church of Perham the next Sunday. I believe it was in those early days of my life that I was taught not to hang on too tightly to "**money**;" that I was just a channel, a canal for the Lord's cash (Mark 12:41–44). Is that the reason I care little about "**money**," whether I have it or not. I know those who can't stand not having money in their pockets on a daily basis. Most days in my year there is literally no money in my wallet. Only on special occasions when I know I will need money, do I carry cash. It is my way of lessening the importance of "**money**" in my life and dealings and resisting the lure of lucre!

For me, it is all about our attitude about "**money**." This simple statute is key: *"No man can serve two masters: for either he will hate the one, and love the other; or else he will hold to the one, and despise the other. Ye cannot serve God and mammon."* (Matthew 6:24) This is the precept that helps us understand Paul exhortation against *"the love of money."* (I Timothy 6:10) God will have no rivals, including gold. God will have no equals, including the exchequer. "**Money**" is a strong and tempting adversary, and we must always see it as such. Like a fire under control it can be useful, but, allowed to get out of control, it will quickly become an inferno uncontrollable. Paul uses the words *"temptation"* and *"snare"* and *"foolish"* and *"hurtful lusts"* and *"drown"* and *"destruction"* and *"perdition"* (I Timothy 6:9) in the context of *"the love of money."* I am happy that Paul says that only *"some coveted after."* (I Timothy 6:10) We don't have to become a slave to silver; we don't have to be trapped by treasury bonds; we don't have to love filthy lucre (I Timothy 3:3). We can use money instead of letting money use us.

I have come to believe through my study of the Bible that God gives man money so that man can use that money for God's glory and mankind's good. Have you ever considered what you are supposed to do with your "extra money?" Most people, including Christians, will say, "What extra money?" Granted, there are some that live from week to week, paycheck to paycheck, but most of us have more than we need. Be honest. Some say put it in the bank for a rainy day. Save, save, save is the word of the Christian advisers including my grandfather, remember? I am not against saving, and I believe it is a precept of the Bible, but not in the standard of the man who put his lord's money in the ground (Matthew 25:24–30). We know of his fate! I have come to believe in investment, not saving. Remember what Jesus said. *"Thou oughtest therefore to have put my money to the exchangers, and then at my coming I should have received mine own with usury."* (Matthew 25:27) Now, before the trust fund managers and the hedge funds directors get too excited, I don't believe the Lord was talking about your businesses. Remember, the rich farmer (Luke 12:16–21) did just that and was condemned. The key for me is this principle from that parable: *"So is he that layeth up treasure for himself, and is not rich toward God."* (Luke 12:21) We must be careful where we invest the Lord's money, and I believe I know where the best investment it.

I believe the best bank is the Bank of Heaven; I believe the best trust fund is to trust in the Lord; and I believe the best insurance is in The Rock. Jesus was clear about **"money,"** it's use and purpose: *"Lay not up for yourselves treasures* [including money] *upon earth, where moth and rust doth corrupt, and where thieves break through and steal* [do you know the number one item that is stolen most on this planet?]: *but lay up for yourselves treasures in heaven, where neither moth nor rust doth corrupt, and where thieves do not break through nor steal: for where your treasure is, there will your heart be also."* (Matthew 6:19–21) After you meet your daily needs and the needs of your family, the best use of your money is to invest it into something that is eternal, that will give you a heavenly return. When we have a willingness to give back to the Lord His money, then we will be rewarded in eternity, and there is no bank or investment firm that can beat the benefits. This is how the Christian gives testimony of the Lord's ownership of his or her **"money."** And when we give *"cheerfully and bountifully"* (II Corinthians 9:6–8), God will reward us handsomely!

Whether we are talking about lucre, wampum, cash, or coinage, the Bible explains without a doubt that **"money"** is something to be taken seriously. We are not to take it lightly thinking that there will be no accountability for our hard-earned cash. Each dollar, every cent, will be asked about in the great judgment of the saints (II Corinthians 5:10). So, the next time you go to your favorite coffee spot and put five bucks down, think if that investment would be better used in an outreach in India. Are you simply building bigger bank accounts for a day of retirement that isn't supposed to come until heaven? Will you leave behind to someone funds that you would have better managed? Then why not plan for that. I love the story of George Muller, the great German Christian who did the bulk of his work in the orphanages of England. He was the man who prayed daily the needs of thousands of abandoned children. It is said that over the years the Lord gave him millions and millions of dollars, but at his death he only had a few dollars in the bank and no property or other possessions. I believe he had figured out God's plan for **"money"** and the use of it. I will close where I started with Paul's classic exhortation, "... *which while some coveted after, THEY HAVE ERRED FROM THE FAITH, and pierced themselves through with many sorrows, but thou, O man of God, flee these things* . . . ." (I Timothy 6:10–11) **"Money"** can be dangerous to your spiritual health, and **"money"** will certainly bring more sorrows than blessings if improperly handled. Use it; every penny, every dime, every quarter, every dollar to the glory of God and to the good of your fellowman.

16.

THE DANDELION DOCTRINE

JUST RECENTLY A YOUNG missionary from our church serving in China was home to report on her first ten years in that fabled land through a new mission's organization called Campus Target. During her presentation she made mention of the title of this article in my ongoing look back at seventy years of life and fifty years of ministry. I will admit I have known of dandelions since birth, but I had never heard of the spiritual concept Alison Chamberland was speaking of. As Campus Target was re-evaluating its outreach to college age Chinese a few years ago, they realized that their original master plan wasn't working as well as they hoped. As they re-thought their approach and method of reaching the young people on China's university campuses, they were introduced the "the dandelion doctrine." Before I explain it in a Biblical sense, let me share something I wrote a number of years ago about the dandelions of my youth. The application will become clearer.

> On a recent visit to my boyhood homestead in northern Maine, I experienced a taste of spring. Despite being ten days before Thanksgiving, there was already a few inches of snow surrounding the old set of farm buildings and homes on the Blackstone Road in Perham, Maine. I had stopped off to visit my 95-year-old grandmother (she passed in 2003), during which time her youngest son Paul showed me some pictures he had taken of the field across the lane that past spring, a field of yellow. My Uncle Paul was (he passed in 2009) an amateur photographer, but a good one. What he captured on film was a sea of dandelions covering the five-acre field. He had picked a bright day for his pictures and had walked halfway into the field taking

the photograph looking back to Gram's house (built in 1922 by my grandfather for his new bride) with the old 1930s potato house in the background. Over half the picture, however, was mustard-yellow dandelions, the color of spring in my hometown, and in my heart. Inspired by this homestead reflection, I returned to my home on the coast of Maine and did a bit of research. I discovered that the name dandelion comes from the French *dent de lion* meaning lion's tooth (Jesus is known as the Lion of Judah in Revelation 5:5). The name was given because of the tooth-like design of the dandelion's leaves. As my grandmother and I talked of Paul's picture, she spoke of the time when my Grandfather Carroll tried to destroy every dandelion on the farm. They were an enemy of good farming, and useless, but to Grandmother Glenna they were food. How Grandmother loves dandelion greens! A bitter weed to most, including this writer, to people like my grandmother and my father (he passed in 2017) it was their first meal in the spring. I thought as Grandmother talked of the value of dandelions that my grandfather (he passed in 1975) would be upset that the few plants that survived his grasp had now multiplied to cover a field just across the road from his beloved home. For me, though I don't like eating them, I stand firmly on the side of those that love the golden-yellow flower. Since my childhood, I have loved to watch the drab of late winter turn yellow with the advent of spring. I stand again on the threshold of nature's hardest season, but my mind through Uncle Paul's photographs have refocused my memory on the spring that is sure to follow when the waysides and roadsides will once again explode in yellow. Despite man's attempts to get rid of this weed including my grandfather (and I have just learned my uncle) that invaded their front lawn and back lawn, the dandelion has remained and will remain because of its unique method of survival. One author on the subject put it this way: "When the fruit is ripe, the head opens into a globe of parachuted fruits, which a puff of wind will scatter far and wide." The dandelion was created by the Creator to survive; it has and it does! Man has discovered over the years a rainbow of artificial colors that brighten our homes and lives. I for one have come to believe that if you want real color, you must take a trip outdoors. My wife often laughs at my basic color ability because I rarely get a shade of color right. Yellow is yellow! A good example of the yellow is a field of dandelions on the Blackstone Road in Perham. Every spring, after the grass turns green, yellow begins to blend its way into the fields and lawns of Perham with the rebirth of the dandelion. Along the Blackstone

Road grows the biggest and most beautiful dandelions in the world in my opinion. For those who see the dandelion only as a weed, think again. They are God's spring flower. Be honest now, wasn't a bouquet of dandelions the first flowers you ever gave to a sweetheart when you were a child? Wasn't it a bunch of dandelions you first presented to your mother or grandmother? Who of us hasn't picked a dandelion and placed it under the chin of a friend to see if the yellow of the sun will not reflect off the yellow of the dandelion? It is sad to me that people spend so much time and money trying to eradicate spring's prettiest flower. (And now I see a wonderful illustration of "the Gospel of Christ.")

What Campus Target and my young friend Alison realized was in order to make their mission a success, they had to take on the characteristics of a "dandelion." In China the gospel is a "weed" to the Communist Party. Since the late 1940s, they have tried to eradicate the pure teaching of Christ, yet, the most populous nation in the world still has a thriving Christian population. Why? The Dandelion Doctrine is to blame as I see now. Who of us hasn't seen the single dandelion of spring sprout through the cold ground against a warm foundation? Yet as the bright colorful plant matures and then fades, the petals turn a whitish color. Then on a breezy day in late spring a puff of wind sends the scores of fine petals to flight. Where they go only God knows, but what we know is by the next spring the one dandelion has multiplied on the side lawn. Give those dandelions a few more years and they will have covered that same side lawn just like the field across from my grandparent's homestead.

Such was the method of the early Church as the small numbers that followed Christ turned into thousands (Acts 2:41 and Acts 4:4) within days of Pentecost. When the Church scattered (Acts 8:1) after the persecution of Stephen (Acts 7), the Church seemed to appear everywhere in the region. I like the way Doctor Luke described it in Acts 11:19: *"Now they which were scattered abroad upon the persecution that arose about Stephen travelled as far as Phenice, and Cyprus, and Antioch, preaching the Word to none but the Jews only."* Campus Target is finding that when they convert a college student, that student leaves for their home at the end of the semester in another part of China. Now, a new seed is planted resulting in a cluster of Christians in an entirely new area. Instead of trying to create a congregation on campus, they are setting the seeds of the dandelion free to blow wherever the Spirit of God directs (John 3:8). I have known of this method all my spiritual life and have been actively involved in prompting its spiritual truth, but now I have a name for it: "the dandelion doctrine." Like the dandelion, the Gospel was created to survive and thrive in the most hostile areas in the world including China. Recently, I was talking to Jessie Lofton, the leader of the children's program known as Child Evangelism Fellowship, about North Korea and the dandelion Gospel that has reached there. (Interestingly, Jessie is another young lady from our church's youth program where Jessie and Alison were in youth group together and now they are spreading the Gospel around the world-they are our dandelions.)

17.

A RELIGION OR THE RELIGION

Alexander Schmemann once wrote: "In the process of replacing the old religions, Christianity became a religion." I, for years of my lifetime that has now reached 70 years, have tried to convince people that Christianity was never intended to be another religion. Jesus never came to institute another religion, but THE FAITH. His intent was never to establish a competing religion, but a new way of living with a newfound relationship with His Father. A 19th century American historian and theologian, Philip Schaff, explained this concept this way.

> That the Christians in the apostolic age erected special houses of worship is out of the question . . . As the Saviour of the world was born in a stable, and ascended to heaven from a mountain, so His apostles and their successors down to the third century, preached in the streets, the markets, on mountains, in ships, sepulchres, eaves, and deserts, and in the homes of their converts. But how many thousands of costly churches and chapels have since been built and are constantly being built in all parts of the world to the honor of the crucified Redeemer, who in the days of His humiliation had no place of His own to rest His head!

Why the 4rd century church fell in love with stone and mortar we know not, but I suspect it had to do with trying to keep up with the other religions. One of our fatal flaws has been this unexplained fascination with keeping up with the pagans, and we have certainly kept up and long surpassed them in promoting our Faith in brick and glass! **In our attempt to establish the religion we have simple become just another religion.**

I have become convinced over the years that God himself isn't against buildings for buildings sake. Did not God instruct Moses to make a building, even if it was simply a fancy tent, in which to seek Him? (Exodus 25:8) Did not Jehovah instruct Solomon to construct the first Temple on Mount Moriah? (II Chronicles 3:1) However, over time the Jew had a tendency to worship the building versus the Lord. Anything connected with God or a miracle of God was open for worship. For me, a case in point is "the brazen serpent" of the wilderness wandering (Numbers 21:9). You would have thought the Israelites would have gotten rid of this accursed object after the terrible plague of snakes, but instead of throwing it away they carted it along with them to Canaan. Then someone, many generations later (700 years later) kept it until they began to worship it. *"He* [Hezekiah] *removed the high places, and brake the images, and cut down the groves, and* **brake in pieces the brasen serpent that Moses** *had made: for unto those days the children of Israel did burn incense to it: and he called it Nehushtan."* (II Kings 18:4) I suggest to you we have done the same with the relics of our faith, especially our chapels, churches, and cathedrals, but for any serious student of the Life of Christ, Jesus came to end the practice of buildings.

In the teachings of Jesus and the instructions of Paul, the new building was His body (Ephesians 1–2) and the new temple was the Christian (I Corinthians 3:16–17). A careful look into the use of the word "church," "temple," or "the house of God," these terms are never used to speak of a building. Since childhood I have been instructed in the simple precept that **"the church is not the steeple but the people!"** Oh, we know the doctrine, but rare are those who live in the reality of this theology. It seems this new concept started around 190 AD when a famous church father, Clement of Alexandria, coined the phrase "go to church." The seed was planted, but there is no Biblical evidence for such a phrase. In the 114 times the word "church" is found in the Bible, it is always used to describe an assembled group of believers. Even the English word "church" is derived from a Greek word that means "belonging to the Lord." Only after centuries of use was the meaning of the word changed. I have come to believe through my study of church history that even Clement was not referring to a church building when he wrote of "going to church." Paul's admonition of not forsaking the assembly of ourselves together (Hebrews 10:25) was in reference to the house-churches of the early Church. The New Testament verifies this teaching in such references as Colossians 4:15 and Philemon 2.

So, when did we make the change from house churches to holy cathedrals? I am convinced that when Jesus came to earth He not only came to take away the temple building, but the Levitical priesthood and the sacred sacrifices. For me, the teachings are clear that the priesthood would go to the believer (I Peter 2:5), not a selected group, and the sacrifices would change (Hebrews 13:15). For nearly three hundred years the new Faith didn't resemble any religion. They sometimes were simply known as "the way" (Acts 9:2) with no established hierarchy or sacrifices. This all changed when the Roman Catholic part of Christianity thought it could compete with the world's religions by doing these older religions one better. Think with me. They did it in three ways: first, by establishing a priesthood of celibate men making them special, erecting sacred structures, and turning the Lord's Table and baptism into a sacrifice. Soon we were burning incense like the pagan, celebrating our holiest days on their holidays (Christmas and Easter), and taking heathen practices and simply changing the object of their worship to Christ. In the menagerie that is now Christianity, what part looks like what Christ intended or the early Church practiced? And for those Protestants who think we changed everything because of the Great Reformation, I would have you note that we just changed practices. We still have our church building, some of them more elaborate and fancier than even the Roman Catholics, and the priesthood of clergy and bishops and elders that rival the Romans. We might have gotten back to the true intent of the Lord's Table and baptism, but at times I wonder if they, too, are not just a ritual, a rite with little meaning to most Protestants.

For me, the crossroad event that changed everything was what happened in the 4th century, and I am talking about Emperor Constantine. I do believe the church building started before him (most Christian archeologist believe the first permanent church building was built in Dura-Europos in Syria about 232 AD), but Constantine would become the father of the church building. (Before he died Constantine would build nine churches in Rome itself, the famous Holy Sepulcher church in Jerusalem, and the Church of the Nativity in Bethlehem). Following his mother's (Helena) pilgrimage to Jerusalem in 327 AD, Constantine began erecting church buildings all over the empire rivaling anything the pagans had done before him. He would set the standard that the church would follow to this day. I would have you consider the edifices the mega-churches are constructing in America today. I have been to Constantine's churches in Jerusalem and Bethlehem, and I left thinking I had just come from pagan temples. There was nothing of my faith there, just another religion, I thought. When the Church began to look at its structures versus its Savior, a change and an influence in the worship took place. Can a person find a building in which the Lord is honored, respected, and worshiped, and maintain a proper spirit? Yes! I believe over the years I have ignored the building I was sitting in and worshiped my Savior in spirit and truth (John 4:24). It can be done, but we must watch carefully lest we see a religion versus the religion, and I mean by "the religion," the one and only way we are to know!

18.

THE COW PATH I NEVER FOLLOWED

Being a six-generation son of a farmer, I am always interested when I read something that reminds me of home and my boyhood. Having been a pastor for 47 years now, I am also interested when something comes along that combines my past with the purpose of my present--preaching (1966 to 2024). Recently, a poem by Sam Walter Foss converged the past with the present as I continue to understand and contemplate the meaning of "threescore and ten." Foss gave his interesting, philosophical poem the title of <u>The Calf Path</u>. I changed it a bit for the title of these thoughts. The reason will become clearer as you read on, but first Sam's words.

> One day, through the primeval wood, a calf walked home, as good calves should; but made a trail all bent askew, a crooked trail as all calves do.
> Since then three hundred years have fled, and, I infer, the calf is dead.
> But still be left behind his trail, and thereby hangs my moral tale.
> The trail was taken up next day by a lone dog that passed that way; and then a wise bell-wether sheep pursued the trail over vale and steep,
> and drew the flock behind him, too, as good bellwethers always do.
> And from that day, over hill and glade, through those old woods a path was made. And many men wound in and out, and dodged, and turned, and bent about
> and uttered words of righteous wrath because 'twas such a crooked path.
> But still they followed, do not laugh, the first migrations of that calf,

and through this winding wood-way stalked because he wobbled when he walked. This forest path became a lane, that bent, and turned, and turned again;

this crooked lane became a road, where many a poor horse with his load toiled on beneath the burning sun and travelled some three miles in one.

And thus a century and a half they trod the footsteps of that calf.

The years passed on in swiftness fleet, the road became a village street;

and this, before men were aware, a city's crowded thoroughfare;

and soon the central street was this of a renowned metropolis;

and men two centuries and a half trod in the footsteps of that calf.

Each day a hundred thousand rout followed the zigzag calf about;

and over his crooked journey went the traffic of a continent.

A hundred thousand men were led by one calf bear three centuries dead.

They follow still his crooked way, and lost one hundred years a day;

for thus such reverence is lent to well-established precedent.

A moral lesson this might teach, were I ordained and called to preach;

for men are prone to go it blind along the calf-paths of the mind,

and work away from sun to sun to do what other men have done.

They follow in beaten track, and out and in, and forth and back,

and still their devious course pursue, to keep the path that others do.

They keep the path a sacred groove, along which all their lives they move.

But how wise old wood-gods laugh, who saw the first primeval calf?

Ah! Many things this tale might teach, but I am not ordained to preach.

Naturally, Foss's poem quickly brought back the cow paths on the Blackstone homestead in northern Maine of my boyhood, distinct trails created by the constant flow of a large Holstein herd as they moved from pasture to milking shed, paths through the hundreds of acres of forest land from pasture to pasture, and tracks from here to there and there to here. Until I found this simple poem with a profound lesson, I never connected the similarities between a cow path and the current course of the Church, but I certainly see it now. It is a proper analogy, an important metaphor for us to learn, and I would like in this devotional on "threescore and ten" to highlight and underline the "moral lesson" because I have been ordained to preach (II Timothy 4:2).

One of the reasons I have missed this insightful observation is that I have never been a "cow path" walker. I have never followed another man's wake. When I was very early in the ministry, I came across this admonition from the pen of Paul in his epistle to the Romans: *"Yea, so have I strived to preach the gospel, not where Christ was named, lest I should build upon another man's foundation."* (Romans 15:20) I was raised in a family, a small community, and a denominational church where it would have been easy to follow a "cow's path." I was set to inherit the family farm started in 1861, but in 1969 I gave up all rights to it. I could have followed into the denomination of my forefathers and settled for an established fellowship with good perks, a good pension, and a good people, but in 1973 I left my home state to start a pioneer work in New Hampshire. I could have followed the denomination path, but for my 50 years in the pastorate I have chosen the independent churches, the out-of-the-way church (including a church on an island off the coast of Maine), and the unorthodox churches to satisfy my calling as a pastor/teacher. Even as a boy I wasn't much for following the established paths. I loved to cut across country and go where others feared to go. I still remember the early criticisms when I told "the cow path" people in my life that I was going to Australia for a summer. But nobody from Aroostook County had ever done such a thing before; it was off the path of the accepted travellers of the region. I went then, and I am still going. (My last trip off trail, out of the track, was to the Punjab in India.)

I hear it all the time that Christians are living by the Book, following the Bible to the letter, and being guided by the Holy Scriptures. Yet very few leave their comfort zone and actually follow the Lord's command to "go" (Matthew 28:19), "love" (Matthew 5:44), "give" (Matthew 5:42), "pray" (I Timothy 2:1-2), "assemble" (Hebrews 10:25), "forgive" (Ephesians 4:32), do I need to go on? We claim we do everything by the Word of God; that the New Testament is our guidebook; and that we will live and die by the Bible, yet, we fail to defend it (Jude 3) in the public arena. We rarely read it (Revelation 1:3) let alone study it (II Timothy 2:15). Let us be honest with ourselves. We are walking the old cow path just like the poem suggests more than we think. I still remember the early days of my calling into the pastorate when I began to examine the Bible in light of my starting a new work in Pembroke, New Hampshire. I was shocked to discover that most of how I was brought up in church wasn't even in the Bible. I had been walking and worshipping in a cow path trod by those who had started the Perham Baptist Church in the nineteenth century. I began to realize that tradition and custom had taken over, and the culture of Perham dictated more the Christianity of Perham than the Bible. What people wore, how they worshiped, and how they lived and acted was more like their founders than their Founder!

Early in my ministry I changed. I got off the old cow path and realized that I would be responsibility to God for what the Bible said. I began to believe what I believed from what I believed the Bible taught, not what I had been taught at Perham or at Bob Jones University, where I went to Bible school. I began to realize that I was to walk an untrodden path, that each of us has our own trail to go. The mistake throughout church history is the often-fatal spiritual flaw of following other men, even men like Calvin, Augustine, Luther—you get the picture. The church did it in the first century (I Corinthians 1:12), and we are doing it today (Jeremiah, Swindoll, Olsten, to name a few). Going it alone is tough and terrifying, but Jesus promised to be with us (Matthew 28:20).

19.

CLIMBING THE WRONG WALL

As I continue pastoring my current church on the coast of Maine into my 70th year, I have observed what is happening to the Christianity of my youth and the Church of my old age. I have come to the conclusion that many will one day come to the conclusion Joseph Campbell came to when he wrote, "There is perhaps nothing worse than reaching the top of the ladder and discovering that you're on the wrong wall!" Could this be a paraphrase of what Jesus said when He asked, "... *Nevertheless when the Son of man cometh, shall He find faith on the earth?*" (Luke 18:8)

I believe I am living in the age of a not-too-silent revolt in the Body of Christ where many are *"departing from the faith"* (I Timothy 4.1) or *"falling away from the faith"* (II Thessalonians 2:3). The old ways of doing church are dying, the old methods of worship have been pronounced dead, and the old Word is being paraphrased and translated to death. These revolutionaries have determined in order to get closer to God and God's first century pattern is to become more institutionalized, more denominationalized with more endless programs and promotions. We have more how-to-do-it seminars, more spiritual growth conferences, more radio and television programs than ever before, and, yet, year after year the average spiritual believer is getting sicker. Don't get me wrong. I believe that there are well-intentioned ministries and churches and organizations and institutions that are trying, but they are climbing the wrong ladder! Instead of the Church we have house churches, market-place churches, school churches, cyber churches, mega-churches, community churches, and a host of others that use the word "church," but are any of them really taking a meaningful step towards the true Church? Are we just repackaging? Are we just playing church? Are we just changing for changing sake? Have we placed our ladder against the wrong wall?

I have become convinced that we are making the same mistakes as our forefathers. Since my early twenties, I have been a student of Church History. I spent five winters actually sharing my finding with a small group of interested students. I have come to believe history, like prophecy (II Peter 1:20), is of no private interpretation. Get two historians in a room together, let them debate a piece of history, and you will get two opinions. Christianity is that difficult to discuss because it seems everybody has their own interpretation of how it used to be and how it should be. The tragedy to me is that most attempts to reform or revitalize the Church have only been "window-dressing." Pick a modern trend over my seventy years, and you will discover whether it is the mega-church trend, the seeker-friendly church trend, the satellite campus church trend, the contemporary church music trend, the small group trend, or the one service a week trend. The result is the same; it is only a trend. Remember the million-man march of the 1990s, Promise Keepers, only a trend. Don't get me wrong. I believe every one of these trends was probably motivated by a sincere heart seeking to help someone or a group of some ones to a better understanding of Jesus, but the result of these attempts is just more evidence to a dying world that we haven't got a clue what we are doing. Jesus was right when He concluded in his parable of the unjust servant, *". . . for the children of this world are in their generation wiser than the children of light."* (Luke 16:8)

The world puts the Church of God to shame because we have forgotten that we don't need the world or the world's techniques or methods to promote the Gospel of Christ. We don't need to set up our local churches on a Madison Avenue format, or a Wall Street (perhaps the wall most are climbing today) style of business! The Church was never intended to be a business, but a rescue mission. I feel the reason for this is that most church members are totally ignorant when it comes to how we got from the 1st century to the 21st century. I feel if we would only get back to the Bible and the Church's history, we would have enough to understand the difficulties we find ourselves in, and with the Spirit of God as our guide we could get the Church out of the mess that it is in. Without failure, a simple study of both will reveal clearly that most of what is called Christianity today and Churchianity today is man-made, the traditions of the "fathers." We have made the same mistake the Jewish people made with their faith. Over time the traditions of men become more important than the commandments of God. I have heard recently a phrase "doing church." The very sound of this makes me think of "works" versus faith. Works-based faith has been on a steady rise since I came into the pastorate 47 years ago. Granted, James admonishes us: *"But be ye doers of the Word, and not hears only, deceiving your own selves."* (James 1:22) Three times in church history "doing" became the model: the period when the church went from local based to central based in the days of Emperor Constantine; the century surrounding the Protestant Reformation (I am writing this article on the 500th anniversary of Martin Luther's famous 95-theses nailing); and the revivalist movements of the 18th and 19th century. Despite the passionate leaders and determined followers, most were ill-informed, emotion-based, and doctrinally weak.

I feel that the results of the last change set the pattern for what we see even to this day, but most Christians have lived in this new normal for so long they think it is the way it always has been, which is not true. Routine has become Biblical because that is all we have known, so, therefore, it must be the way Jesus did it, the way Paul did it. For me, the greatest crime of this "revivalist" movement is the truth that most learned just to go along for the ride. They got on the gospel wagon, they got on the gospel train, they go on the gospel horse, and went along for a ride. The Christian life was never intended to be a ride, but a walk (I John 2:6). People in Jesus day were on a ride until they realized they didn't like where the ride was taking them: *"But though He had done many miracles before them, yet they believed not on Him"* (John 12:37). As long as the boat ride was healing them, feeding them, and entertaining them, they were all for it, but the minute Jesus told them the end (the *". . . hard saying . . . "* (John 6:60), *". . . from that time many of his disciples went back, and walked no more with Him."* (John 6:66) That tells me they were only on a "ride." I have met so many in my walk with Christ that in the end proved they were only on a ride. It's easier to ride something you can get off easily as many are doing today (remember "falling away" and "departing away"); a walk is harder to change. I know there are those who would argue with me on this analogy, but for me the proof is in the results I have been witnessing for my entire lifetime. Despite the Billy Graham crusades, the constant "revivals" from church to church, and the flooding of the air waves with spiritual programing, our country is less spiritual today than half a century ago. Fewer people attend church consistently (my own State of Maine has the least population that attend church on Sunday), and faith as we use to know it has declined.

The tragedy is that the world has changed so we can't go back to the start of the Church (30 AD to 60 AD). Cultures have changed, and we are so far off-track now, it would take a Spirit-filled church-wide course correction to even get us close. For me, I am afraid that most in the Body of Christ do not want a correction; they are content on the rails they are on. I still believe if the Universal Church can't change, the Christian can, and you and I can come to know which ladder we are climbing and what wall we are on and that when the Lord does return there will be a few of us on the right ladder climbing the right wall!

20.

IS THE CHURCH A BUSINESS?

AMERICAN CHURCH HISTORY POSSESSES a great irony, and, for fundamentals, there is no greater irony than the church and business. It has been the work ethic of the average American that has made our nation a world-wide power to be reckoned with, both as a military and economic powerhouse. It has been our amazing economy that has led the earth into the greatest prosperity the world has ever seen, but has the church gone too far in embracing these business standards and worldly philosophies? Let us be honest with ourselves to recognize that American business and the American economy are talked about in sacred, not secular terms now. The successful businessman is seen as divine, the newest innovation as the next "savior" of the world, and Wall Street as the cathedral of worship to millions, and many of them are Christians. Religious revivals, "church planting," evangelism, the Christian school movement, modern mission's organizations, and the building of the modern mega-church, are all achieved today on the ethics of business practices. The business model requires a well laid out plan and well-defined definitions of growth and success. (Christ had one model: Go. See Matthew 28:19–20.) The business model is constantly tinkering with the mechanics, finding new efficiencies, and replacing anything which doesn't contribute to this model of success. (The Biblical model hasn't changed in nearly 2000 years. See Acts 1:8.) Quality is sometimes substituted for quantity (we forget the value of the "one" in Luke 15:1–10), profit for prayer, giving for grace, and, in consequence, there is no room (or needed) for the personal touch (even the Holy Spirit) that is necessary for the Gospel to be tailor-made to a specific individual, or so the current Church models and mentors say. After 2000 years the church thinks it has figured out how to run the church and grow the church and rule the church better than "The Head of the Church." (Ephesians 1:22) We see only cookie-cutter, assemble-line Christians today in most churches; mass production versus individual conversion and development according to the timetable of God. (Acts 2:47) Discipleship, personal relationships, and the freedom to simply hold a relationship with Christ, without a preconceived goal, are things which do not fit the model of success for a church or a Christian as we have come to define spiritual success today. This brings me, in my 70th year, to this question: **"Is the Church a Business?"**

Whatever gimmick or billboard advertisement we can use to attract a crowd is seemingly fair game today. (A case in point, the message board in front of a church in Ellsworth this week promoting "youth nation" simply read "zombies versus humans" Saturday night at 6:00 PM.) Madison Avenue has moved into the church with all of its strategies and techniques and has boosted attendance, giving, and the bottom line of most churches, but is the church any better off? Who cares really whether the promotion is the pastor in a big pink bunny suit, a rifle raffle, a Christian day of running jeeps through the mud, or paying people to come to church though "give-a-ways." I am not prepared to say that those brethren or churches that participate in such things are not sincere or genuine; nor am I prepared to say that we must discard all business practices to make the church efficient. I am not prepared to say how far we have strayed from our Biblical roots in relationship to the work of the Church, but I am prepared to say that we have strayed. I am not prepared to say that the results of nearly 100 years of revivals are true, no more than they are false, but I am prepared to make the statement that if all the individuals of those 100 years had truly and genuinely been saved, then why is the church in the mess it is in today? We are bigger in numbers, but smaller in spirituality. We have more church buildings and property, but we possess far less the properties of the Spirit of Christ. We are certainly richer in things than the forefathers of the faith, but much poorer in our theology. John was right when he wrote of our Church age: *"Because thou sayest, I am rich, and increased with goods, and have need of nothing; knowest not that thou art wretched, and miserable, and poor, and blind, and naked."* (Revelation 3:17) The Billy's (Graham and Sunday) of the church have seemingly led millions to Christ, yet the church has been on a very steady decline spiritually all these years. I am not prepared to state that we practice our faith in insincerity, but I am prepared to say that

IS THE CHURCH A BUSINESS? 89

we have replaced Christian morality and theology and put in its place the ethics and experience of business. We are all too familiar with the tragedy that this replacement has brought to the church. Or are we?

Familiar elements of business have been creeping into the church for years, elements that are without a doubt a product of the business model for economic success in this present world. (BUT CAN THIS BE THE SAME MODEL FOR SPIRITUAL SUCCESS TAUGHT BY GOD IN HIS BIBLE?) Staged and elaborate gatherings called "revivals," (the Bible is very clear that only God can institute a revival, not man--Habakkuk 3:2), with more elaborate rituals of emotional appeal to the heart, has led many into a fevered state of "revival" to be troubled and tested in conscience and mind in the matter of their "eternal salvation." Today, the Gospel is pedaled as a product and salvation as merchandise, again the business model. Some might even give this product away free, but with many strings attached. Genuine spiritual revival has become an expression of enthusiasm, a spectacular, a public event made for television, and now the competing ministers (like competing businesses with similar products seeking the same customer), or evangelists, jealously covet the seeming success of others and seek their own unique "spectacular" product that will draw the masses, make the six-o'clock news, and reap for themselves millions of followers (customers). In short order the "spectacular-spiritual-awakening" and its emotional attachment to their product will result in personal testimonials (the church version of QVC) that will produce other customers and will be promoted as proof of the "working of the Holy Spirit of God." But is this what the Good Lord desired when He left the Church in the hands of a few dedicated followers? Were they to develop a business or a church?

We must at this stage in our examination of the Church and Business pause for a moment to consider the delicate line between public/private soul-searching and the profession of one's faith. Can we all agree that the profession or witness of faith has been abused to the point that it is often taken as a measure of "success" for a particular preacher, evangelist, ministry, or church? We are so apt to define "spiritual victory" in terms which prove to be embarrassing a few short days, weeks, months, or years later when our so-called "convert" is now a black mark on the church's testimony. How many of these "converts" are still in church after a year? How many of these new believers mature in their faith? How many of these aisle-walkers, raisers-of-the hand, signer-of-the-card is still involved in their local assembly as a deacon, Sunday school teacher, or prayer warrior a decade after their conversion? But of course, we avoid the embarrassment by simple pretending that there is no such thing as cause and effect. We did nothing wrong in our method of "making disciples." We are not at fault in our evangelism, and our methodology is sound because we have the model of MacArthur in California, Olsten in Texas, and who can say that Rich Warren and Billy Graham were wrong? We have fallen into the trap our parent church in Corinth fell into that the Apostle Paul had to rebuke: *"Now this I say, that every one of you saith, I am of Paul; and I of Apollos; and I of Cephas; and I of Christ. Is Christ divided?"* (I Corinthians 1:12–13) We are treating Christianity and its Gospel as a grocery store product that sits on a shelf and at our leisure we can go by and buy whatever version or variety that best suits our needs. I ask again. Is the church supposed to be run like a business? Did Christ really want Heinz 57 varieties of churches today?

The problem we have with "church/business" reverts back to the crucial issue between revivalism and evangelism. The church has given way to impulses and imaginations, and without an acknowledgement of this critical spiritual error, impulses and imaginations will continue to define the Church age we are now living through. How else do we explain pink bunny suits, gun raffles, zombie night, and every other gimmick, including the so-called "prosperity gospel," which has been used by so-called evangelical churches to promote this whole "business" of revival and "saving souls" product? This is in my opinion the critical issue of this century, and, unfortunately, our father's generation didn't address it in the twentieth century, and unfortunately, no one, in theological circles, is addressing it in the twenty-first century. We are dealing with talented deceivers who have convinced the church that what works in the world can work in the church. The business model is the best way to keep up church attendance, support mission outreaches, and maintain our status in the world community. As Christ was scathing in His rebuke of the Pharisaical model of his day ("*. . . whited sepulchers full of dead man's bones . . .*" in Matthew 23:27), so must we be as scathing in our rebuke of the business model of the modern church today.

Christ certainly lived in a different age than we do, but He knew that any model of spirituality of man can be both enticing as well as deceiving. As Christ debated the issue with his Pharisaical opponents, we must wage a heated debate with the church experts today on just where they are coming up with these promotions and how they are publishing the Gospel. Our problem is that we want the visible display of spiritual success ever before our eyes, the triumph of both theology and our own self-righteousness and the childish gratification of helping God build the "kingdom." The problem is that we never stop to think about our actions, how our "business" appears to God, and ultimately how it relates to our theology. I use again John's rebuke of the Laodiceans. They saw themselves as successful, but God saw them as a failure. They saw themselves as spiritually rich, but God saw them as spiritually poor. They saw themselves clothed in the white, fine linen of righteousness, but like the fable of the emperor's cloths, we strut about naked, pretending we are wearing the finest raiment in the world. We see ourselves with vision. Oh, how that word is being used for the spiritual inventors and innovators of the church today with their Californian style of worship, their Nashville style of music, and their Hollywood style of preaching, yet God sees us as blind. God's church of the twenty-first century has no value, no vesture, and no vision, and I blame most of it on the business model we are leading our churches with.

Don't get me wrong because I don't have the wisdom to understand how we will ever turn this train wreck around. I suspect, even if we had a 21st century prophet of the caliber of Paul or Peter, they, too, would be ignored and rejected because we now have the data, the statistics, the numbers to prove that the "model" is working. Once again we have forgotten this fundamental method of how God views things: *"For man looketh on the outward appearance, but the Lord looketh on the heart."* (I Samuel 16:7) That is why when we see wealth, He sees poverty; when we see clothing, He sees nakedness, and when we see success, He sees blindness. So, we continue, strutting about with our mega-churches, our revivals, our contrived carnival meetings and services, with the preacher as the barker and our bankrupt theology, with no thought or clue to the simple truth that we have substituted vanity for theology.

So, is there an answer to the dilemma (having no spiritual value, no spiritual vesture, and no spiritual vision) we find ourselves in today? For me, there is only one answer and that is to get away from the business model and return to the instruction given to the Church of the Laodiceans as their only way of restoration: *"I counsel thee to buy of me gold tried in the fire, that thou mayest be rich; and white raiment, that thou mayest be clothed, and that the shame of thy nakedness do not appear; and anoint thine eyes with eyesalve, that thou mayest see. As many as I love, I rebuke and chasten: be zealous therefore, and repent."* (Revelation 3:18–19) The answer to the Church's success isn't Madison Avenue, the Stock Market,

Church CEO's, a business model, but "repentance," a "zealous" return to the "gold-standard" of God. *"That the trial of your faith, being much more precious than of gold that perisheth, though it be tried with fire, might be found unto praise and honour and glory at the appearing of Jesus Christ."* (I Peter 1:7) A "zealous" return to the only garment that really fits the Church of Jesus Christ: *"And to her was granted that she should be arrayed in fine linen, clean and white: for the fine linen is the righteousness of saints."* (Revelation 19:8) A "zealous" return to the farsightedness versus the nearsightedness that now gets all of the church's attention. *"Set your affection on things above, not on things on the earth."* (Colossians 3:2)

For me, the greatest tragedy of this whole "business-model" of the Church today is the sad picture John draws at the end of his letter to the Laodiceans: *"Behold, I stand at the door, and knock: if any man hear my voice, and open the door, I will come in to him, and will sup with him, and he with me."* (Revelation 3:20) I have heard the modern evangelists and pastors use this verse to appeal to the unsaved; how Jesus is at their heart's door seeking entrance when in reality this is the picture of Christ standing outside His Church seeking entrance. A terrible injustice is happening today when "the Head of the Church" is not even welcomed in His own Church. The modern business model doesn't include the Founder (Hebrews 12:2) of the Church. He is not needed any longer because we have a CEO (chief operating officer) called "pope," "archbishop," "ecclesiastical father," "the reverend," or "doctor so and so." A hostile takeover is happening in the body of Christ today, and we have voted out the "Owner" (I Corinthians 6:20) and replaced Him with a figurehead. No wonder Jesus asked, *"Nevertheless when the Son of man cometh, shall he find faith on the earth?"* (Luke 18:8) The answer to our question is "NO!" Christ never intended for His Church to be a business, be run like a business, or be operated by a business model. Jesus never intended His Church to become an organization because He always intended it to be an organism, something that was alive not dead, something that was connected to Him, not disconnected. A clear reading of I Corinthians 12 will verify this concept to an open-minded reader. It is time to simplify and repent and return to Jesus' model, the Bible model versus the business model, and a realization that in Christ and Christ alone we have our beginning and our being.

21.

SHIFTING AND DRIFTING

IN MY NEARLY SEVENTY years on this planet and my over sixty years in the Faith, I have seen a lot of shifting by people on the fundamentals of the faith and a lot of drifting by people in the Faith. Shifting takes place and shifting reveals what one has built one's faith upon. Remember Jesus' classic parable of the two builders, the two buildings, and the two bases? (Matthew 7:24-27) One can make a spiritual application to spiritual sand (Matthew 7:26) and the spiritual Rock (I Corinthians 10:4). If one thinks of the billows of the parable and visualizes these two building on the shore of time, you see clearly that the life built on the Rock will stand and stand up to the billows and the blows of time, but the life built on the sand of this world will first shift off its foundation and then drift away, destroyed, and lost forever. This is my take on the shifting and drifting doctrine.

Paul starts our explanation with these words from his epistle to the Ephesians: *"That we henceforth be no more children, tossed to and fro, and carried about with every wind of doctrine, by the sleight of men, and cunning craftiness, whereby they lie in wait to deceive."* (Ephesians 4:14) Paul was trying to prepare the people of Ephesus against "shifting" and "drifting" by telling them how to avoid this danger. *"And He gave some, apostles; and some, prophets; and some, evangelists; and some, pastors and teachers; for the perfecting of the saints, for the work of the ministry, for the edifying of the body of Christ: till we all come in the unity of the faith, and of the knowledge of the Son of God, unto a perfect man, unto the measure of the stature of the fulness of Christ."* (Ephesians 4:11-13) We live in a day where there is plenty of "shifting with the shift" and "drifting with the drift" in so many areas of the Faith. Paul called them *"every wind of doctrine."* I feel he wrote of this later to Timothy in these words: *"For the time will come when they will not endure sound doctrine; but after their own lusts shall they heap to themselves teachers, having itching ears; and they shall turn away their ears from the truth, and shall be turned unto fables."* (II Timothy 4:3–4) Paul called them *"**the sleight of men.**"* The word "sleight" literally means in the Greek "playing at dice," but at its core it means "to cheat." Paul called them *"**cunning craftiness.**"* The Greek word for "craftiness" is only found once in the Bible, and it means "unscrupulousness." All three descriptions are for underlining and highlighting one thing, *"**whereby they lie in wait to deceive.**"* Remember what Jesus warned about in the last days: *"And Jesus answered and said unto them, take heed that no man **deceive** you. For many shall come in my name, saying, I am Christ; and shall **deceive** many."* (Matthew 24:4–5) Deception will lead to shifting and drifting.

There was a time when the preachers and the people of the Church stood strong against anything and anyone that would question the core tenants of the Faith. Now the temptation is to shift with the political correctness of the age and to drift with the computerized understanding of the first century teaching of the Christ with the twenty-first interpretation of the modern thinking theologian. Besides, we need to be relevant, don't we? God doesn't feed his prophets with ravens anymore, does He? (I Kings 17:6) God doesn't speak through donkeys, does He? (Numbers 22:28) God doesn't swallow preachers with whales anymore, does He? (Jonah 1:17) We have shifted the stories of the Bible to the category of myths and fables, and we have drifted away from reading the Bible literally because, surely, these are only metaphorical and spiritual, aren't they? Something has happened to the average preacher and the average parishioner in this age of conformity, compromise, and co-existence. We have shifted and drifted!

I have come to believe that Paul speaks of this doctrine again in his grand book to the Hebrews: *"Therefore we ought to give the more earnest heed to the things which we have heard, lest at any time we should let them slip."* (Hebrews 2:1) Interestingly, the phrase "let them slip" is explained in the Greek as a leaking ship. Paul was challenging the Hebrews that they needed to hold on to the things they had heard and had been taught and not shift from their teaching and drift from their doctrine. There are a couple of areas that I feel we have done this in relationship to the Lord's example versus what the average Christian has come to believe.

First, didn't Jesus once challenge the Roman government's control over His Promised Land? Think about it. Jesus had the power to change the political landscape in His day, but He didn't because his focus was rendering to Caesar the things that were Caesar's and rendering to God the things that were God's. Why do we today get so involved in the political makeup of our world? We have shifted our focus on the things that are Caesar's and drifted away from the things that are God's. Second, Jesus never once organized a fund raiser or a community supper for the poor. I know this will sound hard in the current climate of today's philosophy, but think about it. Remember Jesus once said: *"For the poor always ye have with you; but me ye have not always."* (John 12:8) Do you remember the context of this statement? Judas Iscariot is alive and well today in these organizations. Individuals that talk and work for nothing other than getting rid of poverty, a noble cause to say the least, but for two thousand years Jesus' statement has proven true. If you can't get rid of it in that long a time, will you ever? Our problem is that this is just one area we have shifted from trying to meet the need of the soul to meeting the need of the flesh, and we have drifted away from Jesus' original commission, which is not to feed the poor, but to *"Go ye into all the world, and preach the gospel to every creature."* (Mark 16:15) (Just a footnote on this point to mention that even Judas didn't want to actually help the poor, but himself [John 12:4-6], as do most in these organizations today.) Third, Jesus never led his disciples in a set-in, or a march, nor did they display placards to pressure the local power to change or deal with some social ill. That is seemingly all the Church is involved today in. Don't get me wrong. I am against abortions, sex trafficking, pornography, hunger, the plight of the refugees, and on and on I could go, but Jesus never led a campaign against any of the ills of His society, and there were plenty. All I know is that in the great spiritual awakening of Church history, like the Wesleyan Revival, the social tragedies of that time were changed not by legislation, education, or reformation, but with the preaching of the Word of God. We have shifted our attention away from the Gospel and drifted with the social gospel.

Shifting and drifting are very comfortable to those that change with the times and adapt to the seasons, but like my father used to love to say, "Even a dead fish can float downstream, but it takes a strong fish to swim against the flow!" Think about it. You have to do nothing to go to hell, but it takes a whole lot of mercy and grace to get to heaven. Remember the prodigal son story (Luke 15:11-32) from one of Jesus' great parables and how he shifted from the father's house to the world and then drifted until he ended up in the pig pen? How did that work out for him? I feel the Church is now the prodigal—rich and carefree, wasting our "... *substance with riotous living.*" Like the prodigal, we have become respectable shifters and honorable drifters in the world. It is time we stand for something or we will eventually stand for nothing. It is time we forget what the world thinks and only follow what God thinks. It is time we check where we are in relationship to the Faith and the fundamentals of the Faith. Have we shifted or drifted?

22.

MY PERSONAL PROVERBS CONTINUE

1- No burns, no blisters, no buttons missing from their coats; no hair loss, no hide singed, no hands burnt; no smell of smoke, no sandals missing, no sign of harm of any kind, such is the complete protection of the Lord (three Hebrew children).

2- When will we stop imitating the priests of Baal in prayer, and start mimicking the prophet of God in prayer--short and sweet and to the point (Elijah on Carmel)!

3- God never quibbles over His instrument of service. If He can use a raven or a donkey, he can use a reluctant person like you or me.

4- If you want to enjoy a rainbow, you first must endure the rain.

5- Government can only give you social security on earth, but God can give you eternal security in heaven.

6- Light has a future, but darkness is nearly finished.

7- To "whitewash" one's sins will never produce "whiter than snow" forgiveness.

8- Our conduct is a direct result of character and creed.

9- Our doctrine will determine our deeds, direction, and dividing lines in this old world.

10- We are not to be kicking down the door, but a simple perseverance in knocking at the door of God's grace.

11-If we persevere in prayer, we will prevail.

12-God is looking for laborers, not loiterers or loafers, for His labor.

13-One minute, one hour, one week, one month, one year, one decade, one century, or one lifetime, our reward will be abundantly paid.

14-Today's modern thinker thinks that order came from some indescribable ooze of eons passed which just happened to creep out of a celestial explosion called the "big bang." Now, that's order?

15-Christ is not only unchangeable, but He is also incredible, inconvertible, incomprehensible, incontestable, and incorruptible.

16-The best way to defeat the devil is to resist, recite the Word, and remember to "Just Say No!"

17-The book of Esther teaches us that we can still trust God even when we cannot trace God. Despite His absence, He is still at work despite His anonymity.

18-It is a dangerous thing to try and explain the unexplainable.

19-It is only fitting that an unknown God would have unknown followers.

20-An insignificant giver and an insignificant gift are only significant to God.

21-It is more important to the child of God to be found faithful than famous.

22-No memorial, no money, and no monument erected in honor; no party, no parade, and no post given as a reward; no fanfare, no fame, and no fortune to the one who saved a city, and we can expect nothing more from this old world. (Ecclesiastes 3:9–18)

23-I believe in death bed conversions because just a few minutes from hell's fire the thief on the cross was plucked from Appollon's bowels to Abraham's bosom, from Purgatory to Paradise, from Hades to Heaven.

24-You don't have to be a seminary graduate, a Sunday school teacher, or a senior missionary to share what you know about the saving truth of Christ. Anybody can, and you can and should!

25-Whether a runaway like Jonah, a fall-a-way like John Mark, or a castaway like Jacob, we serve the God of "the second chance."

26- If you run with the "dogs," you will end up eating with the "hogs!"

27- Jesus never preached a funeral sermon.

28- "The last mile of the way" can be for some the most dangerous part of the way.

29- If we are created in the image of God, and we are, then can you imagine standing before the throne of judgment one day charged with the murder of Christ, the mutilation of Jesus, or the massacre of God? (Abortionist, you will!)

30- The devil's ministers of righteousness look right, sound reasonable, and seem real, but they are liars, every one!

31- God has never and will never change His orders in midstream, alter His commands halfway through, or amend His commission mid-course.

32- "Wait" is a four-letter word to most of us; there is a good reason why they call them "waiting rooms."

33- Will we be caught unawares as the householder was when the thief came? Will we be caught unprepared as the virgins were when the bridegroom came? Will we be caught unexpectedly as the servants were when their master came early? Or will we be caught watching and waiting as Simeon and Anna were when the Lord came suddenly the first time? So it will be the second time!

34- Man develops, plans, and executes his purposes, but God is always working in the shadows for His greater purpose.

35- Patience, not promptness, is a virtue.

36- Our prayers ought to be made "soon after night," "soon after noon," and "soon after nine!"

37- Successful escape versus sensual execution doesn't seem compatible or connectable to the same God, yet they are. (Acts 12)

38- We may have difficulty reconciling Peter's dilemma and John's death, but they are (as with all divinely sovereign issues) examples that God and God alone can and will harmonize them all for our good and His glory.

39- The prodigal might not have been rehabilitated until he got home, but he was redeemed the minute he headed for home.

40-It takes both a horizontal (I have sinned against my father) and a vertical (I have sinned against heaven) confession of sin to get forgiveness for sin.

41-If all we are going to do is rebuild Sodom in our land, put another homosexual watchman on the wall, and continue to practice an ungodly lifestyle, then another storm of fire and brimstone is on the horizon.

42-The only cure for crime and the criminal is Christ, but when you reject the Solution you must live with the alternatives.

43-Biblical wisdom is not to be hoarded or hid, but we are to spend it.

44-Your manners won't save you; your morals won't save you, and neither will your money!

45-Too many people choose temporal blessings over eternal bliss.

46-Sometimes the only mode of victory is flight (Joseph).

47-To mediate on the obscurity of God is to stroll in thought through the valley of uncertainty, but we still are treading on "holy ground."

48-Only when you understand that you can talk to the Almighty will you see beyond the obscure to the obvious found in Him.

49-Try tunneling instead of climbing; the mountain that cannot be climbed may be tunneled.

23.

TRENDISM AND TRENDISTS

I WILL TAKE CREDIT for the title of this article, but not the words in it. **"Trendism"** and **"Trendists"** are made up words from the great American revivalist Vance Havner. I read in one of his books these terms with the caption, "There is no such word, but when I cannot find a word, I want I make one!" What Vance meant by these two words is "the trends of the times" and the people that follow these trends. What has saddened this old pastor's heart is that the Church has gotten caught up in the modern trends of the twenty-first century. I am afraid the Church has the same problem as the rich young ruler: *"But when the young man heard that saying, he went away sorrowful:* ***for he had great possessions."*** (Matthew 19:22) I am afraid the Church has the same problem as the third kind of seed in Jesus' classic parable of "the sower and the seed." *"He also that received seed among the thorns is he that heareth the word; and the care of this world, and **the deceitfulness of riches**, choke the word, and he becometh unfruitful."* (Matthew 13:22)

One of the greatest trends in the American church is materialism. This could be money (I Timothy 6:10–11), but I believe it is more than that as described by the Apostle John in his description of the Laodiceans: *"I know thy works, that thou art neither cold nor hot: I would thou wert cold or hot. So then because thou art lukewarm, and neither cold nor hot, I will spue thee out of my mouth. Because thou sayest,* ***I am rich, and increased with goods****, and have need of nothing; and knowest not that thou art wretched, and miserable, and poor, and blind, and naked."* (Revelation 3:15–17) Note it isn't just "rich," but "increased with goods--possessions. Like the rich young ruler, the Church of the Laodiceans had a lot of stuff, and that stuff was making them spiritually poor. We are drowning in things, just like the world. I despise hoarding of any kind, clutter that fills up spaces and overtakes places. I have pastored the Emmanuel Baptist Church for nearly thirty years now, and it has amazed me how that even the church building can get cluttered. Periodically, I have had to purge the cracks and crevices, wondering every time I do, "where did all this stuff come from?" I have concluded that when the members and others connected with the church have filled their spaces, they simply donate their stuff to the church. I remember one time we had five televisions in the church and two of them didn't even work!

Church people have been bit by the same bug as the world, and Havner defined the bite as **"the pleasure of procuring it, the pride of possessing it, and the peril of what we can purchase with it!"** One of the great teachings our Founder taught, and His followers have ignored through most of history, is: *"And he said unto them, Take heed, and beware of covetousness: for a man's life consisteth not in the abundance of the things which he possesseth."* (Luke 12:15) Jesus followed that statement with the story of the rich farmer and his bumper crop (Luke 12:16-20) with this conclusion: *"So is he that layeth up treasure for himself, and is not rich toward God."* (Luke 12:21) This trend has been seen periodically in history, but, in my opinion, this trend and these "trenders" (my word) have taken the possessing of possessions into an entirely new dimension. What is so sad about this trend is that the leadership of the Church is fostering, teaching, and exhorting the church membership to have more and more possessions, more prosperity, and more "covetousness," the carnal sin of all sins, Satan's sin in heaven (he coveted the throne of God); Adam and Eve's Eden sin (they coveted to be like God); Achan's sin (he coveted the gold and garments); and Absalom's sin (he coveted the throne of his father David).

The greatest danger to the trendist is loving the trend more than loving the truth. The truth is very clear to me: *"Lay not up for yourselves treasures upon earth, where moth and rust doth corrupt, and where thieves break through and steal: but lay up for yourselves treasures in heaven, where neither moth nor rust doth corrupt, and where thieves do not break through nor steal: **for where your treasure is, there will your heart be also.**"* (Matthew 6:19-21) We know from the reading of the rich young ruler's story that his treasure was in his possessions, something more important than following the Christ. We know that the heart of the Laodiceans was in their riches, possessions, and self-reliance, not in the things of God. That is the danger and deception of things; we begin to trust them over trusting the Lord, we begin to love them over the things of the Lord, and we begin to hoard them instead of using our leftovers to help others. I have come to believe that even in going to a church building can become a sin when the pride is in the facility, the beautiful music, the orderly, ornate services, the elegant and clever sermons, the attendance records, and the richness of the interior become more important than gathering with God's people to worship God. I write these thoughts during the Covid-19 pandemic. We are in our third week of a shut-down of all church activities and a shutting out of all people in our building. One of the hopes for me is when we do return, we will have forgotten about our surroundings and have come to the realization that the Church is not a building or the possessions we have, but the Church has always been the people. Remember what Vance said: "Performance without experience is not merely vain, it is downright evil, and instead of being gloried in it should be repented of."

I have come to believe that this tendency towards trendism is another sign of the times when Paul wrote to Timothy of "perilous times" of *"having a form of godliness, but denying the power thereof: from such turn away."* (II timothy 3:5) The current trends and the current proponents of these trends have a "form of godliness" whether through "institutionalism" or "ecumenicalism." I recall a little known Mosaic law that should be applied here: *"Thou shalt not follow a multitude to do evil . . . "* (Exodus 23:2) I know I am a lone voice speaking in a wilderness where the current trends in Christianity have become accepted by the majority, whether I am speaking of the trends in religious music (gospel jazz and sacred boogie-woogie), the trend in our attitude of the Lord's Day (Sunday Football over Sunday services), the trend of professionalism in the ministry (church CEOs and Wall Street marketing), the trend of a popular Christianity (we no longer sing "a tent or a cottage, why should I care? They're building a palace for me over there!"), the trend to a country-club faith and a big shot churchianity (spiritual social clubs and Hollywood preachers), the trend to homogenization of all religions (world council of churches and the brotherhood of Christianity and Islam), and the trend to combine and blend together the Church and the State (whatever happened to *"Render therefore unto Caesar the things which be Caesar's, and unto God the things which be God's." Luke 20:25*).

If one reads the Bible clearly and applies its precepts personally, one will find that the Almighty is not a Trendist! The trends of the world are just that, trends of the world, the world's way of doing its own thing, like before the flood, like the Tower of Babel, like trying to solve the coronavirus on its own without even asking God's help. I have heard no cries for God's help in all of this. The trend today seems to be erasing all lines of demarcation between the world's problems and God. Paul was totally correct when he wrote to the Romans of how it would end in the relationship between God and Man. Read carefully Romans 1:18–32, and you will see and understand "the trendism of the trendists!"

24.

WHAT TIME IS IT?

I AM SO VERY thankful that as I enter my 70th year I have the attitude of the grand, old evangelist Bud Robinson. It seems a group of Bud's friends thought it was time for the elderly man of God to visit America's greatest city, New York. They bought Bud a ticket to the city and a sightseeing tour of the Big Apple. It is recorded that after the big day Mr. Robinson was overheard thanking the Good Lord that he hadn't seen a thing he wanted!

As I write this chapter we have just "sprung our clocks forward" for daylight savings time which often causes me to think that, though man tries to keep track of time and alters time to his advantage, are we really watching God's clock? In one of the great "time" parables of Jesus He tells of the rich farmer that thought he had plenty of time after a record-breaking harvest. He decided to tear down his old barns and build newer barns for the surplus he had gleaned whereby he could retire to a long, pleasant retirement. But while the farmer's clock read "many years" (Luke 12:19), God's clock read "this night" (Luke 12:20). What a big difference! I have been pondering lately just how much time I have left on this planet. Old age does that to you when you realize that you certainly have more days behind you than before you. It has also made me ponder how much time this old world has left. I know there are those who believe that millions upon millions, if not billions, of years have passed and surely there are millions, if not billions left, yet the Bible tells us differently. I often mention in my prayers about either the Lord taking me or coming to get me; I will either depart in the rapture

(I Thessalonians 4:13–18) or depart in death (II Timothy 4:6) and both will be according to God's clock, God's time. The first is unknown to all but God: "*But of that day and hour knoweth no man, no, not the angels of heaven, but my Father only.*" (Matthew 24:36) The second we only know as an appointment: "*And as it is appointed unto men once to die, but after this the judgment.*" (Hebrews 9:27) So, what time is it anyway?

I used the Bud Robinson story to start this article because I want you to understand that all that is in the world today, and the time in which I am living, is getting less and less interesting to me. I am living in the philosophy that "this world is not my home, I am just passing through, my treasure is laid up somewhere beyond the blue!" **It is the time when artists can't paint.** I can't remember the last time I saw a piece of modern art that I liked. There was a time when you knew what the artist was trying to show, but now the question is what is it, what was the artist trying to say? In my book, you are not an artist if the one viewing your artwork must question it. **It is the time when singers can't sing.** I was raised in the 50s and 60s, and, even then, my parents didn't like the music. But today, I know how they felt because I don't understand the modern music, or the musicians. To me, they have no talent, but the talent to scream and shout! Popular music might be popular with the younger generation, but not with me. **It is the time when writers can't write.** I love to read; I am always reading, but I haven't read a modern work in decades. I can count on one hand the number of author's whose books I couldn't put down. Like an old preacher once said after seeing a sign that said "Dirt for Sale" was that it ought to be hung over the paperback bookracks in most bookstores. I would add, seeing most bookstores are going out of business, that sign ought to hang over the internet.

Speaking of the internet, it is time when falsehood, fables, and fabrication has flooded all forms of media. It is a time when myths are making a comeback because most people today despise the truth. Paul told us that such a time was coming when he warned young Timothy: "*For the **time** will come when they will not endure sound doctrine; but after their own lusts shall they heap to themselves teachers, having itching ears; and they shall turn away their ears from the truth, and shall be turned unto fables.*" (II Timothy 4:3–4) For me, the greatest danger is those who use the language of orthodoxy and traditional terminology to speak their lies. It was the great English pastor, preacher, and author Charles Spurgeon that once wrote, "Judas betrayed his Master with a kiss. That is how apostates do it; it is always with a kiss. Did you ever read an infidel book in your life which did not begin with profound respect for the truth? I never have. Even modern ones, when bishops write them, always begin like that.

They betray the Son of man with a kiss!" Everybody today tells you that they are speaking the truth, have the truth, and want you to understand the truth. The problem is that it is their truth. Whether the politician or the preacher, we must be careful in these times to *"Prove all things; hold fast that which is good"* (I Thessalonians 5:21) lest we get caught in a lie that can take us down a hellish path.

One of the greatest blessings of my lifetime was when I witnessed the fulfillment of the end of **"the times of the Gentiles."** There are times and there are the ends of times in God's great time chart of history. Jesus spoke of those times in His great Olivet Discourse recorded twice in the Gospels (Matthew 24 and Luke 21). In that great prophetic sermon Jesus made this prediction: *"And they shall fall by the edge of the sword, and shall be led away captive into all nations: and Jerusalem shall be trodden down of the Gentiles, until* **the times of the Gentiles** *be fulfilled."* (Luke 21:24) The prophecy is clear to me in that Jesus was talking about the time that Jerusalem would be under occupation by the Gentile nations. That occupation started in the BC when the Romans took control in 63 and remained in control until the Arabs took over, and that occupation continued through all the nations that would conquer that land until 1966. The last to possess the city were the Jordanian Arabs, but in "the six-day" war of 1966, the Jews once again occupied their ancient capital and do so to this day. The miracle of the rebirth of Israel in 1948, three years before my birth, was an eye-opener to the world, as have been the numerous wars since when the outnumbered Jews have always come forth victorious. For me, these times just remind me that the Lord's coming is nearer than it has ever been.

So, what time is it? It is time that we wake up to the reality that the time is near for the end of the age, not the end of time because, according to prophecy, when the clock of this age winds down, another clock will start that has 1007 years on its hands, seven years for the Great Tribulation period and a thousand years for the Great Millennium Kingdom of the Christ. Wake up, because another one of the signs of the end is: *"But of the **times** and the seasons, brethren, ye have no need that I write unto you. For yourselves know perfectly that the day of the Lord so cometh as a thief in the night. For when they shall say, Peace and safety; then sudden destruction cometh upon them, as travail upon a woman with child; and they shall not escape. But ye, brethren, are not in darkness, that that day should overtake you as a thief. Ye are all the children of light, and the children of the day: we are not of the night, nor of darkness.* **Therefore let**

us not sleep, as do others; but let us watch and be sober." (I Thessalonians 5:1–6) In another place the Apostle Paul warns: *"And that, knowing the **time**, that now it is high **time** to awake out of sleep: for now is our salvation nearer than when we believed. The night is far spent, the day is at hand: let us therefore cast off the works of darkness, and let us put on the armour of light. Let us walk honestly, as in the day . . . "* (Romans 13:11–13) What time is it? It is time to stay alert, be vigilant and watchful for the signs of the times, ready and waiting for the return of Jesus.

25.

ELITIST AND ENTITLEMENTS IN THE FAITH

WE ARE LIVING IN the age of "entitlement." Certain people groups, religious sects, and wealthy individuals think because they are who they are, or what they have, that gives them the right to some form of entitlement such as special privileges, special homage, or special recognition. Lesbians and homosexuals think their lifestyle should permit them special privileges under the law like the privilege of marriage, something that is clearly taught in Scripture is only available to "a man and a woman" (Genesis 2:24 25). Jihadist Muslims think they are entitled because they believe in the prophet Mohammed, and homage ought to be paid to their Allah; that through their radical fundamentalist belief they have an entitlement, a salvation if you will, if they simply die killing infidel Christians, an entitlement for specific acts or deeds rendered. Some Jews feel they are entitled to eternal salvation simply because they have a covenant with Jehovah, no matter how they dealt with His Son Jesus. Entitlement is the word that best describes these and many more, but how wrong they are. The tragedy is that entitlement has crept into the Christian Church, and there are some who think just because they are a Baptist, or a hundred other forms of Christianity, they deserve something special from God. The Pentecostals believe they are entitled because they can speak in tongues, have a special communication link with the Almighty. The Calvinists think they're entitled because God chose them over others. I am sobered each and every time I read these words from Christ: *"Not every one that saith unto me, Lord, Lord, shall enter into the kingdom of heaven; but he that doeth the will of my Father which is in heaven. Many will say to* me in that day, Lord, Lord, have we not prophesied in thy name? And in thy name have cast out devils? And in thy name done many wonderful works? And then will I profess unto them, I never knew you: depart from me, ye that work iniquity." (Matthew 7:21–23) I believe that Jesus was talking about entitlement, those that think they are entitled because they believe something special, have done something special, or have said something special. The Pharisees thought themselves entitled, and we know what Jesus thought of them!

There is a certain pride and arrogance which creeps into "entitlement" theology. When people think they are better than others, better because of race, better because of religion, better because of riches, whatever, they set themselves up as being "other" or "different" or "privileged." I have always had a problem with "royals;" you know the kind, and they are not only in England. We have the "royal" politicians in America, the Clintons and Bushes come to mind; the "royal" movie stars, Cosby and Ford come to mind, and the "royal" sports figure in our country, like Brady and A-Rod. People seem to love to make "royals," probably hoping one day they can be one, and with the "royals" come entitlements, special rights when they are speeding, special rights when they do something wrong, special rights just because they are "special." What is so amazing to me is that most "royals" don't have the slightest clue of the perilous ground they are walking on, treading over, strolling through. To every "royal," to every "elitist," to every "star" consider these sobering words from the pen of Paul: *"For you see your calling, brethren, how that not many wise [elitist] men after the flesh, not many mighty [rich], not many noble [royal], are called. But God has chosen the foolish things of the world to confound the wise; and God hath chosen the weak things of the world to confound the things which are mighty; and base things of the world, and things which are despised, hath God chosen, yea, and things which are not, to bring to nought things that are; that no flesh should glory in His presence."* (I Corinthians 1:26–29) Those who feel because of their person or position or pomp or prestige they are somehow entitled, are already far down God's choosing list. No wonder Jesus said, *"Verily I say unto you, that a rich man shall hardly enter into the kingdom of heaven. And again I say unto you, it is easier for a camel to go through the eye of a needle, than for a rich man to enter into the kingdom of God."* (Matthew 19:23–24)

The Bible is very clear when it comes to the doctrine of entitlement with verses like this: *"For as many of you as have been baptized into Christ have put on Christ. There is neither Jew nor Greek, there is neither bond or free, there is neither male or female: for ye are all one in Christ Jesus."* (Galatians 3:27-28) And what of this precept from the sermon of Peter to the household of Cornelius: *"Of a truth I perceive that God is no respecter of persons."* (Acts 10:34) Dear English queen (before the great lady died just like anyone one of her commoners, no entitlement at the time of death), let it be known that in the eyes of God you are no better or worse than the maid that serves you. Dear American president, let it be known that in the eyes of God you are no better or worse than the butler than serves you. Dear billionaire of finance, let it be known that in the eyes of God you are no better or worse than your employee that makes minimum wage. We forget that God knows the manner, makeup, and the mind of every man to the point of the base, depraved nature of us all. The common denominator is our original sin, our basic nature and no position, no title, no amount of money can change that fact. The binding power within us, that "infected will" that lives within each of us should cause us to plead for mercy, not expect some entitlement because of who we are or what we are. It is my opinion that American exceptionalism, capitalism, and perfectionism have fostered this belief in entitlement in this land. It has become an essentially American mantra, though many forms exist around the world. I still remember the stereotype I had to combat the first time I went to India. **People from other lands see us more clearly than we see ourselves!**

Another word that can be associated with entitlement is the word "indulgence" because it seems that one follows the other, like Siamese twins. From the overindulgent aristocrat to the greedy banker, when a million or a billion, and now there are some reaching for a trillion, is not enough, the stage is set for those to use their influence and place in society to change things. The Gates come to mind, but what are they trying to change with their billions? I always find it amazing that the corrupt crime boss of Boston still gets the high Roman Catholic Church mass at the end of his life. It reminds me of the story of the rich man and Lazarus in Luke 16:19-31. The rich man was rich and entitled, while Lazarus was just a beggar with the dogs of the street being his only friends. They both died and, though their funerals are not mentioned, I have imagined them in my mind. We know from the rest of the story that the most deserving of the high church mass was the most wretched, filthy beggar in the street, but surely no one would stoop low enough to elevate one so unworthy of such a high honor. The rich man got his "mass" and from hell cries out. The poor man was dumped in a Potter's field and from Paradise rejoices, the religious trappings of an entitlement system versus being carried to Abraham's bosom by angels. In the end which one was the real rich man? In the end I fear for the "royal;" a crown in hell won't make much difference. In the end I fear for the "star;" an Oscar in hell won't change your status. In the end I fear for the "rich" because even a trillion dollars won't get you out of hell. As I work my way through my 70th year, I still see those emulated.

Modern man demands a rational reality created in the image of mankind versus the image of God. Our way and not His way has been at the core of depraved man's ambition (remember the Tower of Babel), thinking himself superior, important, wiser than God. I love the way Paul wrote of this to the Romans: *"Because that which may be known of God is manifest in them; for God hath shewed it unto them. For the invisible things of Him from the creation of the world are clearly seen, being understood by the things that are made, even His eternal power and God head; so that they are without excuse: because that, when they knew God, they gloried Him not as God, neither were thankful; but became vain in their imaginations, and their foolish hearts were darkened. Professing themselves to be wise, they became fools."* (Romans 1:19-22) Entitlement like indulgence is a fantasy of man, a vain imagination to the fool who thinks that God will not notice or even the playing field one day, the rich man's mistake in the story of Lazarus. Perhaps, the worst horror of hell for the "elitist" and the "royal" and the "star" and the "rich" is the reversal of roles that will take place. Remember in life it was Lazarus begging for food at the backdoor of the rich man's house, but in the afterlife it was the rich man begging for a drop of water. From the bowels of hell, the elitist will beg for the basics, the royal will beg for help, the star will trade all his fame for one second out of hell, and the rich will give all his fortune for a reprieve. The wicked and unrepentive are entitled to one thing--separation from God and His Son for time and eternity in a place prepared for the devil and his angels (Matthew 25:41).

There is no rational to entitlement theology, just like there is nothing rational about Islam, or any other faith you choose to consider in the light of spiritual truth. They are all false faiths that only lead their followers down the slippery slope of entitlement that leads to the Lake of Fire. A faith of entitlement based upon our own interpretation will land us in a hot place sooner or later. Isaiah said it best when he wrote: *"For your thoughts [of entitlement] are not my thoughts, neither are your ways my ways, saith the Lord. For as the heavens are higher than the earth, so are my ways higher than your ways, and my thoughts than your thoughts."* (Isaiah 55:8-9) I have a very dear brother in Christ, Mark Honey, who for most of his life has been battling MD, but despite his physical shortcomings is a brilliant thinker. I believe he is the only human being I have met in my life that has a photogenic memory. He says he hasn't got one, but time and time again he remembers something out of the blue that only confirms to me he does. A year back we were having a series of discussion on "original sin," and our debate drifted into this arena of entitlement and rights versus risk and responsibility. Mark has concluded that we are living in an age where it is all about "rights" without any consideration about the "risk" and the responsibilities that come with granted "rights." People of the elitist status want the honor and respect and homage that come with their station, but they don't care to live a life worthy of such rights. There is one word that comes to mind when I think of such privileged people--scandal. The news waves and the newspapers are filled with scandalous stories almost daily, but as the publicity seekers would say, "Any news is good news for them!" Even if that news is bad news in relationship to morals and money.

Any time you get a right, a privilege, and an honor, you must weigh the risk against what is the responsibility that comes with this right. Take for example the rights that come with riches. I am convinced that there is no such thing as "the self-made man." I believe this because of the words in the book of Deuteronomy, *"And thou say in thine heart, my power* [entitlement] *and the might of mine hand* [position] *hath gotten me this wealth* [riches]. *But thou shalt remember the Lord thy God: for it is He that giveth thee power* [position, privilege, and prestige] *to get wealth* [riches], *that he may establish His covenant which he sware unto thy fathers, as it is this day."* (Deuteronomy 8:17-18) When you attain to anything in this world, you must realize that it was God Almighty that gave you that position, that honor, that recognition. There is no "star," no "billionaire," and no "royal" that was not placed there by God. I have come to believe, like nations and politicians, that rich people and famous people rise and fall by God decree: *"And He changeth the times and the seasons: He removeth kings and setteth up kings: He giveth wisdom unto the wise, and knowledge to them that know understanding. He revealeth the deep and secret things . . ."* (Daniel 2:21-22) Even the great medical or scientific discoveries man can't take credit for, or boast about, because without God they would have never been revealed. How many superstars in the fields of science have been exalted, entitled to "stardom" status, and it was really

God? Your title, dear royal, your position, dear politician, your money, dear billionaire, has all come from God and with it a responsibility, not for selfish purposes, but for the glory of God and the good of your fellowman; and then there are the risks!

With rights, riches, and responsibility comes the inherent dangers, for example, these verses to those who would be rich, or those who are rich: *"But they that will be rich fall into temptation and a snare, and into many foolish and hurtful lusts, which drown men in destruction and perdition. For the love of many is the root of all evil: which while some coveted after, they have erred from the faith, and pierced themselves through with many sorrows."* (I Timothy 6:9–10) The common denominator between all the groups I have highlighted and underlined in this chapter is "money." Most politicians have money, most royals have money, most stars have money, and most famous people have money, so Paul's warning is for these "entitled" people. I have come to this conclusion: the last thing you want is for God to dump a great wealth on you, rather a wealth of skills, a wealth of wisdom, a wealth of fame, a wealth of position, or a wealth of riches. Why? Special temptations only come with wealth, and what of "a snare?" Only some "foolish and hurtful lust" are possible if you have wealth! How many are "drowning" today in money? Entitlement can be evil, can cause an evil to come into your life simply because you're entitled. The world would have you believe riches, wealth, money brings happiness, joy, pleasure, security, but the Bible is very clear: "many sorrows" and time has proven this to be true in the life of the entitled.

So in answer to our original question of "why," I conclude with the simple answer of God's Word. If anyone should have felt entitled, it should have been Jesus. He was God. (Philippians 2:6). He was the Creator of the World (Colossians 1:16). He was superior in intellect to any He met (Matthew 12:42). *"But made Himself of no reputation, and took upon Him the form of a servant, and was made in the likeness of men"* (Philippians 2:7). In every aspect of entitlement Jesus did just the opposite: *". . . yet for your sakes he becomes poor . . . "* (II Corinthians 8:9). Jesus didn't think he was entitled even to a home (Luke 9:58). Let's be honest. Few today follow this example of Christ in the area of entitlement. Most are out to get whatever they can, to out play, out last, and come out on top. The world is obsessed with perks, freebies, advances, and attainments that will place them in the now infamous "one percent." Whether superior by race, or riches, or religion, the Biblical answer to our question is clear: entitlement is a doctrine of devils (I Timothy 4:1), not a theology of God (James 4:6).

26.

SOME DISCIPLES JUST STAY HOME

I WAS BORN INTO this world in 1951. I was born again when I gave my heart to the Lord Jesus Christ at the age of seven in 1958. I gave my life to the Lord Jesus Christ at the age of nineteen in 1970. When I finally yielded to the Spirit's call for full-time Christian service, I had aspiration and expectation to a grand ministry on a far off and distant shore, to a strange people with a strange language in a strange place. I thought I had found that place and those people on a 1972 summer mission trip to Western Australia. I found such a place and such a people on a remote mission station with a group of Aboriginal natives hardly removed from their Stone Age ways, but it was there at Warbunton Range on the dusty, dirty Gibson Desert that I learned that some disciples just stay home.

This is why I have always had an understanding and a sympathy for the plight of the demonic of the Gadarenes (Luke 8:26) after his conversion. If a church hymn was ever written for a Biblical character, it was these words by R. H. McDaniel:

> What a wonderful change in my heart has been wrought,
> since Jesus came into my heart!
> I have light in my soul for which long I have sought,
> since Jesus came into my heart.
> I have ceased from my wandering and going astray,
> since Jesus came into my heart.
> And my sins, which were many, are all washed away,
> since Jesus came into my heart.

Remember how Jesus found the demon possessed man after he stepped foot on shore in Gadara: *"And when he went forth to land, there met him out of the city a certain man, which had devils long time, and ware no clothes, neither abode in any house, but in the tombs."* (Luke 8:27) And though Luke doesn't record this before/after image, Mark's account does: *"And they come to Jesus, and see him that was possessed with the devil, and had the legion, sitting, and clothed, and in his right mind . . . "* (Mark 5:15) From wild, naked, and crazy to sitting, clothed, and in his right mind-- what a change! But what came next has always puzzled me.

You know this story well enough to know what happened to Jesus and His disciples after the miracle of the demonic. The Gadarenes would rather deal with a crazy man than the Son of Man. They wanted their pigs instead of the Prince of Peace. They literally threw Jesus out of their country (Mark 5:17). As Jesus and the disciples headed back to the boat that had brought them from the far side of the Sea of Galilee, the converted demonic had a request of Jesus: *"And when he was come into the ship, he that had been possessed with the devil prayed him that he might be with him."* (Mark 5:18) The man was ready, willing, and able to follow Jesus. He had found a friend, a mentor, the Savior, and he wanted to serve Him and follow Him wherever Jesus went. I like the way Vance Havner put it in his classic devotional book <u>By the Still Waters</u>.

> The Gadarene demoniac, now clothed and in his right mind, begs to go along with Jesus. It must have looked romantic and alluring, the Lord and His disciples boarding the ship to cross over the little sea to new places and more adventures. The new disciple wanted to get away from old familiar territory, the scene of his horrible past, and begin anew elsewhere. How interesting to go here and there with this wonderful band and testify in strange places! Above all, he wanted to spend his life with the One who had saved him from such a living terror and had made him a new creature. What disciple would not beg to get away from Gadara and go with Jesus?

My question exactly, both in 1972 and now in 2020.

What an illustration the man could have been to Jesus' ministry. What a testimony he could have delivered at the rallies of the future. What an example of divine grace and Almighty power to demonstrate who Jesus was, yet to the demoniac's simple request Jesus said, *"Howbeit Jesus suffered him not, but saith unto him, Go home to thy friends, and tell them how great things the Lord hath done for thee, and hath had compassion on thee."* (Mark 5:19) What? Go home! What? Stay here! What? Just me? In one of the most shocking conclusions to a Jesus story, the commission was clear. This disciple would stay home. This disciple would minister to his "friends" and "family" (see Luke's version of the commission in Luke 8:39). Oh, he would be working for Jesus, not with Jesus. His was a calling that many of us have struggled with for a long time, the commission not to "go" (Matthew 28:19), but to "stay." Again, I believe Vance Havner understood the tone of Jesus' orders to the demoniac when he wrote:

> But it was not to be. Instead Jesus bid him, "Go home to thy friends . . . " It is not a very glamorous commission, and it might have disappointed some souls. Go back to the old familiar and unromantic grounds where you have been such a hideous character and live down that past; overcome it by your new testimony. Don't run away from Gadara, stay right there and live for me as earnestly as once you did for the devil. It will be hard, for everybody knows what you have been: they will call you names, and some will be slow to believe you, and others will call you a freak, but there is your mission field, you must be my disciple who stayed at home!

His commission, my commission, and yours?

The Gadarene, like me, yielded to the call, the commission, the appointment, and all we ever know about him is this postscript by the hand of Mark, *"And he departed, and began to publish in Decapolis how great things Jesus had done for him: and all men did marvel." (Mark 5:20)* Luke tells us he started in his "own city" (Luke 8:39), but eventually expanded into the "Decapolis," the ten major Greek cities located on the east side of the Sea of Galilee. While travelling in that area with my daughter Marnie in 2010, I still remember the morning we were touring an archeological site of an old church building. The professor from Dallas Theological Seminary that was leading the group said something I will never forget. He told us as we stood in those ancient ruins that according to church records, there was a bishop from Gadara at every major church council meeting until well into the fourth century, and the roots of that faithfulness could be trace back to only one man, the demonic of the Gadarenes! A line from the church hymn <u>Anywhere with Jesus</u> highlights and underlines what the demoniac demonstrated: " . . . **ready as He summons me to go or stay** . . . " Some disciples just stay home.

It was these final words from Vance Havner that warmed my heart in the realization that I like the demoniac had a great commission all these years.

> Do you grow weary of Gadara [for me it has been Maine and, yes, I have] and long to break away to more alluring adventures across the sea? [Yes!] It is a glorious thing to follow the Christ to far lands and strange places. But I am thinking that sometimes it is even nobler to give up fond dreams of high endeavor in more romantic climes and go back home to live down a dark past, proclaiming in dull and difficult circumstances what God has done for one's soul. All of us are smitten with that urge to cross over to better places: "If only I were yonder, how could I preach!" But only a few ever go, and sometimes it is not as romantic on the other side when they get there. Most of us cannot take passage for exciting service beyond the sea. We shall have to stay in Gadara and testify at home. Of course, the Gadarene wanted most just to be with Jesus. What a beautiful evidence of a new affection that he does not want the Saviour to be out of his sight! But more blessed are they who see not, yet believe. Greater it is to labor on in Decapolis, walking by faith and not by sight . . .

As I pass through my 70th year, I see now that the Lord gave me a blessed path.

27.

EAGLES DO NOT FLY IN FLOCKS

SOMETIMES AS I AM reading, I come across a phrase, like the one that has become the title for this article, which jumps off the page, and I say to myself, "That would make a good chapter topic; someday I will write about it!" I will give credit for these thoughts to Vance Havner because it was in his book <u>In Times Like These</u>, published in 1969, that I found this interesting saying. In 1969 I was just finishing high school and heading out into the big world for the first time. Raised on an isolated dairy and potato farm in the North Maine Woods, I hadn't seen much of the world, but in 1969 I left home, never to return, except for short visits. As I journey through this my threescore and tenth year, I find in Vance's proverb a great description of who I am and what I am.

My first stop after leaving home was a four-year Bible college in South Carolina. It was during that stay I joined a boys' society called Basilean. Our mascot was the eagle, and our motto was Isaiah 40:31: *"But they that wait upon the LORD shall renew their strength; they shall mount up with wings as eagles; they shall run, and not be weary; and they shall walk, and not faint."* Despite the fact that the bald eagle was a native bird to my home state of Maine, I only saw the majestic bird a few times in my youth, and, like Vance says, usually alone, sometimes in pairs, and never in a flock. My son Scott was in the United States Army, and one of his duty stations was in Fairbanks, Alaska, where he saw the eagle in huge flocks, but that is the exception, not the rule for this solitary bird. I feel our forefathers were right to choose the eagle as our national bird versus the turkey because can there be a better symbol for liberating freedom than the eagle?

When I think of how far our country has slipped from the moral and political ideals that shaped our country, the eagle must be sad. One of my saddest experiences has been seeing the eagle in a cage, in a zoo, or an animal sanctuary. I still remember the sorrow that came to my heart the day I visited my first zoo in India. In the bird section there was the Indian eagle in a very small cage. I wanted to let it loose. Eagles were created for crags on mountainsides, not cages in big city zoos. Being an avid fisherman, I have had the pleasure of watching eagles in the wild beside landlock salmon streams and bass lakes in the out of the way places in Maine. Each has been a thrill and brought a chill to my soul as I watched the lone eagle just sitting in the highest tree or fishing for supper in the waters where I was fishing. An eagle would never give up his open-space freedom for a cage for security and safety. The tragedy today is that there are a lot of people who covet security over liberty. I remember reading a story many, many years ago of a rancher who found an injured eagle in one of his back fields. Bringing the eagle back to his ranch, he tried his best to fix the eagle. Over time the eagle began to mingle with the barnyard chickens, enjoying the free food, and the pleasant surroundings. As the months passed the eagle's injury healed, but it became content in the barnyard. One morning as the rancher was watching the sun come up from over the eastern hills, a light breeze began to drift across the barnyard, and in a moment the rancher saw the eagle spread its wings. When the sun had escaped the hills and the breeze filled the eagle's wings, the eagle took off. The last time the rancher saw the eagle was when the magnificent creature caught the updraft thermals from off the hill and began to soar higher and higher.

I know why I like eagles! Like the eagle I, too, by my very nature am a solitary soul. I, like the eagle in the last story, had become content, comfortable in my barnyard, but when the time was right I, too, took off to soar in this big old world. Moses also uses the analogy of the eagle in his explanation of how the Almighty got the children of Israel out of the barnyard of Egypt: *"As an eagle stirreth up her nest, fluttereth over her young, spreadeth abroad her wings, taketh them, beareth them on her wings."* (Deuteronomy 32:11) I have taught my congregation often over the years that God's problem wasn't getting Israel out of Egypt; it was getting Egypt out of Israel. 430 years had made the Israelites comfortable in Egypt and until the trials and persecution came, they wanted to stay, and you remember the story well enough that even after they got out, they were always talking about going back (Number 11:1–5). An eaglet will never fly unless the eagle "stirs the nest," and we know sometimes God must do this with us. I write this article on our 24th day at Emmanuel during the Covid-19 shutdown. Sometimes, God has to destroy our comfortable nest, break us away from family and friends, allow sickness and disease to invade our space, or disasters to come so that we can only fly on wings of faith. If God didn't do this in our lives, then our situation could become a cage.

Have you noticed how many of God's great champions were eagles, solitary saints? What about Elijah (I Kings 17), or Micaiah (I Kings 22), or Amos (Amos 1), or Jonah (Jonah 1), or John the Baptist (Luke 1). As Vance said, **"Martin Luther was a free bird in the woods; Erasmus was a fat bird in a cage!"** There has always been a need for those that will buck the trends, go against the tide. My favorite in the list above is Micaiah. He comes on the scene in the days of Ahab for one encounter, then we never see him again. He stood against 400 yes-men of Ahab, and the last we see him he is being hauled off to jail being put on a bread and water diet (I Kings 22:27). The four hundred were fat cats in a cage, and one would think that is where Micaiah ended up, but I believe we can honestly say that though Micaiah was in Ahab's prison, he was not Ahab's prisoner! The Bible doesn't say if he ever got out, but the Bible does say that Micaiah was right (Ahab never returned from the battle alive), making him a prophet, a lone dissenting voice, an eagle.

I have told several people through this coronavirus pandemic that God knew best when He scattered the people at Babel (Genesis 11). As we are learning, this Covid-19 spreads in congregations, congested areas where people live on top of each other. Flocks get diseases that solitary creatures never get. Isn't it interesting that the world has figured out in this pandemic that we need to be more like the eagle, rather than a flock of chicken (probably where the virus came from in China). We are now told to isolate, keep a social distance, be loners and not minglers (my word). Before this crisis it was all about social involvement, group togetherness, and the herd mentality. I know this disruption of people's lives has made many a person crazy (cabin-fever is on the rise), but as for me it has been a blessed interlude to the hectic pace of the modern-day pastor. Oh, do I miss seeing the people and sharing in their lives? Certainly, but this world-wide crisis has reminded me that I am a loner by my very nature, and that I am an eagle. I will close with these words from Vance Havner in the book I referred to at the beginning of this chapter.

What is your cage? Is it a bad habit? Are you a slave of your congregation? You should get your church on your heart but not on your neck! Is it timidity, fear of man? Is it uncertainty, lack of authority? Have minors become majors and major's minors? Has your hobby become a hobble? Get back to the crags! Do not fear to be alone. **Eagles do not fly in flocks.** God grant you to mount up with wings into the glorious liberty wherewith Christ hath made you free and be not entangled again with the yoke of bondage! You are meant for crags, not cages!

So, what is it that has enslaved you, incarcerated your life, and set you into some kind of bondage? Remember what Isaiah said, "*. . . mount up . . . as eagles!*"

28.

GOD'S HIGHWAY PROGRAM

I HAVE BEEN BLESSED to live in the rapid-transportation age. I have read enough to know when the first missionaries left for India it took months, up to seven, to reach that fabled land. I think the longest it has taken me is 32 hours! I can reach my daughter in California in twelve hours or less, but the early pioneers took months to reach the west coast from the east coast. When I go north to visit my mother, it takes about three hours, whereas my forefathers trekked from southern Maine to northern Maine in weeks, many weeks! Highways and superhighways have made life easier. When I was a kid in Perham, there were still many dirt lanes, but even those asphalt free paths were quick compared to the streets of the past. Did you know that God has a highway program? With the coming of John the Baptist (Matthew 3:3) that program was started in fulfillment of these prophetic prophesies from Isaiah: *"The voice of him that crieth in the wilderness, prepare ye the way of the LORD, make straight in the desert **a highway for our God**. Every valley shall be exalted, and every mountain and hill shall be made low: and the crooked shall be made straight, and the rough places plain."* (Isaiah 40:3-4) Doesn't that sound like God's highway program?

Doesn't Isaiah's description of John's ministry sound like a highway project? " . . . **[M]ake straight** . . . " When a highway crew determines the course of the highway, don't they make it as straight as possible? " . . . **[H]ill shall be made low** . . . " Who among us hasn't travelled by a new highway and been surprised by the hills that have been flattened so the highway had no dips? " . . . **[C]rooked shall be made straight** . . . " What about the reconstruction of an old road that had many twists and turns in it, but the new highway now has no curves or corners because the construction crew made the highway straighter than it once was. "... [T]he rough places plain." Who of us hasn't travelled a rough highway (especially in the spring when the potholes appear) or an aged road, and then the road is given a new layer of hot top and the rough highway has become smooth (plain). Surely you understand the purpose of John the Baptist as he was the "forerunner" of the Christ. *"The beginning of the gospel of Jesus Christ, the Son of God; as it is written in the prophets, behold, I send my messenger before thy face,* **which shall prepare thy way before thee**. *The voice of one crying in the wilderness, Prepare ye the way of the Lord, make his paths straight."* (Mark 1:1–3) Jesus is God's highway program to the world.

America has outdone the world in its highway programs and projects. President Eisenhower was impressed with Hitler's autobahn when he was the commanding general of all Allied forces in Europe during the Second World War. When he came home from the war and was elected in 1952 to be our president, he started construction of the national highway system, "from sea to shining sea." Today that system can take anyone quickly from state to state and with very few obstacles unless there is an accident or road repairs. I have travelled from Maine to South Carolina, Texas, Pennsylvania, and just about every other state to the Mississippi. I have been on single lane highways, double lane highways, and triple lane highways. I have been on a few highways in California where there are eight lanes coming and going! But few are on God's highway because *"There is* **a way** *[highway] that seemeth right unto a man, but the end thereof are the ways of death."* (Proverbs 16:25) Did not Jesus speak of these highways in His great Sermon on the Mount? *"Enter ye in at the strait gate: for wide is the gate, and* **broad is the way**, *that leadeth to destruction, and many there be which go in there at: because strait is the gate, and narrow is* **the way**, *which leadeth unto life, and few there be that find it."* (Matthew 7:13–14) Most American's are on a broad way highway versus the narrow way.

Let me share with you some highway construction precepts that can be applied to God's highway, Jesus Christ. In any highway project there is a lot of blasting, and the first crew to come on the scene is the wrecking crew. If the highway is going through a town, often houses are demolished. **1) Highway building is destructive before it is constructive.** When Jesus came, He first had to demolish the Judea religion: *"No man putteth a piece of new cloth unto an old garment, for that which is put* *in to fill it up taketh from the garment, and the rent is made worse. Neither do men put new wine into old bottles; else the bottles break, and the wine runneth out, and the bottles perish: but they put new wine into new bottles, and both are preserved."* (Matthew 9:16–17) Getting rid of the old to replace it with new is destructive in nature. Jesus also said, *"Think not that I am come to send peace on earth: I came not to send peace, but a sword."* (Matthew 10:34) Swords are destructive weapons! Then Jesus said, *"And a man's foes shall be they of his own household."* (Matthew 10:36) Note the context in which Jesus says that he will divide families; very destructive. The hymn writer put it, "Lord Jesus, I long to be perfectly whole, I want Thee forever to live in my soul; break down very idol, cast out ever foe; now wash me and I shall be whiter than snow." Destructive before constructive!

Then you must realize that any 2) Highway building is disruptive before it is constructive. In any highway project there are a lot of things that are disrupted, like travel time between places, schedules, and daily routines. When Jesus came, he disrupted many things and many people. We might say that Jesus was the most disruptive person in history. His birth turned the Roman Empire on its head (Luke 2:1). The news of His arrival disrupted Herod and all Jerusalem with him (Matthew 2:3). Before He was through, He offended just about everybody He came into contact with--his fellow citizens of Nazareth (Luke 4:28–30); his brothers (John 7:3–5); His disciples (Matthew 16:23); the religious leaders; and his own followers (John 6:60–66). Jesus will disrupt your life if you follow Him. He will change your friends, change your habits, and change your schedule. *"Therefore if any man be in Christ, he is a new creature: old things are passed away; behold, all things are become new."* (II Corinthians 5:17) Disruptive before constructive!

Finally, you must realize that any **3) Highway project is expensive before it is constructive.** Surely you have heard of the staggering cost of highway projects, especially if you are going through a city (the big dig in Boston comes to mind). Most highway budgets are shot even before they are half done, but I believe the most expensive "highway" ever built was the Highway of God that takes someone from the depraved, wicked slums of earth to the throne of God in Heaven. Why expensive? Because it cost the Son of God his life: *"What? know ye not that your body is the temple of the Holy Ghost which is in you, which ye have of God, and ye are not your own? For ye are bought with a price: therefore glorify God in your body, and in your spirit, which are God's."* (I Corinthians 6:19–20) The price tag for this highway constructive program was *"Forasmuch as ye know that ye were not redeemed with corruptible things, as silver and gold, from your vain conversation received by tradition from your fathers; but with the precious blood of Christ, as of a lamb without blemish and without spot: who verily was foreordained before the foundation of the world, but was manifest in these last times for you."* (I Peter 1:18–20) Before the beginning of the earth God knew He would have to build a highway of salvation for the crown of His creation, mankind. He paid the price!

29.

IN TIMES LIKE THESE

AT THE WRITING OF this chapter in my "threescore and ten" memoir, I am reading a 1969 book by Vance Havner with the same title as this article. In 1969, I left home for college and never returned, except for a visit or two or three, yes, more. Within months of my departure from my family's homestead in Northern Maine I would start what has turned out to be a fifty-year ministry for me in the service of the King. I think it is worth taking the time to highlight what "**in times like these**" means to each of us, and here is my take on it.

Interestingly, I am also writing these thoughts during the infamous Covid-19, Coronavirus, pandemic, that has put the world into lockdown and "sheltering in place." There is a panic, uneasiness, and a fear I have not felt before in the world around me. Granted, the world has experienced worst pandemics, like the Spanish flu of 1918–20, but now it is in your face because of the advancements in communication. They are counting the numbers of cases and the numbers of deaths worldwide, and, in the States, hourly on CNN. Television station after television station is carrying nothing but Coronavirus news, medical updates, doctor interviews, and preventive tips, which brings me back to our statement, "**in times like these**." So, what times am I referring to?

In our bent to make things easier, more accessible, connected, one world, we failed to see the problem it might create in this category of "a pandemic." Was there a reason for God confusing the languages at Babel (Genesis 11) and sending the people of the world, around the world, in a sense separating them from one another? The world is rethinking and pondering if easy worldwide travel is such a good thing. This virus started in a city in China, but because of all the ease by which people travel around the world today, this virus moved rapidly throughout the world, carried by travelers from nation to nation. So, while the virus is polluting our bodies, the chemicals pouring from our factories are polluting our air, and the messages over the internet are polluting our minds. We live in the most technological time in history, yet we are still vunderable to a new strain of virus? And if we weren't spending our great-great grandchildren's money already, the Congress of the United States just passed a two-trillion-dollar stimulus package, or half the nation's budget for a year, with the nation already twenty plus trillion dollars (at the time of this printing 34 trillion) in debt. We are being devoured by debt, outwitted by a virus, and being gobbled up by panic, and we are paying for it all on money we don't have and will never pay it back.

As I type away at my computer, my dear wife is undergoing a procedure that will drain fluid from her right lung. The doctors feel that it is a side effect of her liver disease called NASH. What is becoming worrisome is this is the third time they have had to do this in 52 days, and the last procedure was only 9 days ago. Her condition is getting worse, but what makes this even worse is that I am not able to be with her like I was the last two times. Our local hospital has been closed to all visitors, no matter what, and we haven't a single case of the Coronavirus in our city or county yet! I am a student of history enough to know that all great civilizations have fallen eventually no matter how big or powerful. I get the feeling that events like Covid-19 are just the opening salvo to the onslaught that will eventually bring our proud nation to its knees. Some say we are different, but I know the Egyptians knew things and how to do things that we don't know even to this day, but they fell. The Greek state was filled with smart statesmen, brilliant philosophers, elegant orators, and amazing artists whose works are still admired today, but Greece fell. Rome is the example most look to as the best of the best in advancement, unmatched until our age, yet it fell under a moral decline that took its material and military progress down with it. Today our leaders are crashing the economy to crush this virus, but what they don't see is, though America is materially wealthy and militarily strong and without a doubt we will probably survive economically and militarily for a time, we are morally rotten to the very core of our society. We have gained the whole world, but we have lost our soul (Matthew 16:26). **"Sad fares the land, to hastening ills a prey. Where wealth accumulates, and men decay!"** In times like these we are lost.

I have come to believe that if you want an unbiased opinion on the state of affairs in our times, all you have to do is read Paul's description of the last days he called *"perilous times:"* (II Timothy 3:1–4) *"This know also, that in the last days perilous times shall come. For men shall be lovers of their own selves, covetous, boasters, proud, blasphemers, disobedient to parents, unthankful, unholy, without natural affection, trucebreakers, false accusers, incontinent, fierce, despisers of those that are good, traitors, heady, highminded, lovers of pleasures more than lovers of God."* Another good read for a description of **"in times like these"** is Romans 1:24–31: *"Wherefore* **God also gave them up** *to uncleanness through the lusts of their own hearts, to dishonour their own bodies between themselves: who changed the truth of God into a lie, and worshipped and served the creature more than the Creator, who is blessed for ever. Amen. For this cause* **God gave them up** *unto vile affections: for even their women did change the natural use into that which is against nature: and likewise also the men, leaving the natural use of the woman, burned in their lust one toward another; men with men working that which is unseemly, and receiving in themselves that recompence of their error which was meet. And even as they did not like to retain God in their knowledge,* **God gave them over** *to a reprobate mind, to do those things which are not convenient; being filled with all unrighteousness, fornication, wickedness, covetousness, maliciousness; full of envy, murder, debate, deceit, malignity; whisperers, backbiters, haters of God, despiteful, proud, boasters, inventors of evil things, disobedient to parents, without understanding, covenantbreakers, without natural affection, implacable, unmerciful."* Our times for sure!

I am living in the theology of my Lord who told us in His Word that **"in times like these"** sin would abound, charity will abate: *"And because iniquity shall abound, the love of many shall wax cold . . . "* (Matthew 24:12) and faith will be practically nonexistent. *"Nevertheless when the Son of man cometh, shall he find faith on the earth?"* (Luke 18:8) Politically, socially, economically, and scientifically these characteristics are clearly seen in our nation and around the world, and I say with Paul: *"But this I say, brethren,* **the time is short***: it remaineth, that both they that have wives be as though they had none; and they that weep, as though they wept not; and they that rejoice, as though they rejoiced not; and they that buy, as though they possessed not; and they that use this world, as not abusing it:* **for the fashion of this world passeth away.***"* (I Corinthians 7:29–31) The great late D. G. Campbell Morgan use to say, "I never lay my head on the pillow at night without thinking that before morning dawns the final morning may have dawned." As do I **"in times like these!"** At the height of the Second World War, a lady by the name of Ruth Caye Jones wrote the words and the tune to a simple hymn with the title <u>In Times Like These</u>:

> In times like these you need a Saviour,
> in times like these you need an anchor;
> Be very sure, be very sure,
> your anchor holds and grips the solid Rock.
>
> In times like these you need the Bible,
> in times like these Oh be not idle,
> Be very sure, be very sure,
> your anchor holds and grips the solid Rock.
>
> This rock is Jesus, yes, He's the One . . . !

30.

WHATEVER HAPPENED TO CHRISTIANITY IN MY LIFETIME?

HAVE YOU NOTICED THAT Christianity is out of fashion in America today, and the name Christian is being redefined and reinvented? In my lifetime our two-thousand-year-old faith and name has been replaced by a spiritual secularism, a godly humanism, and man, not God, has been deified. Doctrines that once were mainstream are out of favor, and teachings that were once a certainty, accepted, and even defined by laws are now questioned and outlawed, even by those that profess a faith in Christ. Historic Christianity has become drab, dull, and discredited, allowing many to discard it to the dust ben of antiquity. 21st century Christianity has become whatever you want it to be, partnered with whatever modern philosophy that at the moment seemingly is in vogue. Those who preach the gospel of inclusiveness, the teaching of accommodation, the doctrine of tolerance, and the theory of acceptance, mock any who will not embrace the current culture of Christianity and the philosophical trends that have rejected the core, fundamental teachings of the Founder of Christianity, the God-man whose name they still invoke in their new religions. In my lifetime this change has taken place and I for one never noticed the pot getting warmer and the faith being cooked until recently. The demonic art of deception has replaced the Godly beauty of truth, and words like discrimination, prejudice, and bigotry only hold meaning when it supports the liberal, humanistic intellectual agenda of those that want to do away with the structure and statutes of Christianity while maintaining the name and image. In a word, in my opinion, and in the observations I have made over my lifetime, hypocrisy has become the national pastime, lies have been turned into truth, and truth into lies by the religious actors (the true meaning of hypocrite) that would change our faith, our Founder, our foundations, and our future. So, whatever happened to Christianity in my lifetime as I near seventy?

Whatever happened to the Apostle Paul's exhortation to the Church at Ephesus: *"There is one body, and one Spirit, even as ye are called in one hope of your calling; one Lord, one faith, one baptism, one God and Father of all, who is above all, and through all, and in you all."* (Ephesians 4:4–6) This has become more than an issue between Congregationalists and Catholics, Baptists and Brethren, Pentecostals and Presbyterians. It doesn't really matter regarding your denominational identity as we have been mixed together into a common word, **Christians**, which in the eyes of most has been relegated to a farce, a fraud, or a foolish faith that is worthless in our modern, civilized, and cultured world. We are too smart, too scientifically savvy to be doped into believing the fables and fancies of a faith based on the short life of a carpenter from Nazareth. A few years ago, I wrote down the foundation of my faith in these words. Maybe they will help you understand why I never questioned what was going on around me:

> I have but a simple country creed, a terrain theology, a "dirt" doctrine, a farm faith. Years ago, in my barnyard boyhood, I decided to stake all that I am or ever hope to be on the teachings of a country carpenter from Galilee. Though I left the Blackstone homestead over forty-five years ago, I still live in its fragrance and faith. When Jesus strolled the back lanes of Judea, He taught through trees and birds and seeds. Perhaps this is why I picked up His philosophy so quickly in my youth. The more I read through His theology, the more I could relate to it through my surroundings on the homestead. When He talked of the sower going forth to sow his seeds, I could see my grandfather and my father doing the same thing. When He spoke of the sparrow and its fall, I, too, watched as the little bird tumbled from the hayloft to the barn floor. When He taught of the trees and their significance to the kingdom, I understood the meaning of the forest because I lived in one. I did and still don't understand everything the Man from Galilee was saying, but I did and do understand His object lessons from my days of walking in the hills and living in the hallows of the homestead. In the complexity of sunlight and shadows, I saw in the darkness of a walk through the cow barn at night just how black sin can be in the human heart, but

I also discovered in the light of the midday, homestead sun, just how brilliant the glory of the Lord can be. As I grew, the pasture parables of sheep and shepherds became for me the same as herds of Holsteins and herdsmen (Yes, I was a cow-boy!). Sheep were replaced by cows. When "green pastures" and "still waters" were mentioned, my mind's eye immediately viewed the Russell Place with its ponds and creeks in pastureland of green fields. (I know now after visiting Israel I had a wrong concept of David's psalm), but for a farmhand from Maine the point was clearly seen, God will provide for his own whether Palestine or Perham. The longer I live the more I am convinced that my real seminary training began long before I went off to Bible school in Greenville, South Carolina. In my boyhood, I spent most of my free days outdoors, whether working in the fields or playing in the forest, I was constantly faced with reality. Life and death were a normal part of life. Long before my first funeral, I had looked death in the eye and learned it was nothing to fear or be afraid of, whether feline or friend, death was just part of life and living. I also learned that the simple pleasures of life were much more rewarding than the worldly passions of excess. To pick dandelions in the spring and to listen to the songbirds in the summer were much more pleasurable than picking up friends and going to the movies. A walk alone along the fence line was far more joyful than a walk through the red-light district. I have come to the city now to pastor, but my creed is still well established in the lessons I learned from the land as a lad and the teaching from the trees I learned from my teens. Today I preach an outdoor kind of faith to an indoor kind of world. It's time we as a society retrace the steps of the Master and learn His country creed and conduct.

Besides, hasn't there been uncovered enough evidence that Jesus was really a liar, a lunatic, a leader that was denied and betrayed by his own disciples. I for most of my life was so focused in proclaiming this Christ, I didn't notice that my faith was being destroyed in the mainstream media, in the institutions of religious training, and in the pulpits of the great churches, cathedrals, and chapels of the land. The destruction of our faith has taken place both by assaults from without and with attacks from within. (Jude 4)

So, whatever happened to the simple child-like faith of a farmer's son from Perham? Over my lifetime the traditional Christian practices and beliefs of my America have faded into the background as a highly motivated, fully educated, easily mobile, and worldly society has taken over our American culture. Once upon a time there was no shopping on Sunday (now Thanksgiving Day has become Thanksgetting Day). Once upon a time there was prayer in school (now armed guards must protect most schools). Once upon a time we could walk through our great cities without fear (now we see terrorists behind every face). We have forgotten that *"Except the Lord keep the city, the watchman waketh but in vain."* Psalm 127:1. Once upon a time we lived under moral laws that defined marriage as one woman and one man (now marriage is defined in whatever terms you want--Bob and Bill as well as Mary and Martha). Once upon a time a baby was safe in its mother's womb (now it is the most dangerous place on the planet for a child). In my lifetime these new cultural elites who set the trends and make the laws have determined that the divinity of Christ is a myth and that divinity itself is now a term for man. They have chosen to throw off and discard any theology which casts a shadow on their innovations, inventions, and ideological actions as sin or sinful. They have dismissed religious faith for personal freedom to do and destroy anything that once was established by a faith that for millennium has stabilized a depraved humanity and a corrupt mankind. This age has chosen to dismiss the orthodoxy of Christianity as something unworthy of an educated, sophisticated, cultured society. Oh, religion is still in vogue, but the more exotic and bizarre the better (why the eastern religions, Mormonism, and Islam, are on the rise in this land). Spirituality is at an all-time high, but spirituality without a taint of traditional orthodoxy. My childhood faith is no longer mentioned unless it is part of a withering critique, a raging critic, or a mean-spirited criticism of my Lord and Savior Jesus Christ.

I have been watching for over half a century the great universities and colleges of our land, the major newspapers and powerful TV networks along with the recognized foundations with the political bureaucracy of Washington, Hollywood, and Madison Avenue dismiss the wisdom and understanding of the faith of Peter and Paul, Augustine and Aquinas, Luther and Luke, John Winthrop and Jonathan Edwards, George Washington, and Abraham Lincoln. The faith of our fathers has been declassified, and we can no longer say that a handful of rotten potatoes is spoiling the whole barrel because the whole barrel is now spoiled, and whether we like it or not we live now in the oozing, festering barrel together. If we are not corrupted yet, we are tainted. Recently, I recognized for the first time why I feel so dirty in this world. The filth of Lot is now the lot of the true Christian of America. *"And delivered just Lot, vexed with the filthy conversation of the wicked: for that righteous man dwelling among them, in seeing and hearing, vexed his righteous soul from day to day with their unlawful deeds."* (II Peter 2:7-7) Are you feeling the vexation yet? Has the filth covered you yet? I have come to believe that, like Lot, our only hope is the rapture or the promise of II Peter 2:9.

When I was 15 (1966), also the year I preached my first sermon (2016 will be my fiftieth year preaching, and my hope was to preach the same sermon on the anniversary of that first message with the same message, and I did), a Time Magazine article was published with the title Is God Dead? As in the Garden of Eden when Satan first caused man to question his God (Genesis 3:1), during my teenage years the Wicked One was bold enough to publish his new battle plan against Christianity, and I quote, **"The notion that henceforward Christianity could flourish only by transforming itself into a more secular enterprise, dedicated to building the kingdom of God in this life rather than preparing believers for the afterlife. In this secularized faith, Christ would be invoked 'as a spiritual HERO** [think Jesus Christ Superstar] **whom even non-believers can admire,' while God and transcendence would be associated with the modern hope for a better future--a hope that would be achieved through progressive politics and enjoyed by a human race that has 'taken responsibility for the world.'"** And now that I look back 50 years, I see that this manifesto has been fulfilled. Mankind has determined that he is smart enough to take care of himself (I write this at the height of the Covid-19 pandemic and not once have I heard a call for a national day of prayer, of repentance, but only that we will figures this out!), and that the planet is his only world, and he needs to care for it (this whole global climate change controversy is part of mankind "taking responsibility for the world"). Jesus is now just another one of the world heroes (Jesus is Islam's second greatest prophet), a good man who did his best and is worthy of emulation as a man, but certainly not as God. Besides, if God is not dead, He is just a being that is "watching us from a distance" (a popular song of a few years ago). Along with the death of God has come the burial of the clearly taught doctrine of the Bible on the depravity of man. Man no longer sins; he only makes mistakes because of disease.

When mankind turned from the supernatural to the natural, from theology to anthropology, and from the Kingdom of God to the City of Man, he had to disregard the sinful nature and depravity of the nature of man. Putting it another way, I have come to believe that the root problem with Christianity today, and it matters not whether we are talking about moderate, liberal, or conservative Christianity, Christianity is no longer God-centered, but man-centered (think of the exaltation of the Pope in the eyes of most today). We have developed a theology of man, and in that theology man is inherently good, not bad; evolving upward versus spiraling downward; capable of improvement and certainly not as Paul taught, *"O wretched man that I am! . . . So then they that are in the flesh cannot please God."* (Romans 7:24, 8:8) Man is only looking to please himself, certainly not God, and this is not the first time in history man has set his own rules and established his own standards. I have been preaching for years that it appears to me that we are returning to the Age of the Judges of Israel: *"In those days there was no king in Israel* [note, not only have we dethroned God we have also dethroned Jesus as King of our lives]: ***every man did that which was right in his own eyes."*** (Judges 21:25) Is not this the philosophy of this age? Surely, you see it, don't you?

In college seminaries and ecclesiastical institutions, pastors and priests began to switch from theology to politics (think the "moral majority") and the central mission of the church became social, not evangelical. We began to abandon the Great Commission for the great compromise. Our new motto is "**creeds divide, deeds unite!**" That is why we only hear about "inclusion," "acceptance," "accommodation," and "tolerance" today. Inclusion will go down as the word of the 21st century if we don't stand up and start re-proclaiming the Word of God as the sole authority in both the secular as well as the spiritual world. Think of it, inclusion of woman as pastors, inclusion of transgender people (another word that will define our age), inclusion of gays and lesbians, inclusion of minorities and immigrants. Inclusion preaches embracing the counter-cultural seeker, skeptic, lukewarm believer, the agnostic, and the atheist into a rainbow that makes nothing black or white, cold or hot, right or wrong. There was a time when you could tell the players without a program, but now a male or a female is hard to define, the black and the white are gray, and right and wrong is up for debate. We have marginalized the precepts and concepts of God to the point they are nearing extinction. We care more for the extinction of a small darting fish, a forest monkey, and a coastal bird than we do the extinction of our historic, orthodoxy faith. When personal improvement and social reform become the priorities of the Church; when soup kitchens and social justice become the focus of our attention in the Church; and when encounters and mysterious happenings become the core of our meetings in the Church, then we have broken one of the fundamental teachings of the Man who put Christ in Christianity: *"Woe unto you hypocrites... ye... have omitted the weightier matters of the law, judgment, mercy, and faith: these ought ye to have done, and not to leave the others undone."* (Matthew 23:23)

To summarize, whatever happened to Christianity in my lifetime, "truth" was sacrificed in the name of accommodation; "Christ" was sacrificed in the name of inclusion; "Faith" was sacrificed in the name of tolerance; and "Christianity" was sacrificed in the name of acceptance. As I watch the state of affairs happening in what has become modern Christianity, I come to the conclusion that we have made a poor choice. We have given away the farm and for what? We live in an unstable world with no historical roots, no firm foundation for morality, and no alternative but total collapse.

31.

A CAUSALITY OF THE CORONAVIRUS WHO NEVER HAD COVID-19

I NEVER IMAGINED THAT one of the heartaches of passing through my 70th year would be a trip through *"the valley of the shadow of death"* (Psalm 23:4—yes, His rod and staff have been a great comfort) with the departure of my dear wife Coleen for Glory Land. Six weeks after I entered my threescore and tenth year, my companion of 51 years, my wife of 47 years, and the love of my life yielded to a liver disease called NASH (non-alcoholic cirrhosis of the liver) and was ushered into the presence of her Saviour and our Lord, Jesus Christ. The irony of her death happened at the very height of the coronavirus pandemic that is still gripping the world and devastating our country's older citizens and the greatest economy on this planet. I shared on the Sunday after her death (April 17, 2020) a message on Facebook's "live streaming" that I recalled well the 1960s during the height of the Vietnam War that every night on Walter Cronkite's evening newscast on CBS that he would share with the nation the death toll of the United States soldiers who had died that day. Often the numbers were in the hundreds, and Walter did that for years on end until the death toll was well over 50,000 into the 1970s! The newscasters of today are doing the same now, but the number of Coronavirus deaths around the country, and especially in New York, the epicenter of the pandemic in America, every day for weeks now have been in the thousands. I said, "What the long and deadly Vietnam War took years to accomplish, the Covid-19 virus will do in weeks!" I have just checked the running score on my IPhone, and we have just passed 45,000 in the United States and 175,000 worldwide, so within days we will match the Vietnam totals in just under two months! (Eventually, the total in just one year was 600,000 in the United States and nearly 4,000,000 worldwide.) So, what did Coleen's death have to do with the Coronavirus?

In a 75-day ordeal which included 8 ultrasounds and cat scans, 26 X-rays, 27 visits to doctor's offices and other medical facilities, including 7 visits to the ER and 4 stays in the hospital for a total of 13 days, six times having at least two liters of fluid taken off her right lung (in her last trip to the hospital, we were actually going in to get the fluid removed for the seventh time), and a Life Flight from Northern Light Maine Coast Memorial Hospital in Ellsworth to Northern Light Eastern Maine Medical Center in Bangor, Maine, because of hemorrhaging and a seizure, my wife's condition came in direct conflict with the shutdown that was taking place, not only in our society, but also in the medical arena. The irony of the day I write this remembrance (April 22, 2020) is that we were supposed to be in Boston visiting a liver specialist (Doctor Gordon) that was supposed to start the process of getting Coleen on a liver transplant list. A week ago, the day I took Coleen into the hospital for the last time, we were supposed to be in Portland seeing our liver specialist there (Doctor Kennedy), but those appointments and several others like that were cancelled because of the Covid-19 virus. The numbers I shared at the beginning of this paragraph don't include the numerous phone calls about my wife and her condition. "Social distancing" had become the norm even when it came to a lady dying, not of coronavirus, but liver failure! And a procedure called TIPS (putting a stent in the liver to help with the fluid buildup) was seen as elective surgery so this, too, was cancelled or put off until the pandemic was over, but my wife didn't have that kind of time as it turned out. I shared with everyone in the medical profession that would listen to me that after this pandemic crisis is over, I believe the medical establishment will discover scores, if not thousands, of patients who never got the Covid-19 virus, but either died because life giving procedures were postponed or delayed resulting in death or a more serious condition developing because of the delays in treatments. Yes, I believe that Coleen was a causality of the Coronavirus without even contracting Covid-19!

I hope that you don't think I am complaining or upset with the medical profession over what has happened to my wife. I believe they did all that they could do under the circumstances and in the current situation. If we could have gotten to Boston or had the TIPS procedure done in Portland, it would not have changed the ultimate outcome. My wife was sick, very sick, and sicker than any of us knew, including the doctors, I believe. Shortly after our annual Christmas trip to Salinas, California, in 2019 to be with our daughter and family, Coleen began a steady decline in her health. She became weaker and more tired. Little did we know the fluid was building around her right lung (a result that fooled the professionals for a while because normally the fluid would build up in the abdomen and the legs), and that her liver was near its end. Her time of departure (II Timothy 4:6) was nearing, and nobody realized it during the final three and a half months of her life. But God knew, and shortly after Coleen passed on the Good Lord told me all about it through a familiar Biblical story in the life of Hezekiah.

The story of Coleen's transfer to heaven actually started in January, 2005, when it was discovered in an annual exam that Coleen had breast cancer. The shock was devastating, but I still remember the first words out of her mouth after she was told the news, "Why not me?" (<u>Why Not Me?</u> is the title of the book I am writing about this experience. I wrote a book called <u>Beyond the Bend</u> chronicling Coleen's and my struggle watching our only son Scott die of liver and lung cancer during a six-month ordeal in 2016–2017. Little did I know the sequel would be written just three short years later!) Over the next eight months Coleen endured three surgeries and seven sickening chemo treatments for one reason that she might live long enough to see our daughter Marnie married (2014 to a wonderful man named Josue) and the birth of our grandchildren Judah (2015) and Elena (2018). As I reread Hezekiah's story, I realized His experience was Coleen's experience: *"In those days was Hezekiah sick unto death. And the prophet Isaiah the son of Amoz came to him, and said unto him, thus saith the LORD, set thine house in order; for thou shalt die, and not live. Then he turned his face to the wall, and prayed unto the LORD, saying, I beseech thee, O LORD, remember now how I have walked before thee in truth and with a perfect heart, and have done that which is good in thy sight. And Hezekiah wept sore. And it came to pass, afore Isaiah was gone out into the middle court, that the word of the LORD came to him, saying, turn again, and tell Hezekiah the captain of my people, Thus saith the LORD, the God of David thy father, I have heard thy prayer, I have seen thy tears: behold, I will heal thee: on the third day thou shalt go up unto the house of the LORD. And I will add unto thy days **fifteen years** . . . "* (II Kings 20:1–6) Coleen got exactly 15 years from the time of her cancer operations to the time she died of liver failure!

The first sermon I preached after my wife's death (48 hours later) was titled "Delightful Desperation," and, though these two words don't seem compatible, they are if you know Jesus as your Saviour. The Lord God was gracious and merciful to take Coleen to heaven so gently; she simply went to sleep and was escorted to heaven by angels (Luke 16:22) and woke in the arms of Jesus (II Corinthians 5:6). I even shared with those on Facebook that the Lord led me to the instruction that caused me to preach that Sunday morning: *"So I spake unto the people in the morning: and **at even my wife died**; and I did in the morning as I was commanded."* (Ezekiel 24:18) My wife has started eternal life (Romans 6:23), but I still have my 70th year to finish, and finish I will until we meet again!

32.

ADDING TO MY PERSONAL PROVERBS

1- Avoid, abstain, and accelerate in the opposite direction when you come across a sin.

2- Secularism, materialism, and socialism mingled with Christianity have turned the average believer into a spiritual zombie. They walk about, they worship weekly, and he or she works for the Lord in a trance-like state. They go through the motions and movements of Christianity, but without the power of God in their lives.

3- The best way to "yield not to temptation" is to have your running shoes on!

4- Our spiritual life is supposed to be like an artesian well, no priming, no pumping, just a continual pouring.

5- What kind of example will you leave when you depart from this world? Will you be remembered for faithfully following the Lord or will you be remembered for faltering near the finish line?

6- God doesn't have to be bribed, bought, or bargained with to gain His favor.

7- Whether lameness, leprosy, or lack of sight, a handicap from God might just be the greatest blessing you get from God.

8- Let us never forget that the God who created the natural world can make the abnormal normal.

9-God is still looking for matched sets who can agree on a course, the cost, and His commission; a duo that can back-to-back fight off all temptations, tests, and trials until the battle is won! (Paul and Silas)

10-Hell is unparalleled to anything we can imagine: unanswered prayer, unsatisfied thirst, unmistakable torment, unforgettable regret, unending suffering, and an inescapable sentence.

11-Today, as you hold on against the onslaught of the wicked one, look over the battlements beyond the advancing hordes, look above the raging battle and battlefield, and see the invisible army of God coming to your rescue (Elisha at Dothan).

12-To destroy the Church, to disorganize the Church, to demolish the Church, would take the destruction of God Himself.

13-When there is strife in a house, somebody had better learn to sing.

14-We must be careful even in victory, lest we yield to pride that will spell defeat in our next battle.

15-Though our body will decelerate as we grow older, our spirit should accelerate as we grow older.

16-When God wants to work something for "good" in our lives, He often allows something "bad" into our lives.

17-Sometimes God gives us "wings," but at other times he gives us "weights." We are just as much governed by God's "starts" as we are by His "stops."

18-Climbing with the wrong mountaineer can be a very difficult climb.

19-Climbing is hard enough without an enemy in the camp. They will slow your accent, they will stop your climb, and they will sucker you into an easier route that will only lead you to a defeat, disgrace, or death.

20-A false philosophy has crept into the Church: "I can do whatever I want with whomever I want whenever I want."

21-Your character will be affected by the character of your companions. Your standards will be touched by the standards of your friends. Your convictions will be molded by the convictions of those you travel with.

22-Love what you do and do what you love!

23- The Lord will recruit. The Lord will draft, but the Lord loves volunteers.

24- I will let the critics criticize and the debaters debate, but as for me, I am here to stress changeability and adaptability in the service of the King.

25- Satan is attacking with all his fury the sick, the suffering, and the straggler. He loves to assault the weak, the weary, the wounded, and the wanderer. It is the duty of the saint to defend the "hindmost" of the Church (think Dan and Israel).

26- It is still trust and obey; it is still faith and works; it is still march and shout; it is still dip and be healed because we must, as those of old, still follow the exact instructions of the Lord if the desired result will be achieved.

27- The expectancy of faith is still a large part of the element of the Christian's success.

28- Weary in the battle, but never weary of the battle.

29- Remember, when we get to Heaven, Jesus won't ask to see your degree or diploma, your medals or medallions, your family tree, or your firm's tribute, but he will ask to see the scars you received in His service.

30- The man who tires of prayer is already defeated.

31- Life is full of trials and tragedies that bring tears, but we should never forget that after God collects our tears, the final thing He will do is wipe away all our tears.

32- What the Church of God could accomplish if its soldiers didn't care who got the stash or the cash!

33- Faith is seeing what others cannot see.

34- The secret of faith is found in the belief of a loving, caring God; that no destroyed dream, that no hopeless hope, that no thwarted time, and that no frustrated future is beyond God's will to work it out for His glory and our good.

35- The secret to a "good" experience during a "bad" time is a merry heart.

36- Win by beginning; nobody wins who never starts!

37-One of the most difficult lessons to learn in life is to know which bridge to build, which bridge to cross, and which bridges to burn.

38-Our desire ought to be to compete as well as complete our spiritual race.

39-A faith that fizzles before the finish had a flaw from the first.

40-Human penmanship, but divine authorship, is at the heart of the inspiration of the scriptures.

41-An "A" No. 1 pastor is an angel, an apostle, and an ambassador.

42-Any climb to God must be an upward accent; ours is supposed to be a climb, not a crawl.

43-So many today in the church have the appearance of attachment to Christ, but fall into the category of "profession, but no possession."

44-We are hearing more about relevance than reverence today.

45-"The last mile of the way" will lead us through a battlefield, not a playground.

46-The devil has tricked us into thinking, like he did the children of Israel on their journey, that we have already arrived, that the battle it over, that the victory has been won and now it is time to play.

47-Defeat is not as fatal as suicide, but pity and pride will convince you differently.

33.

MINISTRY

Eight letters, one word, but contained within those letters and that word is the summary of nearly fifty years of labor for this pastor entering his seventieth year.

Paul encouraged Timothy to "*. . . **make full proof of thy ministry** . . .*" (II Timothy 4:5), something I have tried to do. Paul challenged Archippus to "*. . . **take heed to the ministry which thou hast received in the Lord, that thou fulfil it** . . .*" (Colossians 4:17), which I have been faithfully trying to do all these years. Paul exhorted the Corinthians to give "*. . . **no offence in any thing, that the ministry be not blamed** . . .*" (II Corinthians 6:3), which I have worked hard not to do. I was a very young man (22 years old) when I took up the commission described by Paul in Ephesians 4:11-13 in relationship to the Church: *"And He gave some, apostles; and some, prophets; and some, evangelists; and some, **pastors and teachers** [that's me]; for the perfecting of the saints, **for the work of the ministry**, for the edifying of the body of Christ: till we all come in the unity of the faith, and of the knowledge of the Son of God, unto a perfect man, unto the measure of the stature of the fulness of Christ."* I know that the word "ministry" means something different to every minister and that every ministry is different depending on what the Good Lord has called you into. But with Paul I can boldly proclaim, *"**Therefore seeing we have this ministry, as we have received mercy, we faint not.**"* (II Corinthians 4:1) Over the years I have watched many a fellow minister fall by the wayside because of some sin, while others have given in and given up seeking employment in other areas. I, like Paul, can only praise the Lord for His mercy and grace seeing me through the many obstacles and various pitfalls of the ministry called "the pastorate" through this half century of ministry.

As Paul closed his first epistle to the Corinthians Church, he wrote these eye-opening lines: *"I beseech you, brethren, (ye know the house of Stephanas, that it is the firstfruits of Achaia, and that **they have addicted themselves to the ministry of the saints**,) that ye submit yourselves unto such, and to every one that helpeth with us, and laboureth."* (I Corinthians 16:15-16) Note the word "addicted." It is the only time the Greek word *tasso* is used in the Bible. It means simply "to arrange, or to set oneself." Paul was saying that the house of Stephanas had arranged themselves to minister to the saints; that they had set themselves to minister to their fellow believers. Fifty years ago, I also did that and continue every day that I wake to the same purpose of who will I minister to today? It is the actions of my Lord and Saviour I mirror in the ministry. Remember what Jesus told His disciples when they were arguing over who would sit where in the kingdom and who would be the greatest: *"For even the Son of man came not **to be ministered** unto, but **to minister**, and to give his life a ransom for many."* (Mark 10:45) I believe that I was called to minister, not be ministered unto. Have I had to be ministered to over the years? Certainly, but I much prefer to minister. It is in my spiritual DNA to minister, not to be ministered unto.

There is nothing that can destroy a fellowship quicker than when members of a fellowship begin to think of only themselves, like John and James did in the reference in the last paragraph or the disciples as individuals did in Luke 9:46: *"Then there arose a reasoning among them, which of them should be greatest."* Note in both cases how quickly Jesus recognized the dangerous foe and took it squarely on and eradicated it. There is no place in any ministry for the proud and arrogant, the self-important, or those who see themselves as superior to other brethren. The tragedy is that this danger can happen even in the most pious and polite church situations or circumstances. Why? The natural man seeks a crack to worm his way into a place where he is seen as more important than another and, in turn, turn a ministry into something about him, what we might call self-justification. So many in the ministry have lost sight of the primary purpose for ministry: *"For as touching **the ministering to the saints**, it is superfluous for me to write to you: for I know the forwardness of your mind, for which I boast of you to them of Macedonia, that Achaia was ready a year ago; and your zeal hath provoked very many. Yet have I sent the brethren, lest our boasting of you should be in vain in* *this behalf; that, as I said, ye may be ready."* (II Corinthians 9:1–13) Paul feared, even in the best of places, a problem might arise that would stop their ministry to the needs of saints.

So, after fifty years of trying to minister after the example of Jesus and the instructions of Paul, what do I believe are the most important aspects of **"ministry?"** I will share them in the order I believe of importance in my (and yours) service for the Lord:

1. **The Ministry of Forbearance.** *"With all lowliness and meekness, with longsuffering, **forbearing one another in love**."* (Ephesians 4:2) I believe this is the most overlooked virtue in ministry, tolerating in others what you will not tolerate in yourself. There is too much "my way or the highway" in the ministry.

2. **The Ministry of Faithfulness.** *"Moreover it is required in stewards that a man **be found faithful**."* (I Corinthians 4:2) Faithfulness to a flock, faithfulness to the Word, and faithfulness in one's calling no longer seems important. To stay and just be faithful. In an almost 30-year pastorate and an almost 50-year ministry, I have learned sometimes God just wants you to stay when it is easier to leave. Just be faithful. God will do the rest!

3. **The Ministry of Freedom.** *"For, brethren, ye have been **called unto liberty**; only use not liberty for an occasion to the flesh, but by love serve one another."* (Galatians 5:13) I am ashamed to admit that I was a legalist in the early days of my ministry, but through the Bible I recognized that I am not another man's master, even as a pastor, that I can't be a spiritual dictator in anything (I Peter 5:3).

4. **The Ministry of Forwardness.** *"I speak not by commandment, but by occasion of **the forwardness of others**, and to prove the sincerity of your love."* (II Corinthians 8:8) The basic meaning of the Greek word we translate "forwardness" is "speed or haste." For me, this translates into the ministry of the urgency of time. Like with the preaching of the Word we are to be *". . . instant in season, out of season . . . "* (II Timothy 4:2), so are we to be ready to minister at any time or place.

5. **The Ministry of Forgiveness.** *"And be ye kind one to another, tenderhearted, **forgiving one another**, even as God for Christ's sake hath forgiven you."* (Ephesians 4:32) This is sorely lacking in pastoral leadership today, both the forgiving of oneself and the forgiving of

others. I still know pastors who are holding grudges against former parishioners. We stop forgiving when Jesus stops forgiving!

6. **The Ministry of Forgoing.** *"Look not every man on his own things, but every man also on the things of others."* (Philippians 2:4) The word is to "overlook" things, but I use it to overlook your things for others. Thomas a' Kempis once said, "Never think that thou hast made any progress till thou look upon thyself as inferior to all!" I still say "the golden rule" is the best rule (Matthew 7:12).

7. **The Ministry of Fellowship.** *"And they continued stedfastly in the apostles' doctrine and **fellowship**, and in breaking of bread, and in prayers."* (Acts 2:42) This is why we named my first ministry the Pembroke Bible Fellowship. We must get back to the doctrine of I John 1:3, 6–7, the fellowship with God and each other.

34.

NOT AN IDEAL BUT A DIVINE REALITY

How many times in Church history has a group of believers tried to create the ideal local assembly? They have tried isolation, legislation, and excommunication to make the perfect church, yet in each case, in time, the experiment has failed or just died out for lack of members. It started with a dream, a wish, a desire by someone, male or female, thinking they had come up with the right scheme, the proper plan, the perfect pattern, a definite idea of what the Christian church should look like, be like, act like, live like, and worship like. But in time and over time these spiritual schemes, every one of them, and I am talking about those that are in the world and working today, did fail and will fail, even though the participants don't realize it now, and few saw it then. Why the average believer is so susceptible to the disillusionment of others, the dream world of leaders, the rapturous experiences of certain saints, and the lofty moods of the brethren, I don't know, but what I do know from Scripture is the Church is not an idea, but a divine reality.

What we forget is that our God, unlike human beings, even Christian beings, is not a God of emotions, feelings, impulses, but a God of truth, pure truth, divine truth. This reality came to me when a series of verses jumped off the Biblical page at me: (1) Acts 2:47: " . . . *And* **the Lord added to the church** *daily such as should be saved.*" (2) Matthew 16:18: "*And I say also unto thee, that thou art Peter, and upon this rock* **I will build my church**; *and the gates of hell shall not prevail against it.*" (3) Ephesian 2:22–23: "*And hath put all things under his feet, and gave him* **to** *be the head over all things to the church, which is his body, the fulness of him that filleth all in all."* Only when the Body of Christ, and I mean each member of that Body, realizes that it is the Lord's Church, He is building it, and He has all dominion over it and that it is not our dreams or schemes that will move it or motivate it, only then, will we see the divine reality that is the Church. We have lost focus on the real Church because of the buildings, chapels, and cathedrals that have distracted us away from the real reality of what the Church is in relationship to the body of believers. I think it is as simple as how Paul described this truth: *"While we look not at the things which are seen, but at the things which are not seen: for the things which are seen are temporal; but the things which are not seen are eternal."* (II Corinthians 4:18) The average Christian has lost his or her eternal vision in relationship to the Church, to the temporal vision of what the Church should be. If our sight is just temporal, sooner or later the Church will collapse in our sight to a non-essential identity in our lives. Is this what is happening in the Church as we witness many in mass *". . . depart from the faith . . . "* (I Timothy 4:1) and *". . . falling away . . . "* (II Thessalonians 2:3)? Every believer whose dreams or schemes are injected into the Church will be a hindrance to themselves and others in seeing the divine reality and divine purpose for the Church.

Does God still give visions (Hebrews 11:1)? I believe He does, but false visions can be very dangerous. How many visionary dreamers have turned proud and pretentious to the point that it is either their way or the highway, i.e., taking the local church into a graveyard in Guyana (Jim Jones) or a wipeout in Waco (David Koresh)? I believe that God hates such visionary dreaming, men who create a visionary ideal community of believers demanding that the community church be realized by God and by others even though the Biblical standards and statutes stated by the One that established the Church in the first place are not followed or practiced. People like this walk into a local assembly and demand their ways be adopted, setting up their own rules and regulations, and setting themselves up as judge and jury over God's people. I believe Peter warned of such when he penned this in his first epistle: *". . . Neither as being lords over God's heritage."* (I Peter 5:3) Oh, at first people flock to these dreamers, but in time only a few remain and the ideal begins to fall apart and the dream becomes a nightmare for those that remain until a poisonous cup of Kool-Aid and a fiery end is all that is left to the ideal. They missed the reality because they got their sight on the vision, on the dream, instead of the Lord.

Jesus had and has already laid out the foundation for the divine reality that is the true Church in Himself. Again, it was only as these Scriptures jumped out to me as I read and studied the Bible about the Church, did I not see a dream, a vision, or an ideal but Jesus' reality for His Church: (1) I Corinthians 3:11: *"For other foundation can no man lay than that is laid,* **which is Jesus Christ***."* (2) Ephesians 2:19-22: *"Now therefore ye are no more strangers and foreigners, but fellowcitizens with the saints, and of the household of God; and are built upon the foundation of the apostles and prophets,* **Jesus Christ himself being the chief corner stone***; in whom all the building fitly framed together groweth unto an holy temple in the Lord: in whom ye also are builded together for an habitation of God through the Spirit."* I believe any church that starts with a man, or a woman or eventually has more focus on a person rather than the Christ, will sooner or later fail. That is why I am against anything in the church that highlights and underlines anyone or anything above the Christ. I believe in Pauline Theology, but I catch myself every time I use the words because in reality it is Jesus' Theology that Paul received during his three years studying at the feet of Jesus (Galatians 1:17-18). I believe basically in Calvinistic Theology, but I choose not to use Calvin's name because I believe it detracts from recognizing that all John Calvin compiled was just Jesus' Theology. We live in a world where many of the important, successful preachers, evangelists, and missionaries are known by name better than the Christ. I still remember back in the 1960s when the Beatles brought on a great controversy when they claimed they were more popular than Jesus. No such conflicts today with the myriad of Christians and non-Christians who think that it is all about them, whether the Pope of the Roman Catholic Church or Joel Osteen of the Protectant Church. Who rises in defense of Jesus Christ anymore in this arena? I am trying!

When did the leaders of the churches come to believe that the congregation they led, the flock they pastor, or the community of believers they minister to, is theirs? Granted, like the pastors of the seven churches of Asia in Revelation 2-3, there are messages to be delivered, but *"the mystery of the seven stars which thou sawest in my right hand, and the seven golden candlesticks. The seven stars are the angels of the seven churches: and the seven candlesticks which thou sawest are the seven churches . . . These things saith he that holdeth the seven stars in his right hand, who walketh in the midst of the seven golden candlesticks."* (Revelation 1:20-2:1) Note carefully where the pastors (angels) are and where Jesus is (midst). The congregations have been entrusted to us at best. They are still His flocks,

His congregation, His community of believers and not ours or any others. The Church of the Living God is a gift which we can't claim; it is His. Only Jesus knows the real state of the Church, how far before its completion, who is in the true Church, and who is on the outside: *"Nevertheless the foundation of God standeth sure, having this seal, The Lord knoweth them that are his . . ."* (II Timothy 2:19) What appears weak and trifling to us, what appears broken and failing to us, and what appears strange and separated to us, seems different to Jesus. Remember Jesus' rebuke of John because he rebuked someone for sharing the Christ, but he wasn't a disciple (Luke 9:49)? Should we be rebuke?

35.

WHAT DO YOU DO WHEN GOD TAKES AWAY YOUR HEALTH?

The topic for this "threescore and ten" article started in October 2014 and cumulated in April 2020 with the passing of my wife. Over that span of time the issue of health has been a constant subject because until that fall in 2014 I had been in very good health as were the members of my family. Things changed dramatically with me, then my son Scott (who died of lung and liver cancer in 2017), and finally my wife being diagnosed with a serious liver disease in 2019. With Scott, we only had six months before his departure to glory and with Coleen just a year before her journey to heaven. My situation and the sicknesses of Scott and Coleen provoked the question stated above, what part does the Good Lord play in our health?

To say that I have been a healthy individual for most of my life would be an understatement. Other than three bouts with kidney stones, an injury or two, and the rare struggle with the flu, I have been blessed throughout my sixty-nine-old-life with good, if not excellent, health. Few have been the days that I have been laid up for very long with an illness or sickness, and, as for accidents, very few. Perhaps, up until the autumn of 2014, the longest I had been laid aside was a back injury I sustained while working at a chicken company in New Hampshire in the 70s. Even then it took only a few weeks to get back into the swing of my life (a young body heals quickly), including my first pastorate in Pembroke, New Hampshire. Then a second attack with a blown-out disk in my spine during my third pastorate in Eastport, Maine, in the 1980s laid me up for a few days, but I was quickly back in the Lord's work. I have lived most of my life with the philosophy "that I can get as much done on a sick day as a health day!" Even when I felt bad I always seemed to have the strength and drive to "press-on," so to say I have experienced a true physical shortcoming would be a falsehood, that is until I came face to face with this Biblical truth: God not only gives us our health ("... God ... who is the health of my countenance ... " Psalms 42:11 and 43:5), but He can also take it away (Job 2:6) in His divine purpose for our lives.

In what I am going to call the miracle of 2014, I got home from an Alaska adventure just 30 hours before I was afflicted with my fourth kidney stone attack. I had had three attacks producing four kidney stones in a ten-year span covering the mid-1980s to the mid-1990s. In the year of my daughter's graduation (1998) from high school, I had what I had come to believe was my last attack. (How wrong I was!) Over 16 years had passed, and I thought I had conquered my " ... thorn in the flesh ... " (II Corinthians 12:7). When the pain began to grow on a late Saturday afternoon, I thought it was a blood clot moving into my leg. I never thought of a kidney stone because the pain and the area of discomfort were different than the other three. Why did I think it was a clot? I had just travelled over 12,000 miles in cars and planes in just 17 days. In Scott's car alone we had driven over 2600 miles touring Alaska and over 4800 miles traveling from Fairbanks, Alaska, to Ellsworth, Maine, in just three and a half days! Surely it was a clot from all that sitting. But it didn't take the doctor or nurse at Maine Coast Memorial Hospital very long to discover that I was indeed having another kidney stone attack. I had even driven myself to the hospital because my wife was still in California visiting our daughter (Coleen decided that driving back to Maine from Alaska wouldn't be as fun as checking out where her daughter and new son-in-law were living), and my son was off visiting some Maine friends (Scott had just finished his eighth year in the United States Army and was home for a month before beginning his career in the Army Reserves in North Carolina). Needless to say, Scott was surprised when he came home to find a note on the kitchen counter stating that I had gone to the hospital in great pain. The miracle was clear. I could have had the kidney stone attack at anytime and anywhere and to have had the attack in Alaska or Canada wouldn't have been fun at all, so I have come to believe it was the Lord changing our minds (our original plan was to take a week to ten days to drive home and our first planned path home was by way of Montana [fishing] and North Carolina [golf] before back to Maine) to come directly home, straight across Canada. *"The steps of a good man are ordered by the Lord: and he delighteth in his way."* (Psalms 37:23) God knew and was gracious to get me home before He took away my health, and this time He really took it away!

At the original writing of this article, I have just passed the eight-week mark in the ordeal of 2014. X-rays revealed that I had three kidney stones, two in my right kidney and one in my left kidney. Over the next two months I would have three procedures to get rid of the stones. The first two stones I named Esther and Ezra. I have named all of my stones because they are like delivering children, except they are the ugliest children you would ever want. (I love to tell the story that took place after my first kidney stone when I told my wife the pain was worse than childbirth pain, and my proof was a lady in my church at the time that had just had her first kidney stone, but she had an interesting perspective on the subject because she had also delivered seven children. I asked her when I visited her which was worse, and she said she would have seven more children before she had another kidney stone.) For those interested, the first four stones were Adam, Bernice, Caesar, and Dan. Doctor Curlick, my urologist, even took pictures of the twins from my right side because they came out easily with a method of going in and removing them with a cystoscopy which I'd never had done before. The last, Festus, was the size of a quarter and had to be blasted in a procedure called lithotripsy. I had had that procedure before without any problems. It was the first lithotripsy (yes, the stone was so large it took two attempts to mash it up into small enough pieces so that I could pass them on my own) that got me in trouble. Unknown to me or the medical personnel at Maine Coast, I got a hospital staph infection while having that procedure done. Ten days later I experienced the worst chills and hot flashes I had ever endured and a fever over 103. Again, I found myself in the emergency room at Maine Coast Memorial Hospital, and this time I wasn't leaving with a few pain pills and an appointment to see a urologist!

I was shocked when the attending physician told me she was moving me up into intensive care. I had visited plenty of patients in the ICU, but this was going to be my first visit as a patient and little did I know that the visit would last six-days! I tell people all the time that I visit people in the hospital in the hopes my visits will be enough and not very long. There is a big difference between going in and coming out to going in and staying awhile. I was a very sick boy, the worst of my life! It was eventually revealed that I had a kidney infection which was very bad, and very close to going septic (getting into my blood stream). Not only did the infection affect my kidney and bladder, but my blood pressure went haywire (70 over 40), and my sugar spiked (199). To top it off, my heart went out of rhythm! These were areas of my health I had never had a problem with before. To make a long illness short, I would spend a total of 10 days in the hospital. When I was a freshman at Bob Jones University, I got chicken pox and spent nearly two weeks in isolation, but I was only sick for a couple of days, just contagious! Then there was the pain in passing all that gravel after the last lithotripsy, including another trip to the emergency room for the "good stuff;" my drug of choice is now Toradol. I would miss 25 days of work in September and October and for about as many days I have been on half-days. I had never had a stretch like this in my life of not working. It would take another two weeks before my final (hopefully-as this book goes to bed I am again facing another extended time dealing with the after effects of a kidney stone, so it appears that this will be a lifelong 'thorn in the flesh seeing that I have been dealing with them for 40 year, the year is 2024) X-ray and a clean bill of health from Doctor Curlick. I had never been so tired in my life, and for over a month I couldn't get out of my own way. I didn't feel like going to work, and when I don't feel like going to work, I AM SICK! I slept 16 to 18 hours a day, sleeping in late and taking afternoon naps. I still remember when one of my deacons called and told me that I was being "benched" for at least two weeks. In my 47 years in the pastorate that had never happened before or since (till 2024). Everybody knew I was sick and needed time to rest and recover, and so I have, but what has this spiritual "workaholic" learned about the question that began this chapter?

    I think I had taken for granted my health. What John "wished" for Gaius, *"Beloved, I wish above all things that thou mayest prosper **and be in health,** even as thy soul prospereth"* (III John 2), has certainly happened to me. I knew only good health. Some might say today "good genes," but I come back to the point I began this article with and that being **God is my health,** God is your health. Health is in the hands of God and no one else. They say or try to teach us that we are the guardian of our health by what we eat or don't eat, how we exercise or don't exercise (I Timothy 4:8), what our family medical history is or isn't. The medical profession has gotten proud in its belief that it has figured out the health issue. What they don't like for us to know is that ultimately they are limited, very limited, in the science of health despite their wonder drugs (I got some of them during my ordeal and I am thankful), amazing procedures (I experienced some of them during my illness and am thankful), and highly skilled workers (I had only the best of care and the people who ministered to me were exceptional and I am thankful), but, no matter who or what, I still believe it was the Great Physician that gave me back my health. Who gave man the knowledge to create these drugs, these methods to minister to the body? I am thankful for all the help by my fellowman, but I am going to give God the glory because *" . . . I will restore health unto thee, and I will heal thee of thy wounds, saith the Lord . . . "* (Jeremiah 30:17) This is exactly what happened to me.

I discovered this verse from the pen of Jeremiah and the mouth of God as I pondered on my questions of why now, why this, and what was I to learn? *"Behold, I will bring it health and cure, and I will cure them, and will reveal unto them the abundance of peace and truth."* (Jeremiah 33:6) If I felt anything above and beyond the pain and discomfort of my illness, it was the peace of God and the truth that God was still in control. I have walked too long on this pilgrimage not to have learned that in good times or bad times, "in sickness and in health," I can still trust in my blessed Saviour. He is my witness when I say I never doubted, cried "why me," or stopped believing that this was just another chapter in His purpose for me. Was I in agony? Yes, at times, but not soul agony. If anything, I prayed more, thought of Him more, and focused on what is really important in this world. The world passed me by and carried on, and I saw again that I am not really needed in this world; that the church will carry on without me. Was I missed? Certainly. I received some wonderful cards and letters and drawings (the papers from my church kids were the best!). It was confirmed to me again that working for Christ is an honor and a privilege, but not a necessity because sometimes *"We looked for peace, but no good came; and for a time of health, and behold trouble!"* (Jeremiah 8:15)

There was no worst time in our church year for the pastor to be sick and laid-up. September is the beginning of our new Sunday School year and Awana year. It is the time I begin my Evening School classes, not to mention all the other regular weekly meetings of the church. Besides, I had just missed three weeks to take my summer vacation to visit Scott in Alaska and travel back to Maine with him. The church had already listened to guest speakers for nearly a month, and here I was away again, if only across the street. For one of the few times in my life and in the life of my ministry, I was asked Joab's Biblical question, *"Art thou in health, my brother?"* (II Samuel 20:9) And for the first time in decades I had to admit I wasn't and wouldn't be for a while. So, as I lounged around and mediated on this period of poor health, I thought of these Biblical answers to the question above. **First, you must accept it as from God.** You must recognize that God is the author of both good health and bad health. God gave Satan permission to affect Job with boils. I believe as with "the keys of death" (Revelation 1:18), God has the keys of health firmly in His hands. Nothing, including death itself, can happen to you unless first God gives permission. Let us never forget, what God takes away He can also restore (read Job 42). I believe He has restored my health, and He can take it away at any moment, but still God is to be praised. **Second, you must apply the grace God supplies.** The story of Paul and his "thorn in the flesh" is for me a story about health. Even though we don't know exactly what Paul's alignment was, God was clear in His will: *"And He said unto me, My grace is sufficient for thee: for My strength is made perfect in weakness."* (II Corinthians 12:9) One of the longest lists on Wednesday night prayer meeting is our "chronically ill" list. For such a small church, we know and have so many that seemingly have been afflicted with a permanent sickness, permanent until the Lord takes them home where they will be eternally healed. Not only Paul's thorn, but Jacob's hip (Genesis 32:32), and Timothy's stomach problem (I Timothy 5:23) fall into this category. Can God heal? Certainly. Does God heal everybody on earth? No. That is why we must accept His grace during an illness, either for a short time like I experienced or a long time like others have experienced. **Third, you must appreciate the Goodness of God.** What good comes out of any sickness, illness, kidney stones, or loss of health? One of my core beliefs has been for most of my life Paul's classic precept, *"And we know that all things* [including kidney stones and staph infections] *work together for GOOD to them that love God, to them who are called according to His purpose."* (Romans 8:28) It is easy to apply this principle when the sun is bright and you are walking in perfect health, but can you apply it in an ICU room, a time in which you think you are dying because the pain is a 10 and climbing? It is then we must come out of the physical and apply the spiritual concepts of our faith. Faith, trust, and confidence aren't just for the sanctuary and the prayer closet. They are also needed for the hospital room and the operating room. Sometimes, for the saint even "a sickness unto death" (Scott and Coleen) is good (Revelation 14:13). I learned this during my two-month infirmity.

As for the toughest question of all, the Lord's rebuke of a spiritual "workaholic." One of the most difficult lessons of my life has been *"six days shalt thou labor."* I was raised on a 24–7 farm, and I have carried that philosophy over into my work for the Lord. I believe I was shown again that God's people don't need a 24-7 shepherd because they seem to do well when he is away. The shepherd needs a break on occasion, and, if he doesn't take it, it will be forced on him! I have learned I would rather take a vacation to California or North Carolina than in the ICU unit of Maine Coast Memorial Hospital!

36.

OF AND TO AND THROUGH AND TO JESUS CHRIST

DIETRICH BONHOEFFER ONCE WROTE: **"Christianity means community through Jesus Christ and in Jesus Christ. No Christian community is more or less than this. Whether it be a brief, single encounter or a daily fellowship of years, Christian community is only this. We belong to one another only through and in Jesus Christ!"** I believe the Apostle Paul summarized this concept up best when he described what Bonhoeffer was trying to say by these words: *"For of him, and through him, and to him, are all things: to who be glory for ever. Amen."* (Romans 11:36) This is a lesson I learned over the years of ministry as I head into my 70th year.

I have been one that has been blessed with "a daily fellowship of years" with a group of brethren in Ellsworth, Maine, for 30 years now. Oh, I have had plenty of "brief, single encounters" over the years, those quick, memorable meetings with a brother or sister in Christ in which our time together was brief and singular. I still remember after a very long flight from India, after one of my short-term mission's trips to the subcontinent, I met a young Christian man from Canada as we passed through a New York airport together. As He waited his flight to Toronto, Canada, and I waited my flight to Bangor, Maine, we talked and shared of our common faith in Jesus Christ. It was a few minutes with a total stranger that felt like two old friends had met together again. He left when his flight was called, and I waited a few more minutes for my flight to be called, yet there was a sad separation because I knew and he knew that we wouldn't meet again until the rapture or on a golden street in heaven. Yet, the fellowship was sweet, the conversation was heavenly, and the communion was in Jesus.

First, this communion, this fellowship is *"of Him."* There are several factors that connect us to the Christ in a communal way. Without the Christ there is a natural discord between God and man, man and God, and man and man. The peace and harmony that now exists in these relationships as demonstrated through the fellowship at Emmanuel is because of the Christ. Paul put it this way in Ephesians 2:14–18: *"For He is our peace, who hath made both one, and hath broken down the middle wall of partition between us; having abolished in his flesh the enmity, even the law of commandments contained in ordinances; for to make in himself of twain one new man, so making peace; and that He might reconcile both unto God in one body by the cross, having slain the enmity thereby: and came and preached peace to you which were afar off, and to them that were nigh. For through* [of] *Him we both have access by one Spirit unto the Father."* Without Jesus we would never have come to a true knowledge of the Father, experienced the presence of the Spirit, and finally never shared in the common fellowship of the Church, the members of the Body of the Christ. The way was blocked by our own sin and our natural depravity, but because of what Jesus did we are now bounded together in the Church of God. It is all *"of Him"* for without Him we can do nothing (John 15:5) and are nothing.

Second, this communion, this fellowship is *"through Him."* How often I have said over the years as I have tried to teach "the whole counsel of God" (Acts 20:27) that the only common denominator between the pastor and the flock was the Christ. How does a hundred individuals from a myriad of backgrounds and upbringings ever gather together in the sanctuary of the Emmanuel Baptist Church on a Sunday morning? Some would say that we are all from Maine, but we are not. One of the newest members of our congregation is Howard Lewis, a man born and raised in the south, who in the last few years forsook his southern roots to retire to the coast of Maine. I don't know if you know how strange that is, but most people retire to the south from the north, not the opposite. Yet, here we are, total strangers just a few years ago, now worshipping and ministering together (Howard plays the guitar, writes his own songs, and sings, and just a few weeks ago led the music service during our morning worship service) and all through the redemptive work of Jesus Christ on Calvary's tree. We have people of different races, people of different social status, people of different ages, yet we unite because Jesus Christ died for us all. Our connection is not through the color of our skin, or through the amount of money in our bank account, or through the years we have spent on this planet. Our connection is through the Christ, for through Him we are all made one through Him: *"For ye are all the children of God by faith in* [through] *Christ Jesus. For as many of you as have been baptized into Christ have put on Christ. There is neither Jew nor Greek, there is neither bond nor free, there is neither male nor female: for ye are all one in* [through] *Christ Jesus."* (Galatians 3:26–28) Amen and Amen!

Third, this communion, this fellowship is **"to Him."** Remember the words to Fanny Crosby's classic hymn, **"To God be the glory great things He has done! So loved He the world that he gave us His Son, who yielded His life an atonement for sin and opened the Life-gate that all may go in!"** Have you ever asked yourself why Jesus deserves *"to whom be glory forever?"* For me, it is because Jesus was willing to take on our flesh, our nature, and ultimately our sin so that we might eventually be *"in Him."* Where He is, there we will be (John 14:3), and, though we have a spiritual fellowship now, *"that which we have seen and heard declare we unto you, that ye also may have fellowship with us: and truly our fellowship is with the Father, and with his Son Jesus Christ."* (I John 1:3) We will one day have an eternal fellowship. So why shouldn't all glory go to Him? Without Him, there would be no salvation, no Church, no hope of eternal life (Romans 6:23). This is why Jesus taught: *"Let your light so shine before men, that they may see your good works, and glorify your Father which is in heaven."* (Matthew 5:16) This is why Paul taught: *"Whether therefore ye eat, or drink, or whatsoever ye do, do all to the glory of God."* (I Corinthians 10:31) Crosby ended each of her stanzas of <u>To God Be the Glory</u> with these fine words: "Praise the Lord, praise the Lord, let earth hear His voice! Praise the Lord, Praise the Lord, let the people rejoice! Come to the Father through Jesus the Son, and **give Him the glory,** great things He has done!"

I had been the pastor of Emmanuel Baptist for many years before I recognized the importance of the name of the Church. That reality came to me about the time that many of the well-established and some of the biggest churches in central Maine began to change their names. A trend that started on the west coast has become a way to get denominationalism out of the Christian discussion and to focus more on the Church. So, places like Bangor Baptist Church, probably the biggest church in the area, became Crosspoint Church, or sometimes just Crosspoint. At first, I was troubled because of the removal of the word Baptist because I have been a Baptist all my life. Ultimately, I began to see that not only were they removing anything that told who they were (and the simple placement of "cross" before anything in my opinion is worse than telling people you are a Baptist Church), but it made me realize just how important it was for us to maintain the name "Emmanuel." If a church is not **"of Him,"** being run **"through Him,"** and ultimately all glory going **"to Him,"** then what were we gathering for? Why are we even doing what we are doing?

37.

THE EMMANUEL COMMUNITY

I HAVE BEEN PONDERING and observing for nearly 30 years now "the Emmanuel community" in light of the classic precept from the Psalms that states, *"Behold, how good and how pleasant it is for brethren to dwell together in unity!"* (Psalm 133:1) If Emmanuel was my first church, my conclusions probably would be different, but after being a member of four other churches I have come to the conclusion that I want Emmanuel Baptist of Ellsworth, Maine, to be my last church even in my 70th year.

We take for granted now the wonderful relationship of a group of believers living together in graceful harmony and blissful peace, the feeling that Jesus is living in the midst just like He promised: *"For where two or three are gathered together in my name, there am I in the midst of them."* (Matthew 18:20) And despite the fact we are surrounded by a multitude of enemies, we fear not because: *"Ye are of God, little children, and have overcome them: because greater is he that is in you, than he that is in the world."* (I John 4:4) In our nearly three decades together, we have certainly had our ups and downs: *". . . our flesh had no rest, but we were troubled on every side; without were fightings, within were fears . . ."* (II Corinthians 7:5). We had disappointments and times of despair, but through every crisis and the separation from the pillars of the church through death (I have buried a generation of patriarchs and matriarchs, the founders of this assembly), yet the faithful core of Christians of this fellowship have stayed tight and together, forbearing and supportive, friends among friends, "roses and lilies" in the garden of Christianity.

Each week we witness the visible assembly of the members of the Body of Christ that gather at Emmanuel. It is through the wonderful grace of God that we are allowed such an experience here on earth, a foreshadowing of the great gathering at the Rapture of the Church (I Thessalonians 4:16-17). After travelling to India five times now, (7 now at the time of this final edit) I know that not all believers get or receive that blessing, a blessing the American church has taken for granted for most of its existence. An event took place near the spring of 2020 that reminded us as a church just how quickly and unexpectedly that privileged fellowship could be disrupted and even taken away for a while. It was the infamous Coronavirus, better known as Covid-19! For the first time in my 47 years as a pastor I voted with the deacons of Emmanuel to shut the door of the church to parishioners and strangers. Over the decades I have had to call off a service here or there because of a snowstorm, but rarely more than one at a time, so for the first time in my ministerial life I was a pastor trying to figure out how to pastor without the bodily presence of my flock.

Through that experience I learned just how much the visible fellowship of believers was, what a blessing to not forsake "*. . . the assembling of ourselves together, as the manner of some is; but exhorting one another: and so much the more, as ye see the day approaching.*" (Hebrews 10:25) When the crisis was over, I was shouting with the Psalmist when he wrote, "*When I remember these things, I pour out my soul in me: for I had gone with the multitude, I went with them to the house of God, with the voice of joy and praise, with a multitude that kept holyday.*" (Psalm 42:4) This is the result when a group of believers become a community of believers. I have always found joy and satisfaction gathering with the saints, probably because at a very young age I was taken to a community church in my hometown of Perham, Maine. Many young people came to a place where they despised going to church. I can't remember ever not wanting to assemble myself with others of like precious faith. I learned early that it was far better to be "*. . . a doorkeeper in the house of my God, than to dwell in the tents of wickedness.*" (Psalm 84:10) I was taught and came to believe and practice: "*Blessed is the man that walketh not in the counsel of the ungodly, nor standeth in the way of sinners, nor sitteth in the seat of the scornful. But his delight is in the law of the LORD; and in his law doth he meditate day and night.*" (Psalm 1:1-2) And the best place to do just that is to assemble with a community of Christians in a designated place, like the sanctuary of the Emmanuel Baptist Church in Ellsworth, Maine, where our community of believers comes together.

The physical presence of our group of believers is a source of incomparable joy and an indescribable strength for me and, I believe, for most that assemble at Emmanuel. As Paul was about to die, locked in a Roman jail, one of his last wishes was that Timothy would come to him (II Timothy 1:4) so that they might see each other face to face again. In what I believe was Paul's first epistle, his desire was that "... *night and day praying exceedingly that we might see your face* ..." (I Thessalonians 3:10) As John was writing his second epistle, he simply stopped writing because: "*having many things to write unto you, I would not write with paper and ink: but I trust to come unto you, and speak face to face, that our joy may be full.*" (II John 12) It is not wrong for the Christian to desire the physical presence of other believers. We should not be ashamed to acknowledge and testify to the truth that to be in the presence of our brothers and sisters in Christ is a wishful thing. God created man as a body, and early on Adam learned just how lonely it could be surrounded by animals but without the touch and companionship of another human being (Genesis 2:19–25). One of the heartaches I experienced during the great Coronavirus "sheltering in place" was the absence of fellow believers and the sudden departure of my dear Coleen; how I miss our fellowship together. I missed going to see Mark Honey in his nursing home room in Bangor. I missed gathering with the prayer ladies during Wednesday afternoon. I missed seeing the kids at Awana on Monday or the study group on Friday night and my dear shut-ins in their homes. Sundays were the worst for me. You talk about a fish out of water. Sunday is my "holyday" and to not see Miriam (the youngest of my flock) and not see Joanne (the oldest of my flock) and all those dear saints in between was difficult. I was surprised just how difficult it was!

I have come to believe that that unspeakable gift of assembly is one of God's great unsung graces for His Church, and now I know it is a privilege that can be unexpectedly taken from us. Don't get me wrong. I believe that God was in charge and in control of the Coronavirus, that He allowed it to come upon us. At first, I thought it was just a warning to the world that they better get ready, they better repent, because worst plagues were coming, but in the end, it became personal for me, a rebuke that I had taken my community of believers for granted. I am determined to cherish each and every assembly in the future. I am going to count them a blessing each and every time I gather with the saints. I am making a conscious effort to appreciate every unexpected encounter with a brother in Christ, whether at church or at the Wal-Mart. And I praise the Good Lord for the wonderful gift of assembly, another chance to gain entrance into the fellowship of believers, and, no matter how brief the visit, I am going to have a grateful and thankful heart that my dear Lord and Saviour created the Church for such "... *fellowship* ... " (Acts 2:42). Dietrich Bonhoeffer in his classic book <u>Life Together</u> wrote: "Communal life is again being recognized by Christians today as the grace that it is, as the extraordinary, the 'roses and lilies' of the Christian life." I have come to believe we have such a life in the fellowship and assembly we call the Emmanuel Baptist Church, my church of a lifetime.

38.

IGNORING THE PAST

It was the 20th century Spanish philosopher and poet George Santayana that gets credit for coining the phrase: **"Those who cannot remember the past are condemned to repeat it."** Is this not what Jesus was saying to the Pharisees when he asked: *" . . . Why do ye also transgress the commandment of God by your traditions?"* (Matthew 15:3) The Pharisees had forgotten their historical past by creating a modern version of their faith in Jehovah in which their father's traditions were more important to them than God's commandments. A student of history since my boyhood and a student of the Bible since my young adulthood, I have come to the realization that what Santayana wrote is as true of the world as it is of the Church. I am at the end of a five-winter look at Church History. I started with nearly twenty, but I will end with a dedicated half dozen. I find very few in the Church of God interested in knowing how they got here, let alone understand the mistakes of the past lest they be repeated. I have come to believe in the philosophy of Soren Kierkegaard: **"Life is lived forward but understood backward!"** I have come to believe that everything that happens now can be understood from the past. Our future will be flawed unless we come to grips with the errors of the past, including the Church's past. Remember, it was the wise man Solomon who wrote: *"Is there any thing whereof it may be said, See, this is new? It hath been already of old time, which was before us."* (Ecclesiastes 1:10) So, in order for me to be a profitable pastor for my "church of a lifetime," I must look back. Perhaps, this is the reason for this series of observations after nearly seventy years of life and nearly fifty years in the pastorate.

As with Jesus during his stay on earth, his biggest opponents came within the Jewish religious community and in particular the Pharisees and the Sadducees. I can be honest and say that my greatest obstacles have come from within the Church versus outside the Church. I for one have not had too many difficulties with the world, but my brothers and sisters have been challenging, to say the least. I have found that my brethren fall into the same two categories as the Pharisees and the Sadducees. The Pharisees were those that loved to add to God's Words, like their traditions, while the Sadducees loved to subtract from the words of God by rejecting whole segments of Scriptures, like the resurrection and the existence of angels. These groups fall under the curse of Revelation 22:18–19: *"For I testify unto every man that heareth the words of the prophecy of this book, If any man shall add unto these things, God shall add unto him the plagues that are written in this book: and if any man shall take away from the words of the book of this prophecy, God shall take away his part out of the book of life, and out of the holy city, and from the things which are written in this book."* Interestingly, these are the very last words God gave us except for John's benediction. I have found the same thing in ministering to people. They either want to add something, like the beat of a song, or they want to ignore something, like *". . . Let every man be fully persuaded in his own mind."* (Romans 14:5) The Church is falling into the same mistakes of the past. We are either adding a myriad of manmade rules and regulations and rituals (human traditions and human truths to the Faith), or we are completely removing or rearranging clearly taught doctrines from the Faith by our own revising of Scripture for our time.

I have come to believe that it is a dangerous practice to either add or subtract because both will eventually dilute and damage the authority of the Scriptures. In the end we break the fundamental fabric that has been the glue that has kept the faith the Faith for all these two thousand years. Granted, over the two millennium of church history mankind has tried to bury the truth of God's Words under mountain after mountain of tradition. Humanity has tried to weaken the teachings of Jesus by the teachings of men, even good men like Augustine, Calvin, and others. It amazes me that the pure, unadulterated Word of God has managed to survive, but as I have come to learn through Psalm 119:89: *"For ever, O Lord, Thy Word is settled in heaven,"* God's precepts and concepts will endure *". . . to all generations."* (Psalm 100:5) Oh, has the Word been compromised by some and changed by others and ignored by still others? Certainly, but it will in the end be fulfilled. Jesus predicted: *"For verily I say unto you, Till heaven and earth pass, one jot or one tittle shall in no wise pass from the law, till all be fulfilled."* (Matthew 5:18) Those that ignore the past ignore the past at their peril, but those who ignore the Word ignore it to their destruction. What did Jesus say to the Sadducees when confronted with the classic trap of the woman who had seven brothers for her husband? *"... Ye do err, not knowing the scriptures..."* (Matthew 22:29) In the end ignorance will not be bliss!

For those of us who believe the Bible does contain the best instruction in matters of the church, yes, better than church history, we have only the first century church to look back on. I believe the first church started out pure and genuine, but it was not long before it was tainted and turned. The original organism (a living, Spirit-breathing institution) was Holy Ghost filled with Christ as the Head of the Church. The early functions of the Church as the Body of Christ reacted naturally and morally as a spontaneous outpouring of the Person of Christ. Despite Christ's departure, the coming of His Spirit was the motivation that set the movement on a course that has not been altered. Even through the ups and downs of church history the true Church has been maintained. The tragedy is that what most people see today is not the image of Christ, but the manmade image of a manmade organization that is far from the organism Christ intended. That is why the Bible reveals in the Revelation that in the end there will be both the True Church and an apostate church at the same time. This is why we need to look into the past and shed the light of the Word of God on these two groups to determine which one is real, and which one is false. Remember, the Apostle Paul wrote of the difficulty when he said: *"For such are false apostles, deceitful workers, transforming themselves into the apostles of Christ. And no marvel; for Satan himself is transformed into an angel of light. Therefore it is no great thing if his ministers also be transformed as the ministers of righteousness; whose end shall be according to their works."* (II Corinthians 11:13–15) The apostate church is playing a good game and looks real enough, but returning to our original precept of the adding and subtracting of Biblical truth the churches are easily revealed.

I for one am glad that at an early age I was given the perimeters of theological truth, historical doctrine, and Biblical narrative as the tests one must perform to *"prove all things; hold fast that which is good."* (I Thessalonians 5:21) I am glad I was taught to look back (note: not to go back-Luke 9:62) into the past and learn from the past and see the mistakes of my forefathers and the errors of my fellow-believers and try with the grace of God not to repeat either. What I haven't seen in the America church I have witnessed in the India church. When people are born again and begin to follow the teachings of Christ, the same indwelling, Spirit-filled characteristics of the first century Church emerge naturally. All we must do is get out of the way and allow God to work. Our problem is that we more often than not get in the way of God's natural purpose for His Church, something I have tried to avoid in my church into my seventies.

39.

EMBARRASSED BY ITS IMPLICATIONS

A.W. Tozer: "Many of us Christians have been extremely skillful in arranging our lives so as to admit the truth of Christianity without being embarrassed by its implications." Paul taught clearly: *"Therefore if any man be in Christ, he is a new creature, old things are passed away, behold, all things are become new."* (II Corinthians 5:17) Christians, however, are becoming good at disguising the "old" as "new" and making a new lease on life look like a lease on a new life. The twenty-first century Christian isn't the first to do this. Jesus had trouble with some of his earliest followers (John 6:60–66), and we know about the early believers like Ananias and Sapphira (Acts 5) and Simon (Acts 8). When will we learn that we must embrace Christianity, implications and all? When will we take as a compliment the title "peculiar people" (Titus 2:14)?

It is time for every believer to throw off the image of a "go-getter" and be seen as a "stand-stiller" (Psalm 46:10 and Exodus 14:13); to take off the Madison Avenue suit and be seen in "the fine linen" (Revelation 19:8) of the righteous; to evangelize, not as a high-pressure salesman of Christianity, but as an example of the believer (I Timothy 4:12); and one that loses the world and gains his soul versus gaining the world and losing his own soul (Matthew 16:25–26). We are living in a church age that believes that the rich, the wise, the mighty, and the noble will gain heaven's gate, yet, the Bible suggests just the opposite (Matthew 19:23–24; I Corinthians 1:26; Revelation 3:17). We have failed to take seriously James' admonition: *"My brethren have not the faith of our Lord Jesus Christ, the Lord of glory, with respect of persons. For if there come unto your assembly a man with a gold ring, in goodly apparel, and there come in also a poor man in vile raiment; and ye have respect to him that weareth the gay clothing, and say unto him, Sit thou here in a good place; and say to the poor, Stand thou there, or sit here under my foot-stool: are ye not then partial in yourselves, and are become judges of evil thoughts? Hearken, my beloved brethren, Hath not God chosen the poor of this world rich in faith, and heirs of the kingdom which He hath promised to them that love Him? But ye have despised the poor. Do not rich men oppose you, and draw you before the judgment seats? Do not they blaspheme that worthy name by which ye are called?"* (James 2:1-7) It is time we take to heart James' admonition!

The day the Church welcomed in the "bluebloods," the "intelligentsia," and "the plutocrats" the makeup of the Church changed. The greatest attack on the Church came when Constantine decided he could use the cross of Christ to his advantage without realizing the implications that would have. There was a time when the Church had no VIPs, and now that is all it seems to want, people with a name, people with money, people with influence, people who are embarrassed by the implications of a true and pure Christianity. I am amazed how many people are embarrassed today by Jesus and Jesus' teaching. "Surely, Jesus didn't mean that" is what I am hearing today. Who wouldn't want the rich young ruler in their church? (Matthew 19:16-22) He was moral (kept the commandments), he had money (great possessions by which he could help build the church sanctuary), he had manners (respect for Jesus), and he was manly (young, could give his life to the Lord). Yet he rejected Jesus' call because he was "embarrassed by its implications." This young man fell into the category of those who wanted something from Jesus (the young man wanted eternal life) but was not willing to accept the responsibilities that came with following Jesus (Luke 9:57-62). Paul seems to teach that those who are not embarrassed by Christianity's implications are the *"fools"* and the *"weak"* and the *"base"* and the *"despised"* (I Corinthians1: 27,28), and the *"peculiar"* (I Peter 2:9).

It has become strange to me that any Christian who has read the Bible and lived among Christians, would find it peculiar that a believer wouldn't want to live in this world without the things this world thinks indispensable. Jesus taught clearly in my opinion that wealth, possessions, and things are not important (Matthew 6:25-32). I like what an old saint said after visiting the Vatican: "The Church can no longer say, 'Silver and gold have I none!'" (Acts 3:6) The tragedy in this is that no longer can the Church say: *"In the name of Jesus Christ of Nazareth rise up and walk."* (Acts 3:6) There was a time when the average Christian travelled very light, but now we have so much baggage one wonders at the Rapture will we be too heavy to fly. Who teaches in the Church anymore *"sell all you have, and give to the poor, and . . . come and follow me?"* (Matthew 19:21) Instead, we are teaching get all you can and become as rich as you can, forgetting the warnings of I Timothy 6:10 and Luke 12:15. Even the Church has joined the world in a maddening scramble trying to get as much cash as it can, to rise in some form of spiritual sophistication, political power, and personal prestige. Any believer that can swim against such a stream is a true Christian, and he or she will find that they are numbered among the few and among the group bucking the tide heading for their heavenly home.

One of the other embarrassments that takes place when the real implications of Christianity are revealed is the "separation" issue (II Corinthians 6:14–17). There was a time when the world and the Church were like oil and water, but now it is all about fraternization, mixing, infiltration, involvement, and permeating. I love the new theology of "leaven" that started in the 1960s with "the Jesus people," how we are to leaven the world with our Christianity; how we are to join the cocktail parties (sipping ginger ale of course), the country clubs (just for the golf, of course), the civic circles, and the social protesters, to get our names out there. The tragedy of the 60s was the tragedy of Lot (Genesis 19) and the trauma of Obadiah (I Kings 18). Instead of leavening them, they leavened us. I think F. B. Meyer summarized this failing best when he wrote: "There is not a single hero or saint whose name sparkles on the inspired page who moved the times from within!" The great inventor Archimedes believed in the philosophy that he could move the world if only he had a point outside it where he could place his fulcrum. We as Christians must still believe in this truth, outside, not inside. The story of Lot proves you have very little leverage in Sodom, and the same was true of Obadiah--very little leverage inside Samaria and Ahab's palace. How much did Billy Graham change the White House inside the White House? (Remember Nixon was president at the height of Billy's influence, and how did that turn out?) The problem is while these tried to reform their Sodom or Samaria, Sodom and Samaria were rubbing off on them.

"In the world, but not of the world" has been the philosophy of the true Church for 2000 years. This is the purpose of the Church, and we the Church can't be embarrassed by its implications on our lives, our living, or our lifestyles. Education, legislation, and reformation must be enacted from the outside, not the inside. Ultimately, we are commissioned to evangelize, not Christianize, one of the great mistakes of the modern missionary movement. God is taking out for Himself a people (Acts 2:47) to place in His Church and, as in the days of Jesus' earthly ministry, some are entering and some are refusing to enter the Church. God allows individuals to choose, but there will always be some, even after my 70 years, that will become embarrassed by the implications of faithfully and reverently following the commands of Christ as He taught them.

40.

TRANSPARENCY IN CHRISTIANITY

WITH THE CURRENT TREND in Christianity escalating towards the promotion of our faith by an evangelist clothed in an Easter Bunny suit, or a pistol-packing preacher promoting Second Amendment rights with a second birth religion, I feel it is time we see the lack of true transparency in Christianity today. The use of the Easter Bunny as a means of evangelism is as bad an idea as inviting Elmer Fudd for a rabbit stew lunch, hoping that Elmer would provide the hare knowing full well that Mr. Fudd couldn't hit the broadside of a barn with a howitzer. Even before Elmer Fudd could pronounce his meal "absolutely de-wishous," the gigantic pink rabbit with the shotgun has escaped his rifle-sights to promote himself as someone else and all in the name of Christianity. We need only to hold many of today's entertaining evangelistic practices up to the light of the Bible to see just how utterly corrupt and bankrupted these modern promotes have become. Last summer I sat on the porch of the parsonage talking and counseling a couple and their son from Vermont. They shared the tragedy that was unfolding in their church because of an evaluation by a well-respected church-consulting ministry that helps churches find out what isn't going right. Their ultimate conclusion was to do what it takes, whatever it might take, to bring people into the church; standards and morals and Biblical principles and precepts are no longer the governing line of the Church. California and Texas Christianity promoted by the Olsten's and Warrens of the Church have so watered down the faith some of us have trouble recognizing it when we see it. It reminds me of the local fellowship that does just that even if it is Easter egg hunts and fuel oil give-a-ways! 21st century evangelism and Christianity has degraded itself to the day of Tetzel when he sold his "eternal" indulgences around Europe in the marketplace as a carnival barker. Christianity has divorced itself from its own theology (Acts 26:26: *"For the king knoweth of these things, before whom also I speak freely: for I am persuaded that none of these things are hidden from him;* **FOR THIS THING WAS NOT DONE IN A CORNER.**") and in a society rampant with narcissism and materialism. All we have left is a fake faith, hope disguised as a pink rabbit, and grace dispensed at the hand of a Winchester. Shakespeare couldn't write a tragedy any sadder than this transparent-less form of Christianity of today. I have watched the Church with sadness into my seventh year.

As Paul stood before King Agrippa and made a "defense-of-the-Faith" (Jude 3), he highlighted and underlined the truth that Christianity had never been a secret society; it had not developed in a corner, nor was its truths taught only in a closet. Jesus had always been transparent, and He instructed his followers to be always outward and public, honest and straight forward at all times, never hiding anything. The verse I have printed in the last paragraph as the basis for this theology because this doctrine is the focus of this article and the focal point of my current topic, speaks of *"these things"* and *"this thing."* I believe what Paul was referring to was the Church and Christianity. King Agrippa wasn't ignorant of what was happening in his kingdom. During the earthly life of Christ and in the early life of the Church "transparency" was the adjective that described the movement best. Jesus taught, preached, and healed openly. He was not ashamed to proclaim His Father's message publically. He didn't say one thing to get the people to listen then another thing afterwards. He got in trouble almost immediately with his transparency of the Faith: *"Many therefore of his disciples when they heard this, said, This is an hard saying; who can hear it? . . . From that time many of his disciples went back, and walked no more with Him."* (John 6:60, 66) There is lots of *"departing"* (I Timothy 4:1) and *"falling away"* (II Thessalonians 2:3) from the Faith still today.

Paul wrote to the Corinthian Church: *"But if our gospel be hid, it is hid to them that are lost."* (II Corinthians 4:3) There are many ways to hide the Gospel even when you are promoting the Gospel such as raffles, luncheons, bingo, yard sales, and buzzards to name a few. Our local brother calls their fellowship and ministry "The Gospel" yet they hide it in entertainment events, promotional give-a-ways, and images of the preacher that are to draw people in so they can hear "The Gospel." My question is a simple one: "If you really believe in the power of the Gospel, why do you need anything else such as the chance to win a car or motorcycle or a night dancing with the stars to promote it? For Jesus the Gospel was enough; for the early Church the Gospel was enough; for Paul the Gospel was enough, so why isn't it enough for us? Is the evangelist or pastor using the objects of his own culture for his end or God's? Guns, rabbits, and Santa Claus, the objects to another end, might be admirable if not for the impression it makes on the Gospel. *THE END HAS NEVER JUSTIFIED THE MEANS, THEN OR NOW.* Jesus was always upfront and straight on with everyone He met. So, did the early Church trust in the conviction of the Spirit versus some clever promotional trick to get people saved? From our first day as a Church (Pentecost) ours has been an open faith, an honest faith, a tell-it-like-it-is faith. (A popular misconception is the Church was started in the privacy of an upper room. Compare Acts 2:1 and Luke 24:53. It is my belief that the Church began at Temple Mount in the midst of the Jewish celebration of Pentecost publically.) It happened openly!

We live in an age in which religious extremism, entertainment evangelism, and spiritual gimmicks has resulted in a mass spiritual slaughter, not the evangelism of many innocent victims who thought they were coming to a give-a-way and found themselves in an evangelistic service. I still honor the young Child Evangelism Fellowship worker who will knock on doors to invite kids in a neighborhood to a five-day club refusing to call the event anything other than a Bible Club. We think we are accomplishing something when we, under disguise of something else, get someone into our evangelistic meeting. If we have lied to them once, how do we know that when we tell them about Jesus they won't think we are lying to them again? Why is it necessary to tell anything other than the truth of what we are doing? I hear it all the time, "If you tell them you are having an evangelistic service, nobody will come!" We are haunted by an empty room, only two to a DVBS or nobody showing up to a Gospel film. We have forgotten our responsibility is to plan, prepare, promote, and present. It is the Spirit's job to bring them in. (So, which is worse? Getting a confession of faith by twisting an arm or by the end of a sword?) Sharing of the Gospel to one really seeking Christ is better time spent than to the 99 that really don't want to be there. Glitz and glamour and gimmicks will only hold them so long; the Gospel is the only thing that will keep them through eternity.

It is one thing to have a spiritual vision for one's Lord, and quite another thing to carry this vision through. I am always haunted when I write of such things of the exhortation of Paul in Romans 14:10: *"But why doest thou judge thy brother? Or why doest thou set at nought thy brother? For we shall all stand before the judgment seat of Christ."* I am convinced my brothers in Christ are sincere in their desire to win people to Christ, but I am equally haunted by what an old deacon of mine said many, many years ago: **"What you win them with, you win them to!"** I am convinced that is why we have so few mature Christians today. So many other factors now figure into the makeup of the average believer of the 21st century (when they got saved, their age in Christ; where they got saved, a crusade, a Sunday school class, home with a parent; what was a part of their salvation experience, soul stirring conviction, emotion, a suggestive friend or family member). They might be a child of the King, but they are living more like a friend of the world (James 4:4). It is good the Lord knows His own (II Timothy 2:19).

Nearly 120 years ago a book was written by a man by the name of Chafer. In his book called <u>TRUE EVANGELISM</u> he was speaking out against the contemporary evangelist and notable Christians of his day. The more I read this small booklet, the more I see what Chafer was writing about is happening again. A century and more has passed, but the desire to be non-transparent is still raising its ugly head. Chafer wrote of how the mass promoters of Christianity in his day were delivering a man-centered message focusing on human obligation, calling people to make a decision without placing the emphasis on what Christ had done for them at the cross; presenting duty rather than sacrifice (even a sacrifice after salvation-Romans 12:1–2). In so doing the evangelist, the preacher, the missionary was neglecting the fact that salvation is a miracle of divine intervention versus an act of man. He also condemned the methods being used to promote the Gospel as being unscriptural and spiritually detrimental to the true salvation of a soul. The demand made for a public act of standing, raising a hand, walking an aisle could produce a false sense of assurance when no salvation had happened. There is only one Biblical assurance of salvation and that is "a changed life afterward." Jesus taught you shall know them by their fruits (Matthew 7:20). Paul taught that the old would go and a new would come (II Corinthians 5:17). The danger in all of this is the mixing up of whether or not it is the response to the Gospel or the Gospel causing the response? His conclusion was that man was getting in the way of true evangelism.

It is now my observation that in the Christianity I live in, the same is happening again. Instead of the call of the Father (John 6:37), it is the call of the preacher, the evangelist, or the missionary. Instead of the conviction of the Spirit (John 16:8), it is the plea or the urging of the preacher, the evangelist, or the missionary. Instead of the coming to Christ (John 3:14–16), it is the coming down the aisle, the coming to the front of the church, the coming to speak to the counsellor. Chafer wrote: "Fundamentally then, the personal element in true soul winning is more a service of pleading for souls than a service of pleading with souls." The task of every born-again believer is to be as transparent as he can to his unsaved relatives, friends, or neighbors. In our zeal to see people saved are we missing the mark by concluding that anything goes? I am still reminded of the saying by that dear deacon so long ago. His words have come home to haunt the church that entertainment and only entertainment will appeal to some believers. Christian comedians, Christian entertainers, Christian musicians are in great demand today, but the Bible is still clear that it would be through the foolishness of preaching salvation would be wrought (I Corinthians 1:18) and not 50 minutes of entertainment and 10 minutes of Gospel.

Needless to say, Chafer had his critics after his little book came out. Interestingly, Chafer once was a part of that great evangelistic movement in Church history. He, too, had been caught up in the excitement and enthusiasm of those grand days when revival swept the country and parts of the world. Then he took a good look at the Bible and the methods of Christ and the early Church and found them in some respects on opposite sides of the issue. It was then he decided to break from his friends and share what he saw. I find it hard to bring to light what I see as a disregard of scriptural standards by my brothers and sisters in Christ, but there is something going on in Christianity today that has lowered the standards to a level that sometimes it is difficult to tell a Christian from a non-Christian. When you see as much beer and wine in a grocery cart of the believer as the non-believer; when you see the standards of dress indistinguishable between the saint and the sinner; when you hear the use of "God" and "My Lord" as commonly proclaimed in a secular conversation as in a spiritual conversation, something has gone wrong. A case in point came to my attention just a year ago when I received a letter. One of our church members wrote to the local public school district in relationship to a situation that happened at school during the Christmas season. The writing is self-explanatory:

> "My daughter brought home a picture book that she said was done by the entire class entitled, "Christmas around the world."
> Upon opening the book, each page represented a different

country with pictures and a caption on how they celebrated Christmas. Several countries were listed as Mexico, France, and Germany and yes the United States. The following celebrations were also clearly illustrated; Ramadan-a Muslim religious celebration, Diwali-a celebration held in India, and Hanukkah-a Jewish religious celebration. But here's where I take issue. When the page describing how the United States celebrated Christmas, the creators of this "project" decided that Santa Claus and the Christmas classic "The Night Before Christmas" was traditionally how the United States celebrated Christmas. What? Is this even remotely historically accurate? Are we now teaching our kids to believe in Santa Claus? Where is the true meaning of Christmas? I know we live in a world of political correctness and you are not immune from the constant barrage from the public anytime this sensitive area rears its ugly head. But come on, this one doesn't even pass the straight-face test! It honestly left me just shaking my head in disbelief. You found it important enough to illustrate by what most people would describe as religious celebrations in other countries, so as not to offend those religions, or those who choose to celebrate those religions, but when it comes to the United States you chose to spit in the face of Christians the true meaning of Christmas (except the half-witted attempt when illustrating the country of France). I strongly feel that you should be able to illustrate a baby in a manger without the fear of indoctrination. Apparently indoctrination wasn't a problem with Ramadan and Hanukkah? Where is the "level playing field?" It offends me and my seven year old that the Christmas story can't be included. If you disagree with all that I have said may I offer you one more solution in which we could agree, and change the title of the project from "Christmas Around the World" to "Pagan and religious holidays celebrated around the world in December?" Perhaps, then everybody's concerns would be satisfied."

My dear friend was right: transparency. Why call it something that it is not? Why try to hide the truth, cover the reality, and mislabel the doctrine? When will we realize that transparency in Christianity is what Jesus taught and the early Church practiced?

Why does our faith have to hide behind a rabbit, a pistol, and a man in a red suit, a fanciful poem, and a giveaway? Jesus said it as clearly as any: *"Ye are the light of the world. A city that is set on an hill cannot be hid. Neither do men light a candle,* **and put it under a bushel,** *but on a candlestick; and it giveth light unto all that are in the house. Let your light* *so shine before men, that they may see your good works, and glorify your Father which is in heaven."* (Matthew 5:14–16) What are you hiding your faith behind?

41.

WHAT A PREACHER SHOULD BE

I HAVE BEEN A preacher for longer than I have been a pastor. I have been ministering the Word of God for longer than I have been a minister. After nearly seventy years and fifty-five of them involved in preaching or preparation for preaching, I feel I have some ideas on the subject that I would like to pass along to those who might find my concepts interesting. America needs good preachers today. We have pastors galore; we have spiritual CEOs without number, and we have Bible teachers of all shapes and sizes in respect to Biblical knowledge, but preachers are rare, few and far between. Don't get me wrong, there are aplenty that preach or at least attempt to preach every Sunday, but the down-to-earth, Spirit-filled, Bible-based preacher is rare and almost extinct. I feel it is all because nobody is taking seriously today Paul admonition to the Christian at Corinth: *"For Christ sent me not to baptize, but to preach the gospel: not with wisdom of words, lest the cross of Christ should be made of none effect. For the preaching of the cross is to them that perish foolishness; but unto us which are saved it is the power of God."* (I Corinthians 1:17–18) Oh, we have some very artistic speakers we call preachers today. We have spiritual entertainers we call preachers today. We have able communicators we call preachers today, but like Paul warns about they preach with "words of wisdom." They speak because of how they were trained, how they practiced, and what they know their congregation wants to hear, but God's preacher doesn't fit into any of these neat categories of clergy. God's preacher defines definition, and he can't be cataloged!

For me, men like Elijah, Amos, John the Baptist, Jesus, and Paul were the prototype for what God saw in His preacher. We could go way back to some of the early preachers recorded in the Bible, men like Enoch and Noah. *"And Enoch also, the seventh from Adam, prophesied of these, saying, Behold, the Lord cometh with ten thousands of his saints." (Jude 14)* Was Enoch's sermon a prophecy, yes, but, in order to get that message across, he had to preach it, proclaim a sermon that has yet to be fulfilled. *"And spared not the old world, but saved Noah the eighth person, **a preacher of righteousness**, bringing in the flood upon the world of the ungodly." (II Peter 2:5)* You talk about a rough, tough crowd. In 120 years of preaching Noah only led seven people to his God and salvation (Hebrews 11:7), and they were all members of his family. Why? Because the message was a difficult one, and Noah wasn't willing to compromise on the message to get a few more conversions on the boat! Noah lived in a day where numbers didn't count, but we live in a day where it is all about the numbers. Today, Enoch and Noah wouldn't be seen as successful preachers. Why? Because they never drew many to believing the message.

Think with me for a minute on the thought of what the great preachers of the past became: Elijah became public enemy number one in the land with a price on his head; Amos became an outcast in his own country belittled by the religious elite of Bethel; John the Baptist became a guest, not at Herod's banquet table, but Herod's jail, and he would eventually lose his head because he preached a sermon entitled It is Not Lawful for Thee to Have Her! (Matthew 14:4) Jesus would be crucified, and Paul would be *"in labours more abundant, in stripes above measure, in prisons more frequent, in deaths oft. Of the Jews five times received I forty stripes save one. Thrice was I beaten with rods, once was I stoned, thrice I suffered shipwreck, a night and a day I have been in the deep; in journeyings often, in perils of waters, in perils of robbers, in perils by mine own countrymen, in perils by the heathen, in perils in the city, in perils in the wilderness, in perils in the sea, in perils among false brethren; in weariness and painfulness, in watchings often, in hunger and thirst, in fastings often, in cold and nakedness. Beside those things that are without, that which cometh upon me daily, the care of all the churches." (II Corinthians 11:23-28)* Sound like any preachers you know today?

The preachers of the Bible were given more to solitude than sociability. They preached when they were called to preach, but rarely did they socialize with the establishment. The men we have just mentioned all lived solitary lives in one respect or another. Granted, they all were eventually found in the palace, in the city, among the crowds, but none of them were the backslapping, political preachers of today that hobnob with the world they are suppose to be warning of coming judgment. The true preacher of God is not at home in this world because this world is not his home! The preacher is supposed to be a loner with a difficult message from heaven itself. And unlike the modern preacher who like others in other professions seek only time served and retirement to a warmer climate, the true preacher can never retire. As the saying goes, the pastor is put out to pasture, but the preacher dies in the pulpit. Why? Because there will never be a time that a preacher shouldn't preach. He was called to be a preacher, and I will challenge you to find me a Biblical preacher that retired before death. I thought of the preacher Jonah who didn't like the sermon, but, when he tried to retire to the south of Spain, the Good Lord chased him down and sent him packing to preach his sermon to Nineveh. For me, it isn't the preacher that is important, but the message from God!

If a preacher ever becomes popular, he will probably get in trouble with His Master. Jesus said that *"no prophet is accepted in his own country"* (Luke 4:24), and I say the same is true of the preacher. I have heard of exceptions to this rule, but they are rare. Oh, the next generation might build the preacher a shrine, but, as in the days of Jesus, the generation that built the sepulchers were of the same lineage in which their fathers killed the preachers (Matthew 22:27–29). Why? Because the true preacher is on better terms with heaven than with the earth. Again, do you see Elijah scraping at the feet of King Ahab and Queen Jezebel like the preachers of today at the White House? Do you see Amos bowing to the King of Israel or the priest of Bethel? Surely, you know that there was no love lost with Herod and Herodias and John the Baptist. Who among the elite both of religion and politics didn't hate Jesus? And what of Paul? The preacher has but one focus, delivering the message. Regardless of the circumstances, the situation, or the congregation, nothing hinders or delays the delivery of *"Thus saith the Lord,"* even when the sermon isn't "politically correct" or "socially acceptable" as is the landscape I am facing today.

I like Vance Havner on my last point: **"The preacher must needs have the heart of a child and the hide of a rhinoceros! The problem is how to toughen his hide without hardening his heart. That combination can be achieved only by the grace of God."** In order to achieve such a balance in the preacher's heart he must get alone with God. Didn't Elijah in Cherith? Didn't Jesus in Nazareth? Didn't Paul in Arabia? Only when the preacher allows the Holy Spirit to mold him and fashion him into the tough, soft preacher he needs to be will the preacher become the preacher God wants him to be. Rough and rugged on the outside, but tender and mild on the inside. I believe these words from Jesus are for everybody, but in my personal experience they are really needed for the preacher: *"Come unto me . . . Take my yoke upon you, and learn of me; for I am meek and lowly in heart: and ye shall find rest unto your souls. For my yoke is easy, and my burden is light."* (Matthew 11:28–30) Only God can make you the preacher you ought to be.

42.

A LIFETIME OF PROVERBS

1- Sodomy is sweeping and spreading across our land because this abomination is being approved and applauded from the pulpits of our churches.

2- Do you have a Nehushtan (the brazen serpent Moses lifted up), an ephod (Gideon's idol), an idol, a jawbone (rabbit's foot) still hanging around your life; something that you periodically get out and bow to it, or rub it for good luck; something that is but a symbol of some great spiritual victory from your past? You need to get rid of it!

3- The tragedy today is that we have more people seeking advice from the National Enquirer than enquiring after the Lord; seeking advice from a horoscope than the Holy Word.

4- To vindicate the holiness of God, to vanguard the purity of the saints, and to verify the truth of the Bible are the only reasons we should go to war against our brethren.

5- I have seen my father plant many a crop of potatoes on the family farm in Maine, but I never, ever saw him reap carrots!

6- Attack before being attacked. A good defense is a good offence!

7- You may be a child spiritually, you may be a coward naturally, or you may be disabled physically, but "deep inside the armor of God" there is a peace, a power, and a protection against the Goliath of your life.

8- If you first surrender to God, you will never have to surrender to any foe or force again.

9- To Caleb, hope was spelled h-e-b-r-o-n; how do you spell hope, maybe h-e-a-v-e-n?

10- No Christian can stop growing older, but he or she can avoid growing colder.

11- If you are in the practice of making vows to God, you need to be very careful because you never know what or who might be coming out of your door next (think Jephthah!).

12- Carelessness and carefreeness will turn victory into defeat!

13- God hates haste and waste.

14- Successful tactics against one's enemy are: a clear objective, a continual offense, and a complete occupation.

15- Wounds on the Christian soldier and scars on the spiritual warrior are a "Badge of Courage" that ought to strengthen you in the fight, not scare you into flight.

16- An easy life isn't necessarily God's blessing; it might be Satan's trap.

17- "Idleness is the devil's workshop," or so they say, and Satan had a big factory in Sodom.

18- An earthly accident only furthers a heavenly purpose.

19- We have traded in Christian standards for human values, and we have gotten a very poor bargain in return!

20- All of God's purposes are eternal purposes, and His will is an everlasting will.

21- A suffering saint will always attract "Job's comforters" just like "roadkill" attracts a flock of crows.

22- The world is "waxing worse and worse," and the Church is "falling away" from its "first love." End times must be near?

23- Today, the sentry is sleeping, and the sentinel is snoring when they ought to be shouting and sounding the alarm.

24- The Christian soldier can never be overcome or overwhelmed when the Lord is on his side!

25- Ordinary becomes extraordinary when grace and God combine with a man of God.

26- With a holy cause and a holy course and a holy corps, we, too, can have confidence in our Captain and our comrades.

27- "Pride does come before a fall," and defeat can't be far behind.

28- Too many parents today would rather have their children successful in Egypt than bound for the Promised Land, and you can't have both!

29- Overlook the major and you get liberalism; over stress the minor and you get legalism.

30- There is no bed so soft, nor sleep as sound, as a clear conscience.

31- Political correctness has caused the Church to tolerate anything lest it gain the reputation of being intolerant.

32- We are to get to the middle of God's grace, not muddle around in the mess that is in the world.

33- It is time we escape the misty lowland of this world to the majestic "Lordland" of the "higher ground" experience found only in Jesus Christ.

34- Many preachers today are as straight as an arrow theologically, but without a bow of enthusiasm. What good is it? If you cannot shoot to the heart of the soul, what good is a straight arrow?

35- A spiritual hymn or chorus without a message is like a bird without wings. If the song only keeps you earthbound, if it doesn't make you soar to the heights of God's glory, what good is it?

36- Too many people spend most of their time on a kind of spiritual trapeze swinging between one spiritual high and another. They never seem to realize that ours is to be a daily walk with God in the marketplace of the world. Swinging from our hands and toes in some super spiritual service might impress some, but living an ordinary Christlike life will impress God. Many need to come down from their Pentecostal trapeze and walk with God and man.

37- Too many people today worry about getting more of the Holy Spirit when they ought to allow the Holy Spirit to get more of them. As a great saint once said, "We can have all of Him, if He can get all of us."

38- We ought to talk to God before we talk about God.

39- I will not debate with you the doctrine of eternal security because we have Lot and Demas to consider. All I know is that, when we saw these men last, they were both walking in the wrong direction.

40- I will not debate you on the issue of Calvinism versus Arminianism because the Bible is clear to me; we ought to pray as if we were Calvinistic, and we ought to preach as if we were Arminian. We ought to believe as if it all depends on God and work as if it all depends on us.

41- Have you ever noticed that Jesus never speaks of unanswered prayer because He knew that all prayer is answered prayer in the will and ways of His and our Father.

42- Some say, "Prayer changes things," but I say that prayer changes us.

43- "Like a mighty tortoise moves the Church of God, brothers we are treading where we've always trod" goes a line from an adapted hymn stanza. The tragedy is that such rhymes often find fulfillment.

44- Situations in life are like feather beds, very comfortable if you are on top of them, but very uncomfortable if they are on top of you.

45- That which costs nothing is worth nothing.

43.

THE STUB OF THE SWORD

If you have never read the life of Amy Carmichael, I would encourage you to find her biography and be blessed. What a lady of faith who ministered to my favorite country outside the United States, India. Amy's last years were terrible years of suffering, but despite her physical shortcomings she ministered up to the end and in a very unique way explained through this simple poem how she did it: "What though I stand with the winners, or perish with those that fall? Only the cowards are sinners, fighting the fight is all. Strong is my foe, who advances, snapped is my blade, O Lord; see their proud banners and lances, BUT SPARE ME THE STUB OF A SWORD!"

When the minister enters his 70th year, there are handicaps and weaknesses he never had fifty years ago when he was at the top of his physical and mental strength. There are those who feel that at seventy, one should retire, take his pension and life's savings, and enjoy the good life. I know this is the popular opinion of most in the ministry now, but as for me I want to go out like Amy Carmichael and my dear mentor Vance Havner who also wrote on this subject in his book Peace in the Valley in 1962 (Vance would live until 1986). He started his article with this story:

> The famous evangelist, Billy Sunday, preached in his heyday to great multitudes all over America. Before the age of microphones and amplifiers, he shouted at the thousands in his big tabernacles. Then he grew old and times changed. His crowds were smaller. The multitudes went after other attractions. But Billy Sunday was faithful to his charge to the very last. In his cracked voice he preached the same old gospel until his last

sermon in Mishawaka, Indiana. Gone was the vigor of his prime. Gone were the crowds. Billy's weapons were worn and broken, but he finished the fight with "the stub of a sword," as it were. Like Paul, he was faithful to the faith, to the fight, and to the finish.

As I read that I thought to myself that Billy Sunday was doing nothing differently than what his Lord and Saviour did.

We often forget that Jesus didn't always draw the crowds. At the first, the people flocked to the miracle-worker that spoke like no other man, but even in this it says: *"But though he had done so many miracles before them, yet they believed not on him."* (John 12:37) Then when Jesus' message got tough to believe, even His most devoted followers began to leave: *"Many therefore of his disciples, when they had heard this, said, this is an hard saying; who can hear it? When Jesus knew in himself that his disciples murmured at it, he said unto them, doth this offend you? What and if ye shall see the Son of man ascend up where he was before? It is the spirit that quickeneth; the flesh profiteth nothing: the words that I speak unto you, they are spirit, and they are life. But there are some of you that believe not. For Jesus knew from the beginning who they were that believed not, and who should betray him. And he said, therefore said I unto you, that no man can come unto me, except it were given unto him of my Father. **From that time many of his disciples went back, and walked no more with him.**"* (John 6:60–66) And I think you all know the end of the story of Jesus because when Jesus preached His last message, He was hanging on a cross with few in the congregation. Weak and weary, broken and bruised, forsaken and fainting, with only "the stub of a sword" left.

I like how Vance explains this condition:

> Battling with the stub of a sword is the test of God's soldier. It is not too difficult to battle well when the freshness of the cause thrills us and the exhilarations of life are full and strong. When we are at the peak of our usefulness, appreciated and seeing the fruit of our labors, our armor unbroken, our weapons keen, we tingle with the zest of combat and are anxious for the fray. But age and disease and changing times may take their toll, and we may finish with only the snub of a sword. How to make that last chapter the best in the book, how to finish the course with joy, how to defeat the enemy with broken weapons is life's last and perhaps finest lesson.

And so there it is, how to stay useful and effective in the 70th year of one's life.

If Jesus ended that way, so did the Apostle Paul. Surely, you remember the glory days of Paul when he expanded the Church throughout the Roman Empire, when miracles and mighty messages moved the masses in the great world centers of power and influence. Perhaps, no one ever achieved more in mission's work in such a short time, but how did it all end? Old (Philemon 9), frail (II Corinthians 12:7-9), and languishing in a dark, damp, dingy Roman prison. The crowds are gone, his friends have left (II Timothy 1:15-16), and all he wants is a coat and some writing material (II Timothy 4:13). So, did Paul give in or give up? No! It was then Paul used "the stub of a sword" (Ephesians 6:17), and he started writing. Oh, Paul had written before, but now he writes his famous "prison epistles." (Most talk about four, but I have come to believe there were at least five with a possible sixth: Ephesians, Philippians, Colossians, and Philemon are the recognized ones, but I think you can add II Timothy and Hebrews to the list.) And think with me, what he produced in the last mile of the way, in his old age, and with just the end of his pen is still blessing and inspiring the Church of the Living God to this day. I believe in what Jesus taught His disciples: *"Ye have not chosen me, but I have chosen you, and ordained you,* **that ye should go and bring forth fruit, and that your fruit should remain***: that whatsoever ye shall ask of the Father in my name, he may give it you."* (John 15:16) Paul's fruit has remained!

As I write this article, one of my best weapons has been removed from my arsenal, that being the death of my lifelong companion, co-laborer, and wife, Coleen. Like Jonathan's armourbearer (I Samuel 14:13) she always had my back. I feel sometimes like old Abner being pursued by the younger Asahel (II Samuel 2:19-22) after a tough battle, yet I remember well the outcome of that confrontation: *"Howbeit he refused to turn aside: wherefore Abner with the hinder end of the spear smote him under the fifth rib, that the spear came out behind him; and he fell down there, and died in the same place: and it came to pass, that as many as came to the place where Asahel fell down and died stood still."* (II Samuel 2:23) Abner used the back end of the spear, the stub end of the spear, if you will, to win the fight. Vance ends his article with these encouraging words: "If this little message finds you with a broken weapon, take heart. You are in illustrious company. The battle is the Lord's, and He asks only that you be faithful 'when all the challenge leaves the hours and naught is left but jaded powers.' Now is the time to prove your mettle and endure hardness as a good soldier (II Timothy 2:3). What matters most is not the condition of your equipment, but the state of your heart." Amen and Amen!

So as for me, I am determined to press on (Philippians 3:14) with the arsenal that I have left, with the stamina that remains, and the skills that I have learned over the long fight. I might not be as swift as Asahel, but I am wiser. I might not be as strong as Asahel, but I am more skilled. I might not be as young as Asahel, but I am here, and he is dead! I love the old proverb: ***"For to him that is joined to all the living there is hope: for a living dog is better than a dead lion."*** (Ecclesiastes 9:4) You might just be surprised what God can do with an old warrior because I am finding it isn't the healthy, vigorous, or well-equipped who are carrying on the fight today, but the old guard that have been in the trenches for decades. They are still faithful and still fighting with broken weapons. I am one!

44.

THE MASTER'S MINORITY VERSUS THE MORAL MAJORITY

IN MY LIFETIME AND into my 70th year, I have been confronted by the two competing Christian philosophies highlighted and underlined by the title of this chapter. Who am I, a simple country pastor to question the teachings of some of the biggest names in Christianity during my life? Surely the very success of these men stamps upon their teachings that they were right and what I am about to write is wrong. I really don't know where this obsession started; the desire to believe that somewhere in the masses, the population, there are enough people on our side to make us the majority, or where the inferiority complex came from that despises the word "minority?" When twice-born people try to emulate once-born people, there will arise a conflict of conscience and confliction that will result in confusion. After a half a century of competing with the world, the Church has become troubled and alarmed that what they have been told by their spiritual leaders over the decades is now proving to be untrue; we are not in the majority, and we never were! We are not the top religion of the world by numbers and even in the moral issues, the cornerstone of the social gospel. We have lost in every battle to legislate Biblical morality, the sanctity of life and marriage between one woman and one man comes to mind. So, where did the enlightened leaders of this "majority" philosophy miss the boat? What did they fail to see in the teachings of Jesus Christ?

First, I believe those who promoted and proclaimed "a majority" missed a simple three-letter word in Jesus' instructions, few. This verse is from Jesus' famous Sermon on the Mount: "*Because strait [hard] is the gate, and narrow is the way, which leadeth unto life, and **few** there be that find it.*" (Matthew 7:14) In one of Jesus' first messages He taught that His way would be entered by the "few," not the many, by the minority, not the majority. I have come to believe that this precept applies to any aspect of Christianity, whether a doctrinal teaching or a moral philosophy. For years I have watched the politicians use and abuse Christian voters to get them elected without once actually changing a moral law. I, too, was pulled into the belief that a certain politician could change the moral condition of our country, but over the years I have only watched as the moral character of our land has consistently declined, falling further and further into the immoral gutter of immorality and wickedness that we were once ashamed to even speak about, but now is mentioned in common communication. We are outnumbered and outshouted today, and the only voice being heard is the majority voice, and we are not it!

Second, I believe those that teach and train others to believe in "a majority" missed a simple three-letter word in Jesus' teachings, few. From one of Jesus' famous parables of "the kingdom," this verse: "*So the last shall be first, and the first last: for many be called, but **few** chosen.*" (Matthew 20:16) Granted, the majority is called, as a matter of fact, all are given a charge to follow Jesus. Jesus commanded His disciples to "*. . . Go ye into ALL the world, and preach the gospel to EVERY creature.*" (Mark 16;15) Even in my own experience of sharing the Gospel for over 50 years, I have given the invitation to many, but only a "few" have responded to the salvation provided by Jesus Christ with His death on the cross. Surely, the likes of Billy Graham would verify that despite the multitudes that have come forward in his mass evangelistic crusades, the "few," not the many, responded; the minority, not the majority, accepted the invitation. According to what I heard, the Billy Graham Association published that Billy led millions to Christ, but in a world where there are billions, millions are not a majority, just a minority.

Third, I believe those that practice and preach that there is "a majority" of moral people that will standup and testify of Jesus' doctrines have missed a simple three-letter word in Jesus' theology, few. From one of Jesus' observations of His generation, I feel this verse also speaks about my generation: "*. . . The harvest truly is great, but the labourers are **few**: pray ye therefore the Lord of the harvest, that He would send forth labourers into His harvest.*" (Luke 10:2) Few will respond to the Gospel, and few will call on the Gospel, and now we know that few will proclaim the

Gospel. So how do you get a majority out of these teachings? It starts with a few called, then fewer still will answer the call, and the fewest of them all are those that do believe and respond but will not serve. We are living in a day where the servants of Christ, even in the Church of Christ, are few. I talk all the time about the faithful few even into my 70s. Fewer kids' workers, fewer prayer warriors, fewer deacons or those that qualify to be a deacon, fewer Bible teachers—you get the idea. We live in an age that will be known for the fewest, and yet we have the boldness to proclaim to the world that we are the majority, that there is a moral majority, when we can't even get a majority of church members to come to a business meeting, the prayer meeting, or the town meeting if you want to go secular.

Throughout history there has always been the Master's minority. Before the Flood the majority was the godless, the ungodly to the point that it says: "... *in the days of Noah, while the ark was a preparing, wherein few, that is eight souls were saved by water.*" (I Peter 3:20) There is only one way that the minority ever becomes the majority in Biblical terms, and that is after a major judgment. Noah and his family's minority status was turned into a majority after the flood. Throughout the Old Testament the doctrine of the "remnant" or what I like to call the "few" is also seen. Remember, in the days of Elijah there were only a "few" that didn't bow the knee to Baal (I Kings 19:18), and even in the New Testament this concept is seen in the Church of Sardis where only a "few" had not defiled themselves (Revelation 3:4). We must come to the realization that "minority" is the designation determined for those that trust in the Lord. We will never be a majority in this world because only in the next world will we attain this label.

Getting back to our original focus and that being "the moral majority" of the 1980s and 1990s, even then there never was a moral majority. Even then the low ethical standards seen in politics and in politicians were clearly understood that America had changed its convictions on most moral issues and morality. It was in those same decades that Christianity itself came under attack because the moral ethics of leading church leaders were also suspect by their lifestyles and living practices. The great church scandals made national news that shamed us all, and for us to be preaching to the politicians and persuading the legislators to legislate morally was hypocritical at best and downright dishonest at the worst. We were trying to teach a doctrine that isn't even found in the Bible, let alone in the teachings of Jesus. How wrong was it that after twenty centuries of Christianity, the Church that set out to be like Christ was teaching something and trying to practice something that was entirely un-Christlike. Even the Lord didn't suggest that despite the multitudes that followed Him, He was ever in a majority. Jesus knew the hearts of men (John 2:24–25), and He knew that when the crowds finally understood His teaching, they would abandon Him (John 6:60–66). Christ was content to be in the minority. Why can't Christians? I know many of my fellow believers still have a hard time accepting this theology, but as for me, I have always been in a minority, and I find it encouraging to know that I am numbered with the Lord and that is good enough for me.

45.

THE SCOURGE OF LEGALISM

I WRITE IN MY 70th year of a falsehood that is again finding its way into the mainstream thinking of the average Christian. This wickedness came over from England to our shores on the "Mayflower" through the seemingly righteous teachings of the Puritans. The concept is simple: to establish a righteous kingdom on earth through just laws and the administration of God's people without the bodily presence of the Christ. Those of every religious persuasion have from the beginning dreamed of creating their own version of a righteous kingdom here on earth, and the fanatics of the Taliban are just one who in recent years has tried in various parts on this planet to do just that. It is a delusion I believe of faith no matter what kind of faith you are talking about, that one can somehow or other, create a righteous state, a religious nation, a holy commonwealth through the leadership of the unrighteous, unreligious, or the unholy, no matter how godly or good these men or women appear to be. It doesn't really matter how good or godly or spiritual you may think you are, or they are, the hope, or the dream is doomed, dead on arrival from the start because no man can rule wisely or justly without **"absolute power eventually corrupting absolutely!"** (Remember Cromwell in England?) Jesus is the only one that could have died for the sins of mankind, and Jesus is the only one that can create such a righteous kingdom.

Many got excited during the November elections of 2010. There were those preaching and prophesying that morality was coming back, and that we were on the verge of restoring religious values into the mainstream of society. I for one have lived long enough to observe that even when the righteous are seemingly in control of society *"evil men and seducers shall wax worse and worse, deceiving, and being deceived."* (II Timothy 3:13) It is just another lie of the legalist that wants to force everyone to abide by certain rules (their rules). They believe that education, legislation, and elimination can clean up this evil world. That by outlawing certain vices and habits depravity will somehow be erased. (How did prohibition work out in the roaring twenties?)

I am convinced that as long as we are in this world, without the personal presence of the Christ, we will always see though *"a glass darkly."* (I Corinthians 13:12) Where in the Bible is there a single verse that tells us that we can bring in the Kingdom before the King returns? If it can't be done, won't be done, then why are we jumping on this political bandwagon, this religious movement, this community action to this end? American history, world history, and church history are full of stories of strict religious groups who thought they had established the perfect community, the perfect school, the perfect fellowship, but history eventually revealed the darker side of these movements, and all of them eventually failed.

The problem with the Moral Majority of the 1980s was not one of sincerity, or desire, or right standings and standards. The problem was within every leader and every member, and it did fall no matter the earnest expectations, the fervent prayer, and the active participation in election booths across this land. We voted, and we still vote, for the standards and laws that would make our society better, but how is that working out? Have you noticed that the ungodly and the unrighteous have just as many new laws on the ballot as we do? Until the hearts of the people are changed our country will not change. Legalism by legislation is just as uncertain as any legalistic endeavor ever thought up or for a period of time achieved. If we know from Scripture and history that this formula hasn't worked or will never work until the Christ returns, why are we wasting our prayers, money, and time on it?

I have come to the conclusion it is the temptation and enticement of a certain doctrine known as **"the will of God."** Everybody on the legalistic side seems to understand it, know it, and is determined to exploit it. The problem is always one of mistaking the permissive will of God for the perfect will of God, and people of faith are quite adept at making this mistake. Right now, in Ireland an old curse of the last decades of the Twentieth Century are beginning to re-emerge in the Twenty-First Century: the religious struggle between the Protestants of Northern Ireland with the Roman Catholics of Southern Ireland. When both sides believe that God is on their side and that they are doing what they are doing in the name of God and according to the will of God, some very sad results have happened and will continue to happen as long as this doctrine is exploited and abused and misused.

It all seems so simple to those who feel that they have found the will of God, so clear, so unmistakably correct to believe that it is the perfect will of God for them to kill their neighbor because he or she or they will not conform to the lifestyle, the life, and the living to what they see as godly. How can good people, godly people, misunderstand this relationship to His will? For me, it is simple. Anytime you get the natural man reasoning in the Spirit, you will run into difficulties. Every man, even the best of men, comes into the dilemma with a slant, an opinion, yes, even a prejudice. And that bent will distort "the will of God" every time. That is why it is the arrogance of mankind, even the arrogance of the religious right, godly men and women of conviction, to feel that they have achieved, have been revealed the mystery of the perfect will of God, and rare, very rare, is there a dissenting voice in the group who cautions humility or godly patience.

This leads us back to our original thought. Why are we struggling to accomplish something that is certainly beyond our ability or reach: a perfect world without the Perfect One? Even when Christ comes, and even after he sets up the Kingdom, the world will not be perfect because not everybody will yield graciously to Christ's control. Why else does the Psalmist write this: *"I will declare the decree: the LORD hath said unto me, Thou art my Son; this day have I begotten thee. Ask of me, and I shall give thee the heathen for thine inheritance, and the uttermost parts of the earth for thy possession. Thou shalt break them with <u>a rod of iron</u>; thou shalt dash them in pieces like a potter's vessel."* (Psalm 2:7–9) Just to bring control of this planet and its people, the Lord will have to use force which doesn't sound like a Utopia to me? Then it was the Apostle John that picked up this theme in his Revelation: *"And there appeared another wonder in heaven; and behold a great red dragon, having seven heads and ten horns, and seven crowns upon his heads. And his tail drew the third part of the stars of heaven, and did cast them to the earth: and the dragon stood before the woman which was ready to be delivered, for to devour her child as soon as it was born. And she brought forth a man child, who was to rule all nations with <u>a rod of iron</u>: and her child was caught up unto God, and to his throne."* (Revelation 12:3–5) Even the best of kingdoms, the Millennial Kingdom, will not be a perfect kingdom without fault or failures in the citizens of that kingdom. John would finish his Revelation with these words: *"And out of his mouth goeth a sharp sword, that with it he should smite the nations: and he shall rule them with* a rod of iron: *and he treadeth the winepress of the fierceness and wrath of Almighty God. And he hath on his vesture and on his thigh a name written, KING OF KINGS, AND LORD OF LORDS."* (Revelation 19:15-16)

Why "a rod of iron?" Why not a golden scepter of grace, a wand of mercy, or a baton of love? Because the human race will still have their depraved nature; that bent to sin, that desire to run away from that which is right and righteous? We often forget that after a thousand years with the Christ in a restored planet with better health and plenty to eat, in the end when Satan is let loose from his "fallen" prison (Revelation 20:1-3) the Bible says this: *"And when the thousand years are expired, Satan shall be loosed out of his prison, and shall go out to deceive the nations which are in the four quarters of the earth, Gog and Magog, to gather them together to battle:* **the number of whom is as the sand of the sea.**" (Revelation 20:7-8) How can this be possible? With every advantage, with every law and rule in place, with a perfect, just, caring, and loving leader, the majority will still elect Satan as their desired leader at the end of the age! If "the perfect community" can't be legislated during the Millennial Kingdom, it certainly won't be elected in this present age!

A classic example of these attempts is the Puritans of early America. They had a chance to do it right with a clean start, a fresh slate, and an untouched state to develop their "kingdom on earth." Caught between two precepts, they chose wisely and unwisely; they ruled perfectly and imperfectly; and they revealed their faith to both the mature and naïve. They placed their trust in themselves while trusting in God, and when they thought they were placing their trust in God, they were trusting in their own laws and rules to conform their members to a righteous kingdom. Their kingdom on earth lasted barely a hundred years in its various forms. I have noticed that during this latest surge of legalism the fundamental truth of this movement is beginning to raise its ugly head again. Every legalistic group, small or great, school or assembly, nation or state, which seizes some kind of power in the name of God begins to quietly place controls on what can be said, what can be read, and what can be thought. The Taliban is notorious in this regard, but I remember a similar law at Bob Jones University. The Roman Catholics did it during the Reformation, while the Puritans did it both in England and New England, and yes, local churches and private schools and communist countries have done it, too, and are still doing it to this day. (Do you think North Korea has an open press, freedom of speech, open communications, personal opinions?) Why? How can you control without censorship? When was the last time we grouped these organizations together? Are we so afraid that our Church will be destroyed if we learn what is really going on in the world? I for one trust the Word of God and believe that there is no philosophy, or religion that when compared to our Faith will be chosen above the Faith. I am open to debate, information, and a challenge. This is why I respect those who are willing to take the Bible into the arenas of science (like Ken Ham) or politics (?) or business (like my brother Mike) or philosophy (?). We have nothing to fear to expose our faith to the man on the corner, the professor in the classroom, the businessman on Wall Street, or the politician in Washington. They might want to close us down or shut us up (Covid-19), but our faith in God's Word doesn't need to take a backseat to anyone, any religion, any philosophy, or any political party. Remember what Jesus said in His Sermon on the Mount: *"Think not that I am come to destroy the law, or the prophets: I am not come to destroy, but to fulfil. For verily I say unto you, till heaven and earth pass, one jot or one tittle shall in no wise pass from the law, till all be fulfilled."* (Matthew 5:17–18)

It is a simple lesson of history. Everything is complex, and nothing is as easy as it seems. If I were to put on the mentality I received from my Bible School days and have witnessed periodically in my pastorates, I would shout with the legalists, side with the fundamentalist, and join the Christian Jihad against anything and everything that doesn't follow my line of thinking, but what do I do with Romans 14:5–8: *"One man esteemeth one day above another: another esteemeth every day alike. Let every man be fully persuaded in his own mind. He that regardeth the day, regardeth it unto the Lord; and he that regardeth not the day, to the Lord he doth not regard it. He that eateth, eateth to the Lord, for he giveth God thanks; and he that eateth not, to the Lord he eateth not, and giveth God thanks. For none of us liveth to himself, and no man dieth to himself. For whether we live, we live unto the Lord; and whether we die, we die unto the Lord: whether we live therefore, or die, we are the Lord's."* Do I believe my interruption of the Scriptures is right? I do, but am I willing to side with those that say we must force, imprison people in a set of rules and regulations to keep them pure? I am not! I am talking about religious legalists whose heads are in the puritan clouds, so-called Bible scholars with silly notions about this life and the object of creating their own version of heaven on earth and enforced by false teachers with silly notions of grandeur, the next Peter or Paul, who allow their religious zeal to go terribly and horribly wrong (like Jim Jones). I have witnessed over my years the spiritual destruction of many a saint caught up in this arrogance and pride that I believe is a true offense to the eyes of God and the nostrils of Christ and the ears of the Holy Spirit. (Never forget the lesson of II Peter 1:20.)

It would be a far better approach if we would receive from our religious leaders a proper and honest assessment regarding why and what we ought to be doing while we wait the return of the Christ. We need to spend time wrestling with the contradictions brought about by the conflict that often arises between sincere faith and belief, between one polar-opposite faith and polar-opposite belief. We never seem to get around to these debates and discussions because we are constantly shouting down the other side and planning ways we can capture their minds and control their actions with legislation. It is all about the triumph of faith, the glory of God, the Lord's will, and the wonders of living in obedience to God as we see it! But is this how God sees it?

A few years back I spent the bulk of a year in our adult Sunday school class studying Paul's classic book on this matter of legalism, Galatians. I have come to the belief that the churches of Galatia were the first to face the evil of legalism head on. Through the ministry of Paul many of the Galatians had been set free from the legalism of Judaism by the grace of God and the work of the Spirit, yet, Paul had to write to them with this rebuke: *"O foolish Galatians, who hath bewitched you, that ye should not obey the truth, before whose eyes Jesus Christ hath been evidently set forth, crucified among you?"* (Galatians 3:1) Why would they, why would we, want to go back to a life of bondage after being set free, yet, this is exactly what the legalists want to persuade us to do. The Law failed, yet "a law" is being championed as the answer to society's ills; we are just one law away, one rule short of our Utopia! We are just one piece of legislation away in forming a perfect community, but I ask what legislation? But the Moslems want their laws to rule, and the liberals want their laws, and even the conservatives want their laws! A law, a form of legality is not the answer, and the coming back of the Lord is our only hope: *"He who testifieth these things saith, surely I come quickly. Amen. Even so, come, Lord Jesus."* (Revelation 22:20) Legalism is just another demon trick to distract us from God.

46.

ONE OF THOSE DAYS

THREE MONTHS INTO MY widowhood, I had one of those days. You know the phrase and the meaning behind those four simple words, don't you? It was a day of petty problems, routine and same-old church work, simple decisions to make, and what to wear, the normal vexations of life on this planet. Added to all that, lingering in the background, was my grief, missing my wife, asking what my purpose was, the feeling of loss and abandonment, yes, one of those days in the life of a man who was now alone.

In the midst of my pity party I was brought short when that "still small voice" spoke to my soul and asked, *"What are you doing here, little man?"* (I Kings 19) I felt like I had just been transported to Mount Horeb and that deep, dark, dusty, dingy cave occupied by Elijah. Was I discouraged? Was I fighting despair? Granted, I missed my best friend, but what was I doing in this hole in the ground looking at four blank walls with no hope in sight, no hope of getting out of the depression I seemed to be in. It was then that voice spoke again with these words, *"While we look not at the things which are seen, but at the things which are not seen: for the things which are seen are temporal; but the things which are not seen are eternal."* (II Corinthians 4:18) I was acting as if "one of these days" would last forever. I knew my theology better than that, but I wasn't focusing on my theology. I was focused on my current situation, the unexpected circumstance I was in after the departure of my beloved. It was then I came back to the reality that Coleen's death wasn't the permanent thing, and my grief and loss was only temporary at best.

On top of the death of my wife, my mother, and an uncle, I am also fighting a reoccurring E-coli bacteria that had been my *"thorn in the flesh"*

(II Corinthians 12:7) for six years now. I am in the midst of its fourth major invasion in those six years and the third in the last three years. It is one of those anti-biotic resistant bacteria that can only be treated with certain drugs, mostly IV drugs. I have just finished 16 days, five in the hospital, but it appears it wasn't enough. One of these days all this planning, scheduling, financial decisions, meetings, and health issues will be over and what seemed so important then will be lost in the tranquility and serenity of eternity. I will be with Coleen (my wife), Phyllis (my mother), Wendell (my father), and a whole lot more that I miss. As I often say, I am at a place in my life where there seems to be more over there that I know than over here that I know. It was then I realized that all I need is the Lord's presence and the rest will fall into place until I crossover.

So, what do you do on one of those days? I went back to a core precept that has governed me through the good and the bad and the ups and the downs of life: *"Trust in the LORD with all thine heart; and lean not unto thine own understanding. In all thy ways acknowledge him, and He shall direct thy paths."* (Proverbs 3:5–6) I realized that I was allowing the lesser things in my life to take a central place in my day while putting God in the background, off to the side; I was making God marginal. I had allowed my grief to put God on the sidetrack, the sideline, forgetting to *" . . . seek ye first the kingdom of God, and his righteousness; and all these things shall be added unto you."* (Matthew 6:33) I have come to believe that this challenge is talking about more than food, raiment, and drink (Matthew 6:31). In times of loss we should seek God; in times of despair we should seek God; in times of questions and doubts we should seek God. No matter the time, circumstance, or situation, even on one of those days, we need to seek God, and we know from the Word of God that He is there to help us through one of those days.

I learned long ago, even the best theology is sometimes forgotten in grief, that if we are hidden in Christ and are allowing Him to live His life in us, we have been immunized against one of those days. Oh, we can still have those days as Elijah had and I was having three months into my widowhood, but like with the Meropenam (the drug that takes me from feeling like I am dying to feeling 16 again) that helps me fight my E-coli bacteria, the truth of the Bible helps me fight the cares, the fears, the worries, the doubts, and the grief of this world. So the true immunization against one of those days is knowledge of the One that has promised: *"And we know that all things work together for good to them that love God, to them who are the called according to his purpose."* (Romans 8:28) Yes, even when it comes to the agony of one of those days! The world can't understand why through most of my grief I have been able to press on, preach on, and go on. But for those of us who really do see the eternal behind the temporal, we know "this too shall pass away," and as Vance Havner once wrote: **"A poor light affords a poor view."** As for the Christian, we have a bright light that affords a better view: *"Thy word is a lamp unto my feet, and a light unto my path."* (Psalm 119:105) Amen!

What that still, small voice taught me in the darkness of the cave I was in is that one of those days will soon be turned into one of these days. One of these days all restless nights will pass, and I have had a few of those over the last three months. Not that I worry where Coleen is or mother went, but just an agony of the soul over my loss. I have been telling people that part of the problem is that because of the Covid-19 pandemic I have yet to bury my dear wife, and that troubles me. I know they are only her ashes, but until one properly says goodbye, can we really get over the grief? But one of these days all the griefs that darken our days here will be gone over there. All the regrets that haunt my mind, and I have some, especially not giving Coleen the things she deserved and would have made her life easier when I could have, will pass. All the blunders and mistakes, the heartaches and the pains, the hurts and the blame that once overshadowed everything will all be forgiven, over, removed, buried, and remembered no more.

I have come to believe that Paul lived in this philosophy: *"Therefore judge nothing before the time, until the Lord come, who both will bring to light the hidden things of darkness, and will make manifest the counsels of the hearts: and then shall every man have praise of God."* (I Corinthians 4:5) I will admit I have been trying to judge a few things, trying to understand the timing of God prematurely. I sometimes forget that the view of the temporal is nearsighted at best because we need to be farsighted knowing that God knows best and has worked it all out for our good and His glory. It comes down to what is our perspective on one of those days. Suddenly, when we get our eyes open like Elisha's servant (II Kings 6), the big becomes small, giants become gnats, and the bugaboo and hobgoblins that harass us leave because in reality they were never there, only an imagination that often happens on one of those days. As Vance Havner once wrote, **"The last great day will put everything in order."**

I also came to this conclusion. Why should I wait for the last day when I can claim God's promises now and take the spiritual medicine that can keep my discouragement at bay, just like my Meropenam? God's

Word has the cure for my itch, my torments, and my fever. If God is all that will matter one day, why not live as if He is all that matters today? Someone has said that on Paul's calendar there was circled only two days: "Today and that Day!" So, on one of those days I am looking forward and am in full anticipation and expectation for one of these days!

47.

INSTEAD OF INDIA

Plans had been made for an exciting, ministry-filled forty days in India. The tickets had been bought, the suitcases had been packed, the sermons and lessons had been prepared, and I was looking forward to my sixth trip to the subcontinent, a place I have come to view as my second home. I had been looking forward to my winter trip to Kerala since I was there in 2016. It had been four long years for me, but instead of going to India I went to the hospital with my dear wife. Instead of India I ministered to my dying wife those forty days and with the coming of the now infamous Covid-19 pandemic, my way of ministry and my life would dramatically change forever. But through it all, my dear Lord was teaching me what "instead of India" means.

When one spends hours and days waiting for an X-ray, Cat scans, and ultra-sounds, a fluid removal procedure, doctor's visits, hospitalizations, and all this in just 75 days, one has time to do a lot of thinking, meditating, and pondering "instead of India." It has been amazing to me what you think about in those times, but you don't think about when you're walking around doing what you want to do. I look forward to India for the times of total freedom without a responsibility or care; just going along for the ride as others make your schedule, guide you from meeting to meeting, and take care of your every need and want. Instead of that I was taken through a time where I was responsible for every decision, both my own and another, culminating with the hardest decision anyone can make in this world, telling the medical professions you want them to stop all care for your wife so she can die!

So, after the profound disappointment, the bewildering sadness, the discouraging outcome, the long, slow process of recovery begins. And though I am only in the first three months of that recovery, I realize this is a great time to take a fresh look, take a soul-searching inventory of one's life, with nothing in that life off-limits. I know that I am being supported by prayers all over the world. My church has allowed me time to grieve, and my daughter and her family have moved all the way from California to help me, but at times I wonder if I will survive the ministry, the new start without Coleen, or the trauma the coronavirus has had on the Church and the mission of the Church. Just a few days ago a good pastor friend of mine (same age, in 70th year, from the same county) called to tell me he was retiring after 30 years in the pastorate and 22 years pastoring a church just up the road from mine. He had been thinking about it for a while, but the new normal didn't allow him to minister to people as he had, and he wasn't willing to change. Some say this is only temporary, but for many of us we feel a profound change has taken place, so either we adjust or we get out. I will admit I, too, have thought this is not the way I minister, and I don't like the alternatives. Then to top it off the very day my friend resigned, another church in the area voted to shut its doors. Being in the area for 29 years, I knew the people there, and when they had a Christian school, my kids went there. I knew the former pastor and counted him as a friend and many of the members. What is happening? Instead of India, I find myself at a major crossroad wondering what to do.

One is first tempted to ask the three-word question that often comes up at these times, "Why;" to try to figure out "instead of India," why Coleen got sick, and Covid sickened the world. But through many a trial and tribulation in my life, including the death of children and the death of a church (my very first church dissolved after just six years), I don't ask why any longer; instead of India I seek the lesson the Good Lord is trying to teach me in the change of plans, in the end of life, in the crossroad experiences that have happened, that are happening, and that will happen. And the one thing that has come up repeatedly in the first half of 2020 is that God is not interested mainly in how many sermons I preach because He has taken away many an opportunity only to replace them with other opportunities. In all my disappointment of not going to India, yesterday I got a text from an Indian friend from Orissa (a state on the northeast side of India) who wants me to teach and preach to a group of pastors and evangelists through a modern marvel called Zoom! (At the putting of the book to bed I just finished a 100 of them!) I might not be going to India physically, but I still will be teaching and preaching in India before the year ends. God hasn't put me on a shelf; He is just readjusting the way I minister. Since the pandemic and Coleen's passing, I have started a weekly blog (nearly 500 to date), live stream messages on Facebook (nearing 700), send out weekly e-mail devotionals (over 200 now), and now Zoom. I think Vance Havner said it best with he wrote: **"We are not here to turn out a quota of activities; we are here to glorify God!"** I had gotten in a spiritual rut thinking that I could only glorify God through teaching Sunday school, preaching twice on Sunday (only one service now), going to three nursing homes (all of them has shut me out because of the virus-again at this compiling for the final time I just did my 3300th service in this ministry), and a few other ministries, but now I see that God can change them up. I have come to see Coleen's sickness and the Covid sickness is like what Jesus said to His disciples when He heard of Lazarus' illness: *"When Jesus heard that, he said, This sickness is not unto death, but for the glory of God, that the Son of God might be glorified thereby."* (John 11:4) God has always used strange and mysterious means and methods to get glory, and I have come to believe that He is doing it again.

To give faithful testimony and example in India is one thing, but to give that same faithful testimony and example while your wife is dying is another thing; or to give a faithful testimony and example during a pandemic is yet another thing. Could it be that in God's eyes the glory He gets in these tough and rough times is a greater glory than when you are teaching and preaching His Word in India? As with all periods like this, including my own sickness in this time, we learn again that we are not indispensible. Whether in the hospital, with Coleen, or in the hospital myself (five days in June), the world goes on. The ministry goes on, and though I feel a great hole in my life over Coleen's departure, the world, nor the Church, ever skipped a beat. I have always known that God doesn't need me but has chosen to use me anyway. If I am still here, then my usefulness is not over, and if I must adapt and change to the new normal, then I will to the glory of God and to His cause. I despise technology, but if technology is the only way I can reach and teach and preach in India, then Zoom it is. If the only way I can reach back into the nursing homes is through Facebook, then so be it. If live streaming is the only way I can feed the flock and reach the unreached, then so be it. Do I like it? No! But if my Boss tells me to change, then change I will, and as Vance Havner also wrote: **"You may gain more ground in adversity than in success."**

This might just be the time that God has decided to change His servant and his ministry.

I have come to the conclusion that the puzzling questions of this world and the unanswerable questions of this life are some of the best grounds, the most fertile soil, to grow your Christian character and to be more like Jesus. Everything working out and going well was not the ground that grew the first-century Church, and it isn't the ground that will mature the 21st century Church either. We often start for India but end up in the intensive care unit of the local hospital instead. The detour is of God to take us to a place where we can change and adapt into the servant He wants us to be, now!

(Postscript: so you know my times in India haven't finished, for as I put this book to bed I have returned to India twice more (2022 and 2023) spending nearly 50 more days in that fabled land; visiting former students of KBBC and visiting three more states and a number of unreached people groups. I have written two more books on my trips to India; one published and one ready to be published!)

48.

DISTURBERS AND DISRUPTERS

IN MY OPINION I believe the Church has lost its edge in the world because they have backed down from being the two things highlighted and underlined in the title of this seventieth-year article. The world has tried to portray our Lord and Saviour Jesus Christ as a mild-mannered, soft-spoken Galilean preacher with an accommodating message full of innocuous platitudes that offended nobody and embraced everybody. Sometimes, when I watch these so-called religious documentaries, I wonder if these people are reading the same Gospel I read. Jesus was a disturber and a disrupter from the first day of His life. We overlook this Christmas verse: *"When Herod the king had heard these things, he was troubled, and all Jerusalem with him."* (Matthew 2:3) Jesus had disturbed Herod's plans and disrupted Jerusalem order. How do you not see that Jesus was always in the eye of a storm, whether a social storm, a political storm, or an actual storm.

Jesus provoked such violent opposition from the Sadducees, Pharisees, and the Herodians that those who were bitter enemies themselves conspired together to crucify Him. Even those who were loyal at first abandoned Him when His teaching got too radical for them. Sound familiar? We are living in similar days because segments of Christianity want us to tone down the tough teaching of the Teacher. Oh, much of Jesus' theology was well accepted, but when He started to expose the leaven of the Pharisees (Read Matthew 23), the clamor for His death got louder and louder. And what was true of the Christ was also true of the early Christians. Paul and Silas created disruption and disturbances everywhere they went. Take time to read just the first missionary journey of the pair (Acts 13-14) and note the times they disrupted the status quo which often landed them in jail, or worst, stoning! I love the way Luke put it in Acts 17:6: **"These that have turned the world upside down are come hither also."** That sounds like they were disturbers and disrupters in their day. I am no authority on Church history, but I have read more than most, and, when you follow the saints down through the ages, they were always in confrontation with someone or something that caused great upheaval to the way things were. Instead of unifying, they brought division just like Jesus taught: *"Think not that I am come to send peace on earth: I came not to send peace, but a sword. For I am come to set a man at variance against his father, and the daughter against her mother, and the daughter in law against her mother in law. And a man's foes shall be they of his own household. He that loveth father or mother more than me is not worthy of me: and he that loveth son or daughter more than me is not worthy of me. And he that taketh not his cross, and followeth after me, is not worthy of me. He that findeth his life shall lose it: and he that loseth his life for my sake shall find it."* (Matthew 10:34-39)

This is certainly a teaching many shy away from today because they can't accept the truth that Jesus and His disciples would bring disruption to the world instead of peace, disruption to the family instead of peace, and disruption to society instead of peace. Since Jesus, those who truly follow Him and take up their cross and lose their life in him, Vance Havner says, **"upset the world, divided the people, and incensed the powers of darkness."** But are we doing any of that today? No, we are catering to the world (when the Covid-19 hit who were the first to cave?), we are trying to bring people together into one happy band of believers, and we are making the devil's job easy. You would think that in this day where sin is accepted, immorality is the law, and transgressions against the Almighty are late night show jokes, the Church and every Christian in it would be standing and shouting against these iniquities, but in contrast the world has lost its fear of us and our God. There were days in the past when the world feared our proclamations and the devil fled (James 4:7). We have been convinced we are to be pleasant and getting along with all men. I like the way Paul put it: *"If it be possible, as much as lieth in you, live peaceably with all men."* (Romans 12:18) But, my dear brethren, sometimes it isn't possible because the compromise is too great, and the cooperation is too compromising!

Think with me for a moment when there was a time when the liquor industry feared the Church, but today they go on unchallenged. There was a day the abortion industry feared the Church, but they realized we are a paper tiger. There was a time the pornography industry feared the Church, but most Church members allow it into their own homes. We are no longer considered an obstacle or dangerous to the devil or his demons because when we should be shouting, we are yawning; when we should be disrupting their activities, we are sleeping; when we should be disturbing their lives, we are trying to overlook their transgression. The Church has become full of mild-mannered members with a mild-mannered means, and our enemies know we will only go so far, not wanting to make a scene or bring an attack on the name of Jesus. We no longer create any resentment or ferrous opposition. And despite the entrenched evil that now lingers in communities, we lock our doors and shut our blinds and let it ravage our society with Satan's demonic evil!

I hope, despite my statements so far, you don't believe our primary purpose is to stir up trouble, to even look for trouble as some fighting fundamentalists like to do. But at the same time, we are to be ready with a word (I Peter 3:15), we are to defend the faith (Jude 3), and we are to stand and having done all to stand (Ephesians 6:13). There was a time when the Church was offensive minded, but now we seem to only be defensive minded, reacting instead of attacking. Remember, Jesus promised the gates of hell would not prevail against us (Matthew 16:18). Gates don't attack; gates are attacked suggesting that we are to be offensive motivated versus being content to defend only. Again Vance Havner: **"But when Christianity is inoffensive it is ineffective!"** Jesus went to them, and the Church went to the world, so why are we waiting? As preachers like me have preached for years, there is a different **go** in the **Go**spel. And if we go and tell the Good News of Jesus Christ, we will disrupt some people and disturb other people. That is okay according to not only the example of the Christ, but the experience of the Church.

Most of you will remember this saying: "The man that isn't against anything usually isn't for anything either." I like the way Vance Havner put it: "The world has put up a 'Please Do Not Disturb,' and some churchmen are walking on tiptoes to respect it . . . The degree of intensity with which we hate evil is a pretty good gauge of how much we love God!" I am afraid that I have become one that believes that apart from the return of Jesus, the only possible hope is for the Church to grow a spine and stand up and disrupt and disturb this old world with its righteous teachings and holy life. We need to return to the days of "The Acts of the Apostle" when the neighborhood sees the Holy Spirit as fire, hears the Apostle Peter proclaim repentance, draws the wrath of the religious establishment, gets a few of us thrown into prison, and, yes, a few of us martyred to show the world we mean business. Then this will as Vance Havner said: " . . . stir the community, agitate the ungodly, alarm the workers of iniquity, and enrage the devil!" Anything would be better than being ignored as we are today. The world sees us as unimportant, Satan sees us as impotent, and ungodly men see us as ineffective, so what are we to do? I believe the answer is clear. We need to become disrupters and disturbers!

49.

WHO IS QUALIFIED?

WHEN ONE WATCHES FROM within and from without the development of Christianity for over half a century, and when during those 50 plus years you study and read aplenty of the history of the Church before your half-century plus begins, I believe one gets to the place he has earned an opinion and the right to make an observation. With age comes certain privileges, I believe, and I also believe that is true in the Christian community I have been a part of for 62 years now. I write all that to justify what I am going to write in this chapter. Like with prophecy (II Peter 1:20-*Knowing this first, that no prophecy of the scripture is of any private interpretation.*) and with observations (Romans 14:5-*Let every man be fully persuaded in his own mind.*) of both the Bible and Church history, these are my beliefs.

    Have you noticed that religion (note I didn't say Christianity) is enjoying a resurgence, a boom, and the world is cashing in on the popularity? The tragedy is that modern Christianity is cast in the same shadow with all the world's great faiths. Have you noticed over the years how many Biblical themes Hollywood has dramatized in major movies (The Passion of the Christ, Noah, The Prince of Egypt, to name a few)? Now we have station after station, including a few purely "Christian" stations proclaiming spiritual doctrine 24–7. Television pastors, talk show hosts, and evangelists perform and publish Heniz-57 varieties of Christianity and Churchianity. Even the Christian cults, like the Mormons, now compete, vying for audiences through mass media with Christmas and Easter specials that fill the airwaves. Secular musical groups are now spiritual musical groups, and popular Christian artists are now so popular they have switched into the secular field. Preachers have become politicians; popular religious tunes are used to sell beer, and some of the world's greatest superstars are now giving testimonials of what God has done in their lives. Many in the Christian community think this is perfectly wonderful, proclaiming that a great revival is happening in the 21st century, but is it?

I know that some that read this chapter will think that I am throwing cold water on a hot event; that I am rude and very unchristian to question or disturb the current trend and that my dissenting words are judgmental and downright unloving. Why would I even question what is happening in Hollywood, Wall Street, or even in the White House? Surely, Christianity needs all the help that it can get from whatever source there is so long as the faith is being promoted. But for me, this shows the deep-seated ignorance of the Scriptures that abounds today, a famine according to Amos 8:11, a famine of hearing and believing and practicing the Word of God. I see so much of the sacred things of God being handled by the profane, people who know nothing of true prayer calling for prayer in a crisis; people who go to church for a photo-op to promote some agenda; people who wave the Bible over their heads, self-righteous and pious, thinking they are on the moral high ground because they have a Bible in their hand without knowing what the Bible actually says. These so-called christians have forgotten the core teaching of the Christ when it comes to worship, worship of any kind: *"God is a Spirit: and they that worship him must worship him in spirit and in truth."* (John 4:24) Only the truly born again and consecrated believer can worship, pray, or has the right to wheel the Word of God!

What the world and these would-be believers don't realize is that you can't come into the presence of the Almighty on your own talent, ability, or merit. The Bible teaches clearly that if you are going to come into His presence, then there are certain requirements: *"Who shall ascend into the hill of the LORD? or who shall stand in his holy place?* [1] *He that hath clean hands, and* [2] *a pure heart;* [3] *who hath not lifted up his soul unto vanity,* [4] *nor sworn deceitfully."* (Psalm 24:4) Then the Psalmist adds this: *"LORD, who shall abide in thy tabernacle? who shall dwell in thy holy hill?* [5] *He that walketh uprightly, and* [6] *worketh righteousness, and* [7] *speaketh the truth in his heart.* [8] *He that backbiteth not with his tongue,* [9] *nor doeth evil to his neighbour,* [10] *nor taketh up a reproach against his neighbour.* [11] *In whose eyes a vile person is condemned; but* [12] *he honoureth them that fear the LORD.* [13] *He that sweareth to his own hurt, and* [14] *changeth not.* [15] *He that putteth not out his money to usury,*

[16] *nor taketh reward against the innocent.* **He that doeth these things shall never be moved.**" (Psalm 15:1–5) This isn't perfection because no man is perfect, but there is also an eternity between the most gifted singer and the humblest Christian. The unregenerate and undedicated singer might have the better voice, but the meek Christian with the terrible voice will be heard by God. A classic precept that is always overlooked by the worldly christian is I Corinthians 1:26–29: *"For ye see your calling, brethren, how that not many wise men after the flesh, not many mighty, not many noble, are called: but God hath chosen the foolish things of the world to confound the wise; and God hath chosen the weak things of the world to confound the things which are mighty; and base things of the world, and things which are despised, hath God chosen, yea, and things which are not, to bring to nought things that are:* **that no flesh should glory in his presence.**" God will always look at the heart first.

Today we have the show business professionals singing our hymns and the expert orators preaching our sermons and the Wall Street managers directing our churches, but God is still looking for the common, ordinary saint that loves Him and allows His Spirit to rule in their lives. Oh, the professional christians might stir our hearts and inspire our emotions, but if it doesn't come from a born-again spirit, filled with the Spirit, it is nothing to God. I love the story of the famous orator and the old preacher who were asked to recite Psalm 23 to a group of people. The famous speaker went first and when he had ended the six verses the crowd stood and cheered, clapping their hands for a long time. It was then the simple preacher stood to quote the famous psalm, and when he was through there was no cheering, no applause, but there was not a dry eye in the crowd. The orator asked the preacher what made the difference to which the old preacher said, "You know the psalm; I know the shepherd." A Hollywood version of the Christian life might excite certain emotions and feelings and resolves, but they are surface at best and temporary at best because without a Spirit change in the soul there will ultimately be little change in the life. Your talents might be better than mine, but without Christ they are useless.

I have been witnessing for decades famous christians who bloom today and fade tomorrow. The Church has put great stock in them only to be shamed eventually by them. So, who is qualified? I like what Vance Havner wrote in the early 60s when this trend was starting: **"Only the twice-born and the dedicated can qualify to sing or speak for God. No amount of art is enough unless the heart is right. Some have good** hearts and do not sing with the voice. Some have good voices and do not sing with the heart. True worship means yielded Christians singing in their hearts and speaking in the Spirit. No others can qualify!" The Church has missed the boat thinking the world and the worldly can help us.

50.

SEPARATION OF CHURCH AND STATE?

WE HAVE, OVER THE course of the past 70 years, labored to explore some of the current issues of the modern church in America in an annual "challenge" to the flock of the Emmanuel Baptist Church in Ellsworth, Maine (30 of those years now). We have dealt with such topics as "does a pastor have to give an account to the Church?" or "does the Church still need deacons?" or "has the Church really changed?" or "has the modern mission boards let the Church down?" or "is America still a Christian nation?" This has led me to one of the great debates in both the church and the nation: **"Is the separation of Church and State Biblical?"**

It is not sufficient to simply understand theology as expressed by theologians when dealing with this issue, but we must also understand something about the times and the culture in which this question is being raised. There have been times in history when the Church and the State were the same (like when the Roman Catholic Church was in total control of the western half of the old Roman Empire). Theology on any topic does not happen in a vacuum, nor does it miraculously appear like manna from heaven delivered by an angelic host. Biblical teaching on any subject is the attempt of godly men to understand the written Word of God in light of his time and the important issues of his time, and, make no mistake about this, every theologian who has attempted to tackle such topics as "the separation of Church and State" issue has gotten it wrong as many times as he has gotten it right, and I will not be the exception to this reality.

One of the fears I have each time I attempt to jump into the middle of a social debate that has become a spiritual discussion is the law of unintended consequences. The history of the Church is marred and marked by this law. God intending one thing, but God's men directing His Church in something entirely different. And then I am coming from a totally Western Civilization bias. If I have learned anything from my times in India, it is that the so-called "world-view" is not the western view or an eastern view with respect to God or with respect to the Church. We are often so blind to our own upbringings and culture that we can't understand that God is the only one that really has a "world-view" on any topic. The eternal God is the only one with the foresight and insight into all things and can truly understand and determine the truth about any topic. I can't, only He can. We only have the Puritan experiment in New England to see the benefits and the strengths of a society with a simple official Church, and the pitfalls, embarrassments, stupidity, and hypocrisy of a society in which a single group of people define what faith is and how it is to be practiced. The total of Church history does give us some other examples, but given the times and the cultures these were a part that doesn't help us much with the question at hand in our time and place along the timeline of human history.

Many within the Church who wish to return to some form of one religion rule point to the famous Reformation that eventually split the Church into Catholics and Protestants. For better or for worse, the Reformation gave us a faith of mind and heart, and we cannot turn those consequences back simply because we don't think that things are going in the right direction now. We are, whether we like it or not, victims of our own heritage, our own culture, our own western slant, victims of the law of unintended circumstances and consequences, and the current debate (sometimes very heated) in America and in the Church over separation of Church and State really boils down to a tremendous change in our culture over our more than two hundred and forty years, a change which has for the first time in our history cast aside traditional morals, Biblical values, and Protestant religious beliefs which at one time use to unite Americans. Now these same issues are dividing us, something our forefathers never foresaw or anticipated when they formed our current form of government. Instead of progress, a fifty-fifty split will eventually slow us down, then eventually stagnate us, and finally stop us as we try to go forward as a nation or a Church.

The traditional ethics and religious beliefs, the so-called Judeo-Christian morality of Western Civilization, is no longer valued or practiced by many because we have so many competing religious influences, including Islam, which is changing our nation in ways many of us do not want to see happen or never imagined in our lifetimes would ever see happen. In this land that prides itself in religious liberty, have we already let the cat out of the bag, opened Pandora's Box, and can we, will we, be able to put the genie back in the bottle? Can we ever get back to even a hope of a purely Christian nation, or has that ship already sailed? Were we ever a purely Christian nation anyway?

We have been correct in my opinion in witnessing these tremendous changes in our nation and in the Church, but most of the dramatic changes actually began in the 18th and 19th centuries, some in the earliest years of our land. These facts are often ignored, and sometimes rightly so because the changes we face in our lifetime are simply overwhelming and too profound to behold, recognize, or even accept. We live in a society that doesn't even pay lip service to Christian values and godly ethics, and putting a new president in the White House or putting a new chief justice on the Supreme Court, or swearing in a new Congress is not going to stop the overwhelming flood of immorality and indecency flooding and engulfing our country. I guess the first point I am making in this discussion over the separation of Church and State is that we have bigger issues before us than this.

We have already witnessed the crass abuse of the evangelical vote, the compromise inflicted on evangelical leaders, and the wining and dining of our leading Christian superstars to play along with the political game that is Washington D. C. Whether right or wrong, whenever the Church mixes it up with the politicians on the "Hill," the subsequent disdain and contempt is poured on those of "the Faith" when their "issue" is embraced or rejected. I have come to only one conclusion. Somehow or other, we must get beyond this obsession which has mesmerized us and find a better way to make an impact on the society in which we live. I have a simple suggestion if you would permit me to share my thoughts.

Let us get out of politics (this world is not ultimately our home, and our citizenship eventually will be in heaven-Ephesians 2:19) and setting the agenda for the next president, and simply return to what we were left here to do--not change the "state" we are in but change the "soul" we live next to. We have forgotten Christ's Commission: *"Go ye therefore, and teach all nations, baptizing them in the name of the Father, and of the*

Politics, culture, religion, and the human quest for spiritual identity, expression, and choice has been the inspiration behind this debate and discussion, not the Holy Spirit of God. Where in the life of the Christ or in the ministry of the Apostle Paul do we find one verse on this debate? I find none because in the mind of God this is a non-issue. Is the Holy Spirit at work, certainly! Does God still rise up and put down governments and governors, yes! (Daniel 2:21) Has He ever sought a kingdom on earth, no, not yet! Only when Jesus returns will "... the government be upon His shoulders ..." (Isaiah 9:6) and not until then. I am convinced that we need not see this as a Biblical issue. It should not take any more of our time then the time I have written about to say forget about it and get back to the real issues of life and death, heaven and hell, saved and unsaved.

In the end, we cannot hope to change our culture without reforming ourselves, and this we have repeatedly failed to do. We have missed too many opportunities to make a difference, taken too many stands on unimportant issues which have only isolated us even more (like our dear Puritan brethren of a past age), and failed to practice a faith of love, not with the unfaithful, but with our own brothers and sisters in Christ. As I have been preaching for nearly 55 years, **the greatest hindrance in Christianity today is the Christian!** God forbid that we should actually assist a Catholic priest neighbor to cross a busy School Street (where I live across from the parsonage of the Roman Catholic Church). We must straighten out our own house before we can ever imagine a former America which is now fading rapidly from our memory. We have failed, chronically, to tend to our own dirty laundry, but at the same time are eager and ready to try and clean up the dirty laundry of others first (*"Judge not, that ye be not judged ... Thou hypocrite, first cast out the beam out of thine own eye; and then shalt thou see clearly to cast out the mote out of thy brother's eye."* Matthew 7:1–5). The topic of "the separation of Church and State" is an argument that has been heard by many a generation of Christians throughout Church history. American evangelicals have simply taken the old arguments and put them in a brand-new three-piece suit and wrapped them in a new twenty-first century debate. This issue ultimately is the same old elephant in the room, the same pig in the barnyard, but we have deceived ourselves into thinking that we are original in our approach to the problem, the solution to the problem, and the uniqueness to the problem. The Separation of Church and State is a myth, a fable, a fantasy created by those that wish and hope and desire that there is "no God," no eternal plan, and no coming back of Jesus. It should be a non-starter in our eternal quest to see souls saved, lives changed, and people come to Christ. My conclusion is a simple one. The debate over the separation of Church and State is just another distraction away from the real purpose why we are still here.

51.

BOWING OUT GLORIOUSLY

I HAVE LIVED TOO long in the northern hemisphere not to love autumn best of all the seasons. Oh, I love spring after a long winter, but nothing compares to fall. I enjoyed the arrival of September when I lived on the family farm in northern Maine, and now I enjoy October on the coast of Maine. Both bring with them the cooler air and the glorious change of the leaves. As Vance Havner once put it, "They end the summer in a blaze of beauty!" And for me, the best colors of autumn are found in Maine. I remember when my dear wife and I moved to New Hampshire to start a church in the summer of 1973. As that summer turned into fall, everybody was talking about the fabulous colors that could be seen in the White Mountains, the best of the best, they said. Having been raised in the forests of Aroostook County, I said they must be something, so my wife and I planned a weekend get-away to check the foliage out and see the best of the best! I was never more disappointed than that weekend when I realized the people of southern New England don't have a clue what real fall colors are. Granted, there were color shades of orange, yellow, red and the like, but the brilliant, blazing color was missing. In a late September day I can take you to a ridge overlooking the Salmon Brook Valley and show you the greatest fall scene you will ever see, and I can do that any year, year in and year out. I know many would think I am crazy because of the sights and sites you have witnessed in your life, but I leave the challenge out there.

The advantage I believe northern Maine has over other places is the vast number of trees that tend to come alive with vibrant colors, such as the Sugar Maple, when the autumn woods burst forth in a blaze of glory only the Master Painter could create. (I have travelled by car the entire length of the Alaska Highway in the fall and though there was a lot of color, it was mostly yellow.) Granted, soon after the autumn breezes have done their work, the woods (except for the evergreens) turn barren and naked, but the memory of those colorful few weeks lingers still. My daughter loves fall as well and when she lived in California, I would send her some maple leaves that fell from the front yard tree in front of the parsonage in Ellsworth because there is no color in California! There is nothing better than to take a scenic ride along the back lanes in Maine just taking in the splendor of the spruce trees (green) and the red maple trees next door. And when the sun comes out, the colors are nearly neon for brilliance. I am sharing all this and hoping I have brought to your mind some memories of a few autumns in your life to make this application in my 70th year. Again, I think Vance Havner said it best when he wrote, "We mortals ought to learn how to take the autumn of life. Because the harvest is past and the summer ended, there is no reason why we should turn drab and dull. Even if winter comes and the snows fall, the next thing on the calendar is spring! With the Christian, springtime is an everlasting season. With such a prospect, we have a right to '**bow out gloriously**.'" This is what I want to do.

I know that I am in the autumn of my life without a doubt. Whether early autumn or middle autumn or late autumn, I haven't figured out yet, but fall has descended on my life. The trouble with most is they live with a faulty understanding or anticipation of what an autumn season should look like in their life. Many see it for the retirement that it might bring, a carefree life after a lifetime of labor. Many have found that never happens because for some death comes early and for others the loss of their health comes late. I have been a pastor for 47 years now, and I have ministered to my share of individuals that have moved from the summer of their life to the autumn season. Some do very well, but others fail and fall because they are not willing to "**bow out gloriously**." Instead of enjoying the Indian summer of their lives, they spend all their time worrying about winter (death); instead of living every moment to its fullest, they fret and fear events that may or may not come. Like the women heading for Jesus' tomb on resurrection Sunday, they could only think, *"How will we roll back the stone"* (Matthew 28:1–2). Instead of glorying in the glorious morn, we look to the tomb, a death place, not realizing that the angel has already rolled away the stone, and the angel waits for you to share the great news of resurrection. So many live today under the shadow of death, they fail to see the brilliant colors of life that life has to offer even in old age. I like the psalmist on this: *"They shall still bring forth fruit in old age; they shall be fat and flourishing."* (Psalm 92:14) I love the word "flourishing" because isn't that the perfect word for a maple tree in full fall colors making a final statement of, "I was here, and I will be remembered." I am determined in my final years to be like a maple tree in fall garb.

Jesus taught His disciples that *"Ye have not chosen me, but I have chosen you, and ordained you,* **that ye should go and bring forth fruit, and that your fruit should remain**: *that whatsoever ye shall ask of the Father in my name, he may give it you."* (John 15:16) Granted, leaves are not the fruit of the maple that comes in spring with its sap, but the point I believe Jesus was making is that we are to be productive with fruit that will outlive us. Is there no better time than in the final years to lay the groundwork for some lasting fruit? Instead of fearing old age or wasting old age, let us color our lives with those things that will bless others now and leave them memories that will remind them of the color we left behind. Did you know God has given us a promise for the autumn of our lives: **"And even to your old age I am he; and even to hoar hairs will I carry you: I have made, and I will bear; even I will carry, and will deliver you."** (Isaiah 46:4) I remember when my dear wife Coleen decided that she would no longer hide her greying hair. Coleen always prided herself in her hair, and for her those streaks of grey were not attractive. But the day came she yielded to old age and allowed the natural color of her hair to come out. I will admit I loved the grey. I believe it gave her a distinguished look and a seasoned appearance. She would laugh at me when I complimented her because I don't think she ever liked it. All I know is that the Good Lord did "carry" her and did "deliver" her in the end, and though it was spring when she departed, she "**bowed out gloriously!**"

So, what are my aspirations for this autumn of my life? They are simple, but I hope colorful. I am determined to preach as long as I can. At this writing, I am in my 54th year of actual preaching. I still have plenty of sermons unpreached in my files, and I would like to finish them. I am determined to pastor as long as I can. At this writing, I am in my 48th year in the pastorate, starting my thirtieth year at Emmanuel Baptist Church. I am determined to stay here, my church of a lifetime, until I have nothing more to share. I am determined to write for as long as I can, and to get published as many of my books as possible because I believe this ministry will be the fruit that will remain the longest. I hope my preaching and pastoring will linger awhile, but these books, this book, could stay around for a long time blessing people still unborn. I am also determined to be a colorful example of the believer for as long as the Good Lord gives me grace, so that when my life's work is ended and *"I have fought a good fight, I have finished my course, I have kept the faith"* (II Timothy 4:7), I will "**bow out gloriously!**"

52

MORE PERSONAL PROVERBS

1- The highest reward for any work is not what you get for it, but what you get out of it.
2- *"He must increase, but I must decrease,"* said John. So must Christ, and so must we!
3- Silence is God's way of saying that your supplication is being answered by His sovereignty.
4- Prayer is simple; any child can do it. Prayer is supernatural; it involves the Almighty. Prayer is spiritual and mysterious, a work of the Holy Spirit.
5- Earthly books might be silent concerning your exploits of faith, but Heaven's books will tell a different story.
6- Accommodation with the ungodly might be acceptable to you, but for God accommodation is "anathema."
7- The ministry of "helps" is the most helpful spiritual gift ever given to the Church by the Holy Spirit.
8- Crusades often start in the commonplace and chivalrous acts in courteous deeds.
9- The standard of our greatness will be judged on what we do with "the least among us."
10- You can buy or hire a man's time, but you can never buy time for any man, including yourself.

11- The most melodious musical instrument created by God is the human voice, so why are we allowing all these other musical instruments created by man to upstage the human voice?

12- Songs of the soul in times of sorrow are songs of the season of the Spirit.

13- Come out from the shadows of others and cast your own shadow.

14- Forgiveness is never to be handled statistically, as Peter suggested.

15- Like grass on the other side of the fence, tomorrow seems greener, but rarely is. Enjoy today!

16- God rewards virtue and punishes vice.

17- We live in a stormy world, so I ask, "Which are you: a 'fair-weather' friend or a 'foul-weather' friend?"

18- Rejected by man and received by God is far better than being received by man and rejected by God.

19- Popularity has silenced more preachers than persecution.

20- When others are saying, "All's well; All's well!" you better hear from Jeremiah and Paul, "All is not well!"

21- When in doubt, be merciful.

22- When an earthly soul gets saved, the heavenly angels sing.

23- A good deed without a name is more important than a name without a good deed.

24- If Jesus brings you to it, He'll bring you through it.

25- Prayer is the key to the day and a lock for the night.

26- Prayer is so valuable that God keeps every one of them in Heaven.

27- Christ never intended His Church to be a cruise ship, but a lifeboat!

28- Stand fast; stay faithful!

29- If we explore God's Word only for debate and doubt, then we have journeyed for nought.

30- A sure path to an early grave is to over eat and under work.

31- God has made man to work and work for man.

32- I am not saying "fleece faith" is great faith, but it is faith.

33- Though liberal-minded theologians and narrow-minded scientists dismiss the Biblical account of a universal flood as a myth or a fable, any serious student of either the Bible or science would have to disagree.

34- The lame man of Bethesda thought his continual condition was due to poor timing, little help, and bad luck. Do you think the same of your state?

35- The hopeless will hope in anything they think will help.

36- Our job is to dig the ditch and trust God to fill it.

37- There has been scholar after scholar, generation after generation, who have tried to explain away the "Red Sea Crossing." Some would call it a wind in a marsh, an earthquake making a path, a simple fable, only a myth, but I call it "a way of escape!"

38- How many people have lost their future by eating and sleeping one more night with frogs?

39- God always warns before He wounds.

40- Any part of God's creation can quickly be transformed into a scourge.

41- The "finger of God" brings warning, but the "hand of God" falls in wrath.

42- You ought to take seriously your standing with Christ before you start using His name!

43- We forget that one of our jobs is to put the devil and his demons out of business.

44- We serve the God that just loves to give His servants a second chance, even if that servant is an unnamed woodsman working in an unnamed forest by an unnamed stream using an unnamed neighbor's ax. (Think Elisha.)

45- It is high time we believe in miracles again!

46- Where hospitality dwells, the rooms are always full.

47- Our "prophet chamber" should also be our "prayer closet."

48- Courage is not the withdrawal of fear, but the conquest of it.

49- A fearful person is frightened before the foe arrives; a cowardly person is frightened when the foe appears, but the courageous person is frightened after the foe is conquered lest pride gets the best of him.

50- It is "politically correct" to put "animal rights" over "human rights," but that doesn't make it right.

51- Too many Christians are "paying off" the Lord by their offerings to appease their consciences for lack of service for the Lord.

52- There is no such creature as "a self-made man." We are all made up of the countless hundreds that have touched our lives over the years.

53- Incredible ingratitude is the ideology of our day.

54- If I did have my life to do it over again, I would pick more flowers, take more time for God, and carry a lighter load.

55- Christ's example ought to be our encouragement. He kept His eye on the goal, not the going; He kept seeing the prize, not the process; He reached for the treasure, not the trial, and He embraced the joy, not the journey.

56- If you miss the translation, you will miss the transfiguration.

57- By telling who you love, you can determine who you are.

58- May this day be the alpha of your new life, with the ALPHA of life.

59- Jesus was truly a lion in lamb's clothing.

60- When Christ was mortal, He was still immortal.

53.

GET YOUR HEAD UP

I WRITE IN MY 70th year in the midst of a world-wide pandemic (Covid-19 or the Coronavirus), and you would think that a world living on the verge of the last days, or in the midst of the last days, would do some very serious and sobering meditating on the end of the age. Yet, at the height of the worst this world is acting more like the days of Noah or the days of Lot. Remember our Lord's warning to that last generation: *"But as the days of Noe were, so shall also the coming of the Son of man be. For as in the days that were before the flood they were eating and* <u>drinking</u>*, marrying and giving in marriage, until the day that Noe entered into the ark, and knew not until the flood came, and took them all away; so shall also the coming of the Son of man be."* (Matthew 24:37–39) And then this in Luke 17:28–30: *"Likewise also as it was in the days of Lot; they did eat,* <u>they drank</u>*, they bought, they sold, they planted, they builded; but the same day that Lot went out of Sodom it rained fire and brimstone from heaven, and destroyed them all. Even thus shall it be in the day when the Son of man is revealed."* Mankind seems to be bewildered about the pandemic and certainly frightened, panicky at times and very perplexed at how and why this is happening, but not very concerned about the moral issues of the day. If anything, society is advancing without a pause to bring in an age of such immorality that the past will blush in shame. We shouldn't be surprised at this or even amazed because humanity is blind to the truth (II Corinthians 4:4) and dead in sin (Ephesians 2:1).

What has saddened me most in this crisis is that many Christians are also walking around with a drooping head and a discouraged heart and wring their hands in despair. I think my brothers and sisters know that the world's moral situation and Covid circumstance is entirely hopeless apart from divine intervention by God Himself. Nobody in Washington seems to know what to do, and the United Nations has gone on lockdown. World leaders are grasping at straws, and even many Christians have been infected with this mood. The Church is questioning why doesn't God act; why doesn't the Gospel affect people; and why do the things of this world become more accepted and the truth of Christ more rejected? I think a lot of believers are where John the Baptist was when from Herod's prison he sent his disciples to ask Jesus this question: **"Art thou He that should come, or do we look for another?"** (Matthew 11:3) Remember, John was the one that first pointed out the Christ (John 1:29) and was Jesus' forerunner until he was arrested. What made this mighty man of faith, remember, the greatest of men born of woman (Matthew 11:11), question at the end? My opinion is that John's last days were nothing like he expected. His faithfulness had resulted in imprisonment and eventually beheading. This often happens when believers aren't prepared for bad times, as today. But the answer is not to question with a down demeanor and a dropped head.

We need this challenge from our Lord: *"And when these things begin to come to pass, then look up, and lift up your heads; for your redemption draweth nigh."* (Luke 21:28) Get your head up! Christian brethren, look at the signs of the times being fulfilled almost weekly now and remember this from Christ's lips: *"So likewise ye, when ye shall see all these things, know that it is near, even at the doors."* (Matthew 24:33) Get your head up! I have come to believe that the fearful headlines and frightening newscasts mean one thing to the world and another thing to the Church. We should never rejoice over the world's messes and misery, but we should see these events and happenings from the Lord and a preparation for the end times. If your theology is sound, the end of the age (Matthew 28:20) should mean an end to pain and sorrow, a new body, and being forever with the Lord and loved ones that have gone on before us. I was reading just today of this blessed hope: *"Behold, I shew you a mystery;* **We shall not all sleep**, [or die] *but we shall all be changed, in a moment, in the twinkling of an eye, at the last trump: for the trumpet shall sound, and the dead shall be raised incorruptible, and we shall be changed."* (I Corinthians 15:51–52) Get your head up! A read of the Revelation will reveal the death and destruction waiting over the horizon for this world, but for the believer the rapture is sure (I Thessalonians 4:13–18) before the worst happens. I love Vance Havner on this: "The wise men of this world shake their heads in perplexity, but the humblest Christian with a dollar Bible knows what time it is!" That is why we should get excited about what is happening around us, virus or no virus; possible war in the Middle East or no war in the Middle East (the Ukraine-Russia war was just a year off and the Israel-Hamas war just two years away); Republican or Democrat in the White House; the stock market going up or down. The believer shouldn't be looking for something to happen, but for Someone to come back: *"Looking for that blessed hope, and the glorious appearing of the great God and our Saviour Jesus Christ."* (Titus 2:13) Get your head up dear Christian, get your head up!

Just a couple of days ago I was talking with a young brother in Christ about this very thing. One of the things we were talking about was whether there will be a great revival before the end of the age as some are proclaiming today. I personally don't see it in prophecy (II Peter 1:20) because I have come to believe what I shared at the outset of this chapter and that being the condition of the world before the Lord comes back (II Timothy 3:1–5). I see no hope for a revival with all the departing from the faith (I Timothy 4:1) and the many falling away first (I Thessalonians 2:3), but I also believe this: *"Say not ye, There are yet four months, and then cometh harvest? behold, I say unto you, Lift up your eyes, and look on the fields; for they are white already to harvest."* (John 4:35) The Lord will be adding to His Church daily up until that last day (Acts 2:47) so we should not only be lifting our eyes upward to the coming of the Lord, but we ought to be lifting our eyes outward to those who still need the Gospel, and there are plenty! I believe that we still have time to pluck a few fire brands from the fire and a few souls from the Lake of Fire. We must look up and watch the skies for Jesus' return and listen for that trumpet certainly, but we also need to cast an eye to the harvest fields that are "white" around us for a soul that needs to be saved.

Get your head up Christian! Get your head up believer! If the world is looking for their utopia, their one-world leader, and their do-it-their way then we as believers must see that our hope is better than theirs. I have concluded after five months of this new world order that it is "redemption time" (Luke 21:28) and "reaping time" (John 4:35) and "rapture time" (I Thessalonians 4:17). That is why we need to be looking up: *"Set your affection on things above, not on things on the earth."* (Colossians 3:2) The last thing we Christians ought to be doing today is hanging our heads; we are on the victor's side, and our Lord isn't far away. Paul said it best to the Romans: *"And that, knowing the time, that now it is high time to awake out of sleep: for now is our salvation nearer than when we believed. The night is far spent, the day is at hand: let us therefore cast off the works of darkness, and let us put on the armour of light."* (Romans 13:11–12) Get your head up! The world will try to discourage you, and the devil will always cast doubt into your mind, but the Bible teaches me that ours is a blessed hope and a glorious future and nothing in this world can change God's ultimate plan for the ages. Get your head up brother and get ready for the rapture because our *"redemption draweth nigh!"* Amen and Amen!

54.

WALKING THE WAVES

EVER SINCE I WAS a small child I was told the story of Peter walking on the water, walking the waves! For those who don't know this famous story of the Apostle here is Matthew's (who was in the boat and witnessed it) version of the event: *"And in the fourth watch of the night Jesus went unto them, walking on the sea. And when the disciples saw him walking on the sea, they were troubled, saying, it is a spirit; and they cried out for fear. But straightway Jesus spake unto them, saying, be of good cheer; it is I; be not afraid. And Peter answered him and said, Lord, if it be thou, bid me come unto thee on the water. And he said, Come. And when Peter was come down out of the ship,* **he walked on the water,** *to go to Jesus."* (Matthew 14:25–29) Sometimes, when we ask to get out of the boat, Jesus lets us, but, oh, what courage it takes and what faith is required!

Over the years I have heard many preachers talk about this story in the life of Simon, and many more writers write about this gospel tale. Often the speaker or the writer highlights and underlines what came after Peter stepped over the railing and started his stroll towards Jesus: *"But when he saw the wind boisterous,* **he was afraid; and beginning to sink***, he cried, saying, Lord, save me. And immediately Jesus stretched forth his hand, and caught him, and said unto him, O thou of little faith, wherefore didst thou doubt?"* (Matthew 14:30–31) Simon Peter is an example of the classic *"double-minded man"* in James 1:8. Peter was always either putting his foot in his mouth (Matthew 17:4) or leaping before he thought the situation through (Matthew 16:22). His famous walk on the waters of Galilee verifies this observation on the personality of Peter. There were eleven others in the boat that morning (fourth watch is between three and six in morning) when Peter asked Jesus if he could come to Him. You will note that nobody else spoke up as they were still frightened, but Peter's fear soon turned to boldness (just like the boast in the upper room that he would never deny Jesus; then in the garden his defending boldly the Lord with a sword before he fled with the others), and he made the request. I admire this part of the story for its spiritual daring and physical boldness.

First, I recognize that he didn't just throw his legs over the side of the boat, but he first asked permission of Jesus. This tells me that Peter knew he could never walk the waves without help from the only other person doing it. Peter did this right, asking before leaping. We sing in our churches the hymn <u>Leaning on the Everlasting Arms</u> (Deuteronomy 33:27), but few really do it. Another chorus that I have sung for years is <u>Learning to Lean</u>, but few of us have. Most of us still put more faith in the flesh than in our Lord. In that moment Peter felt the urge to walk, and, whether it was motivated by trying to impress Jesus or the others, we are not told, but we are told that once the command of "come" was given, Peter responded and got out of the boat and started walking the waves!

Second, I recognize that Simon is only the second person who ever did walk on water. It is one of the classic demonstrations that Jesus was God, just like the calming of the storm moments later (Matthew 14:32–33), but for a mere mortal to also do it if only for a few steps is remarkable. Think about the power necessary to do that impossible act. Jesus was God, and God can overcome all natural laws He placed nature under. One of those laws is you can't walk on water, water is a fluid, yet, Jesus did it, but more amazing to me he gave Peter the power to do it as well. That transfer of power was nothing new for we read in Matthew 10:1, *"And when he had called unto him his twelve disciples,* **he gave them power** *against unclean spirits, to cast them out, and to heal all manner of sickness and all manner of disease. Now the names of the twelve apostles are these; the first, Simon, who is called Peter . . . "* So, we shouldn't be surprised by this transfer of ability.

Third, even though Jesus rebuked Peter for his *"little faith"* (Matthew 14:31), we need to be reminded of this teaching of the Christ: *"And Jesus said unto them, Because of your unbelief: for verily I say unto you, If ye have faith as a grain of mustard seed, ye shall say unto this mountain, Remove hence to yonder place; and it shall remove; and nothing shall be impossible unto you."* (Matthew 17:20) Mustard seed faith for me means "the power of little faith." Granted, Jesus admires *"great faith"* (Matthew

8:10, 15:28), but great faith is not the only faith that does the impossible. Peter had enough faith to believe that at his Lord's command he could and would walk the waves of the Sea of Galilee.

Fourth, Peter's failing was that after walking the waves, he started watching the waves: *"And he said, Come. And when Peter was come down out of the ship, he walked on the water, to go to Jesus.* **But when he saw the wind boisterous,** *he was afraid; and beginning to sink, he cried, saying, Lord, save me."* (Matthew 14:29-30) Faith is broken when we take our eyes off Jesus and begin to look around. I have been challenged by this chorus for years now: "Turn your eyes upon Jesus, look full into His wonderful face, and the things of earth will grow strangely dim in the light of His glory and grace." If Peter would have stayed focused, I believe he would have made it those final steps to Jesus. Why I say the final steps is because Jesus was there to save him from drowning. I like what Vance Havner once wrote about Peter: "He may not have walked far, but he walked farther on water than anyone else ever has!" Let us all learn this lesson of focus.

Fifth, and when Peter began to sink, who was there to rescue His drowning disciple? *"And immediately Jesus stretched forth his hand, and caught him . . ."* (Matthew 14:31) Again Vance Havner on this: ". . . the Lord may let you be ducked, but He won't let you be drowned." I guess this is where this whole chapter is heading. In my 70 years I, too, have made some bold choices that have left me drowning because I have allowed doubt to replace my faith. One moment I am walking the waves, and the next minute I am watching the waves! Who of us hasn't done this? Our great act of faith is a bold move on our part, and like Peter we walk a little way in the command of our Lord. Despite the obstacles and dangers, we make it for a while, but then situations and circumstances begin to surround us, and we refocus our attention on them instead of the Lord and His command. I have had my days this year with the sudden death of my wife where I have gotten so caught up in the grief and the loss that I only saw *"the wind boisterous."* I lost focus, and I began to sink into despair, but what grace my Lord had for me when He pulled me back to Himself, just like He pulled Peter up from the stormy waves. Praise God for that grip!

I can't say I have been filled with rejoicing over the years that I have been called outside the boat, especially when I have failed, but years after the events I now feel I can honestly say that I am glad for my experiences when the Good Lord said "Come," and I faced "the boisterous wind" and "the billowing waves." At least for a while I walked the waves with a son dying at 39 and a wife dying at 67. These and other trips on a stormy sea have taught me the lessons I have shared in this chapter. And what I have learned most is that every step on that stormy sea has been a step towards Jesus. Even when I have sunk somewhere between where I started and Jesus was, I have found Him faithful to be there to lift me up and go back with me into my boat: **"And when they were come into the ship, the wind ceased."** (Matthew 14:32) This fulfills Paul's precept: *"if we believe not, yet he abideth faithful: he cannot deny himself."* (II Timothy 2:13) Amen!

55.

IS AMERICA A CHRISTIAN NATION?

I HAVE CHOSEN TO answer this thought-provoking question because of the current political and economic crisis my dear country is in (written during the great crash of 2008 and adapted for my "threescore and ten" book), no doubt, the worst I have experienced in my nearly sixty years (until the Covid-crisis of 2020), being a native of this grand land from birth (1951). Perhaps, we need to ask two questions about our question: first, was America founded as a Christian nation in the first place, and second, what does it mean to be a Christian nation anyway? These are important questions which deserve an honest answer and serious contemplation from a Biblical view, the perspective of a 70-year old!

Based on what I know from American history, Jamestown, the first English settlement in the Americas, was founded as a colony to make money for a company back home in England (maybe that is why we have so much trouble getting away from the pursuit of money). Of course, Jamestown didn't survive long, but Plymouth, the first successful English colony did. It, too, was also founded on similar principles and precepts that boil down to the quest for wealth, but there were among that original group those that were looking for a place where they could worship and raise their children without war, persecution, or religious intolerance. Were they Christians? In my research, I have found Anglicans and Catholics and Puritan rebels of various stripes in the first pilgrims, and some no doubt were the genuine item. Of course, the resident, native Americans all started out as animists. Not until serious evangelism among the natives started were the original "Americans" anything close to "Christian." Some might even conclude that the jury is still out on our original question, but this we know, that within a short time the underlining foundation of "Christian" morality and philosophy began to take hold in this wilderness land across the great ocean. Our early theologians and politicians established government by the people and for the people, and the rise of congregationalism spread until it became the very bedrock of what is American politics and religion today.

What I found interesting in the last presidential election (2008) was the cast of characters that emerged as the front runners. Most of the presidential candidates claimed to be "christians," from a Mormon from Massachusetts named Mitt to a Baptist preacher from Arkansas named Mike. I must admit that my political philosophy has changed over the years (I first voted in the 1970 elections), and despite the use of "christian" a lot by the candidates, I was very confused over the current crop of individuals that would be president. I have been challenged to rethink the very values of voting I once held in such high regard and respect. I will confess I don't think I had much of a choice last year even though my choices all claimed to be "christians." Just because one calls himself "christian," and just because a nation calls itself "christian," does that make either of them Christian? I was literally driven crazy over the last two years (how long the last presidential election cycle lasted) when this line between "christian" and "Christian" was obliterated and blurred during the political debates and discussions until all that was left was the conclusion that everybody is a Christian, and if everybody is a Christian then we must still be a Christian nation.

I was challenged in the last election to choose between the better of the two "christians:" Hillary or Obama; Mitt or Mike; John or Joe, and then there was Sarah, but this was in no way a lesser agony for me and my American conscience and personal responsibility to vote for the next president of our great land. I just wish each of them would have been more honest about what they called "christianity." Why has the leadership of this land concluded that it is important to have the label of "christian" attached to them? If Mitt would have been honest about his Mormonism and just called himself a Mormon instead of "christian," it would have helped me (because I believe that the two terms can't be mixed); if Mike would have been honest about being a Baptist, just called himself a Baptist instead of a "christian' (no, not all Baptists are Christians, and this is coming from a lifelong member of the Baptist denomination). We have just too much paganism dressing itself up in a "christian" dress for me. Didn't Jesus warn about this? *"Beware of false prophets, which come to you* in sheep's clothing, but inwardly they are ravening wolves. Ye shall know them by their fruits. Do men gather grapes of thorns, or figs of thistles? Even so every good tree bringeth forth good fruit; but a corrupt tree bringeth forth evil fruit. A good tree cannot bring forth evil fruit; neither can a corrupt tree bring forth good fruit. Every tree that bringeth not forth good fruit is hewn down, and cast into the fire. Wherefore by their fruits ye shall know them." (Matthew 7:15-20) Anybody can look like a Christian and talk like a Christian without being a Christian, and time will tell the true nature of all these so called "christians."

Just because we can agree with one's social philosophy, like Sarah, does that mean all social conservatives are Christians? If I wanted a Baptist preacher in the While House because I am a Baptist preacher, then this year was my year, yet once again I saw my cherished name (Acts 11:26) clarified and corrected until I wondered if any of these national leaders really knew the connection they were making to the name "Christian." As I watched and listened, day after day, debate after debate, I heard and saw little "Christlikeness." The majority of Americans, Democrats, Republicans, or Independents, have added "christian" to their political label without really being a Christian. If I heard correctly, this election, whether for the presidency, congress, governorship, or a hundred other elected offices, was an election of "christians" against "christians." Is the Body of Christ divided? According to the elitist left-wing media, and the arrogant right-wing media, without question! It is this very conclusion that convinced me that few people in politics or the media even know what it is to be a true Christian, to be a follower of the Christ where the name comes from.

I have a simple argument for this: if it talks like a duck, walks like a duck, then it is probably a duck, but, if it talks like a chicken and walks like a chicken, how can you call it a duck? Paul, in his classic theological book called Romans, made the same argument with his own people, the Jews. They thought because they were of the right race (Hebrew), had been circumcised (a Jewish ritual of the flesh), and had been given the Word of God (the Torah), then they must be God's people (Carefully read Romans 3:27-4:10). Paul argued that it took more than rights and race and rituals to hold the lofty title of being a child of God. John the Baptist made the same argument with the scribes and the Pharisees of his day when they came to his baptism: *"But when he saw many of the Pharisees and Sadducees come to his baptism, he said unto them, O generation of vipers, who hath warned you to flee from the wrath to come? Bring forth therefore fruits meet for repentance: and think not to say within yourselves, we have Abraham to our father: for I say unto you, that God is able of these stones to raise up children unto Abraham."* (Matthew 3:7–9) What I am simply saying, it takes more than a history of Christianity, a nation established on Christian principles and precepts, and the name Christian to make an individual or a nation Christian.

I was born into a Christian family, taken at the earliest of age to a Christian church, surrounded throughout my younger years with Christians, but did any of that make me a Christian? That is "Christian" by association. It seems so foolish when we speak of it this way, yet I challenge you to listen to the newscasts and read the articles in the papers. What are these people, our leaders, saying? This philosophy has found roots, and it seems to grow rapidly during an election cycle. I do find it interesting that now the election is over I haven't heard the name "christian" invoked yet by our president-elect or any other politician who used it during their campaign. Why is it they are only "christians" during the campaign? Is it because it is only a label, and the true value of being one is to get elected? Ever since our dear brother Jerry promoted Christian participation in politics have we been deceived into thinking that these politicians think like us and believe like us and live like us and have our best interests in mind when they finally get elected. George ought to be a clear example of the difference between a "christian" and a Christian.

America did have a great beginning, and so much of that start was inspired by Christians and Christianity, without a doubt. Faith did play an important role in early education in this Land (Where is that aspect of Christianity today? Outlawed!), in government (Where is that aspect of Christianity today? In the occasional prayer breakfast where the prayer is to all gods!), in our American culture (Where is that aspect of Christianity today? Other cultures are protected while the Ten Commandments are taken off the walls and the Christmas tree is outlawed on public property!), and in our philosophical outlook on life (Where is that aspect of Christianity? Football has replaced church services and shopping instead of Sunday School!). Granted, the values of Christianity and the valuableness of Christians made our Land what it has become, the number one and only superpower in the world, but I am afraid we have reached our zenith, found the summit of our success, and now going the way of all former super powers before us. Why? We have exchanged our Christian values with humanism (man knows best); we have decided that we can make our own way without God's help (In God We Trust), and that we no longer need what truly made us a great people (our Judaic-Christian ethic).

I am not saying that any nation can be exclusively Christian because it can't be. There are too many factors to be considered in a land based on democracy (people rule). When there is a theocracy (God-rule) under Christ, then and only then will there be an established Christian nation. Faith, even the Christian faith, was not always practiced in purity, and it was certainly not always practiced without legalism because it was sometimes practiced in arrogance and distain for the freedoms of others, even the freedom not to be a Christian. I must admit that there are some "sects" and "cults" of Christianity that I wouldn't want to live under. We have that great right as members of society to vote, to run for office, to take part in the current political debate, to influence public policy, and to provide examples of faith in action. We should never forget that God established governments, and He is still in charge of them: *"Let every soul be subject unto the higher powers. For there is no power but of God: the powers that be are ordained of God. Whosoever therefore resisteth the power, resisteth the ordinance of God: and they that resist shall receive to themselves damnation. For rulers are not a terror to good works, but to the evil. Wilt thou then not be afraid of the power? Do that which is good, and thou shalt have praise of the same: for he is the minister of God to thee for good. But if thou do that which is evil, be afraid; for he beareth not the sword in vain: for he is the minister of God, a revenger to execute wrath upon him that doeth evil. Wherefore ye must needs be subject, not only for wrath, but also for conscience sake. For for this cause pay ye tribute also: for they are God's ministers, attending continually upon this very thing. Render therefore to all their dues: tribute to whom tribute is due; custom to whom custom; fear to whom fear; honour to whom honour."* (Romans 13:1–7) We have every right, but we must not make the mistake in thinking that these rights are somehow exclusive to only Christians as some of our brethren have preached in the past. We forget that this world is not our final home, even America. I am a proud American. I wouldn't want it any other way or be a citizen of any other country on this planet, but I also have another citizenship (Ephesians 2:19) and another president (King) (I Timothy 6:15) and another country (Hebrews 11:14–16).

So, what are you saying you might ask? What I am saying is that we are not to stake our future on this so called "christian" country or this so-called "christian" government. We are not, and they are not! I doubt that America was ever a Christian country, and I know that sounds like heresy to most Americans, but think through your American history and your Biblical understanding of what it means to be Christian. Oh, there were times in our national history like prohibition when the moral side of our culture tried to legislate morality and Christian values, but we know how that turned out. As long as man has a free will and a depraved nature and the right to choose for himself, and the majority always rules in a democracy, we will never be a Christian nation. I would argue whether the "moral majority" ever existed in this land despite my brethren of the 1980s opinion, let alone Christianity!

Christians do not have all the answers. If we did there wouldn't be Heniz-57 varieties of us, and the answers we think we have may be as wrong as those that advocate killing babies and the marriage of Bill and Bob. Remember, Jesus advocated in His parable of the Wheat and the Weeds that we grow together (Matthew 13:24–30) until the end so we live in one field in America, a field of wheat and tares. It is either or it is both, and we can't change that; it is in America today. We are both Christian and pagan, and evil exists just like godliness exists. It is at the very core of the nature of man to try to define who he is and what he is even when most of the time he is unable to come to a proper definition. I believe the Good Lord left us here in America to restrain evil, resist wrong, and revolt against the rules of wickedness. Can we change any of these things by putting our label on them? Never! Despite this being a brief look into this complicated question, I hope I have provoked you to thought, and that you would consider my opinion as that.

In closing, I do believe that God chose America as His instrument to work through in doing good in the world just as He has chosen Israel, Bohemia, Holland, Switzerland, Scotland, and England in the past (note I have a western bias, but I do believe other nations in the world as well). At different times, God used these lands to protect His Church and His Christians and His Christianity. We have been a blessed and prosperous land because of the Christian truth and the character that was infused into our early culture, but we never were, never have been, and are not a Christian America. We are at best a "christian" land. We have been a secular country from the very beginning because we have voted to be, the people have chosen to be, and in making those choices we have nobody to blame but ourselves in the direction we are heading. It is time to stop voting for the "christian" and start living, acting for the Christ. I don't believe we are in a Post-Christian era in America because I don't believe we ever truly were a Christian land. That is my opinion; now, what do you think? (Romans 14:5)

56.

GIVE ME LIBERTY OR GIVE ME DEATH

OF THE 56 INDIVIDUALS that wrote their names at the bottom of one of the most famous documents (The Declaration of Independence) in world history, I have been most impressed with Patrick Henry. You know the one, "Give me liberty or give me death!" What I know about him and the others, they were not looking for success (most were already successful in their chosen fields), or security (most were already quite affluent financially in their lives), or safety (they were already under the protection of the most powerful nation in the world). So, what did they stick their necks out for?

I have come to believe that they esteemed freedom more important than peace and liberty, more important than safety. When it came to riches versus poverty, they felt liberty with poverty was more important to them than wealth under bondage. How far we have fallen in this country from that lofty aspiration. I am, of course, writing these thoughts during my 70th year which is also in the midst of the Covid-19 pandemic. How quickly has the new majority of this land shown their colors? Instead of King George it is Governor Mill's dictating rules and regulations that for a time even took away our freedom of public worship. As I write, we are still forbidden to sing in church publically (we are still singing, one of the few times in my life I have defied the government), but I am afraid we are getting closer and closer to Peter's edict, ***"Then Peter and the other apostles answered and said, We ought to obey God rather than men."*** (Acts 5:29) We have arrived at a place where most in our free land are more concerned with the byproducts of freedom rather than the cost of freedom, the price that must be paid by every generation to be truly free. We know now that most Americans would sacrifice in a moment their liberties for their health and, I am afraid, their wealth. We have discovered through this crisis that what matters most is the economy and the national health, and that we maintain our position as the wealthiest nation in the world. Surely, we see now that the chief end of most is to have a bigger house, a bigger income, and a bigger job so that we can "eat, drink, and be merry" and live a long time! How did that work out for the rich farmer (Luke 12:16–21)? For me, this period in our history is just another example of "the days of Noah" and "the days of Lot." (Luke 17:26–33)

I like the way Vance Havner put it in a 1962 book: "We have lost the love of liberty that risks everything, even life itself, to be free!" We have forgotten in this pandemic that death is a part of life which I have learned very well in this my 70th year. I have watched two church members and three family members die in just six months of this year. Whether by Covid or a liver disease, what difference does it make? They are still dead, and no rule or regulation will bring them back. All I see is an amazing decline this year in the decaying of our democracy and the continual shouting of the mobs for a welfare state versus a free state. People want to be taken care of whether in their health or their wealth. We are paying people more to stay home than they could get working, and we are promising them a vaccine that will keep them safe. We all know there is not enough money in the world to pay everybody, and behind Covid-19 will be Covid-20! Men like Patrick Henry staked everything on a kind of freedom seen very rarely in world history, and since his generation other generations have made the greatest sacrifice to keep that freedom, including my son, but today all that people want are the benefits of that freedom without the sacrifices. They are interested in the fruits, but care little to defend those fruits.

What has disturbed me most about the results of this coronavirus outbreak is not the affect it has had on my country, but the affect it has had on Christianity. Of course, Jesus taught us that in Him we would find an amazing freedom: *"If the Son therefore shall make you free, ye shall be free indeed."* (John 8:36) A peace of heart, a liberty of the soul, and a freedom of mind and action are just a few of the liberties we enjoy now in Christ. The benefits are both earthly and eternal, but I noticed, and I will confess that I was just as guilty as most, how quickly I caved to the community pressure to conform to the certain wave of governmental regulation thrust on us because of the Covid crisis. We, like the world, have switched our priorities from peace, liberty, and serenity to wealth and health. Even before the Covid crisis the Christian bookshelves were being flooded with volume after volume on how to be happy, feel secure, and of course prosperity. The theologians of the church have been replaced by the self-help experts with little scripture and a whole lot of worldly philosophy. I was given a 138-page book by a parishioner just last week about how to be a happy Christian in a sad world. In the entire book there were only three Bible references and of the three only two actual passages and not even the verses were quoted. We have turned our faith over to the self-help gurus of the world.

Today we have so many attracted to the faith who want the blessings of Christianity without the Christ of Christianity. They want forgiveness of sin without repentance; they want peace of mind without righteousness; they want joy without confession; and they want happiness without the Spirit. Just like Patrick Henry realized that there could be no liberty without death so, too, most of us had to come to the realization that there could be no spiritual freedom without the death of Jesus Christ. Oh, the byproducts of that death on Calvary two thousand years ago are amazing, but today most want the byproducts without believing in the death. Just like those early Americans had to die to self to ensure a free land so, too, must we die to self, deny self, and dedicate self to Christ (Luke 14:26–27, 33). In Jesus' text regarding principles to discipleship (Luke 14:28–32), He mentions "counting the cost." Patrick Henry and the others had to count the cost before going up against King George, but in the end they decided that liberty was worth the cost. I am afraid that if this generation was faced with the same situation, we would still be under control of England because few today would pay the price. Just like there are few today in the Church that would pay the price our forefathers paid in the Faith. If we buckled under the current persecution (I believe at first our governor required her rules on all, but when she opened the bars before the churches, I was convinced she was out to get the Church!) then what will we do when the real persecution comes?

I think I have found the answer to why them and not us, both in America and in Christianity. The early Americans were so caught up in the concept of democracy, they didn't see or care how much it cost. The early Christians were so caught up with Christ, they didn't see or care how much it cost. Many early Americans didn't live long enough to enjoy the benefits of freedom. Many early Christians didn't live long enough to enjoy the benefits of spiritual freedom. No wonder it was "a shot heard around the world," and no wonder they "turned the world upside down." (Acts 17:6) I again like Vance Havner on this: our problem today is "we are so occupied with the marginal that we live on the periphery!" Americans should live or die for liberty, just like Christians should live or die for Christ (Philippians 1:21). If you are challenged either with your American freedoms or your liberty in Christ, would you say like Patrick Henry, "Give me liberty or give me death?" I think the time is very near when we will have to choose either or both!

57.

THE INTERNET GENERATION

I couldn't write a book on my 70th year without writing a chapter on the advancements of technology in my lifetime and how much I despise most of it. I have just leased my third car from Honda and, though I love the car, the handling, the gas mileage, and the ride, I despise the technology with each new version of basically the same car. This last car is the worst of the three because they have thrown so much computer control into the car including automatic brakes, lane control, and distance controls. It has taken me three months figuring it all out, and I know new issues will arise in the future. I would be one that would be content with a basic car without all the gadgets, a car that I was totally in charge and control. So, whether cars or appliances, phones or computers, though some things have made my life simpler, most have complicated my life because I am not geared to this lifestyle or living. I really do prefer how it once was over how it is now, but there is no going back because this is the internet generation.

In just the last few decades we have been inundated with a flood of computer advances, cheap now, so mostly everybody can afford them, and mostly thrown away. They are coming out with new phones so quickly most people trade their old phone in for the latest model whenever it comes out. Phones have become status symbols, like a cup of coffee. What use to take a day to find in the library or a few hours in a book, with the internet it is now almost instantaneous, and if there was only good on the internet that would be one thing, but all the evils and all the wickedness accumulated by man over the millenniums is now available in an instant.

Oh, has the internet provided access like never before? Certainly, but as I have been asking for years, does the good of it outweigh the bad of it?

Today I write my thoughts during the Covid virus and the return to school. America is at its wit's end trying to figure out how, under the current situation, classroom learning can happen. The answer is remote learning, education through the internet. If this generation wasn't already the internet generation, the generation to come would be because now everything of importance seems to be connected with this form of communication. And with this format of education there will be easier ways for humanism to program the next generation into the social morals and political manners the world wants to promote. The current wave of popularity of the internet is symbolic of a deeper evil than we think. There was a time when life had to be lived and understood through example and interaction with others. Now it is virtually everything. Some people never leave the screen to enjoy a walk. I was watching a commercial just last night of an exercise treadmill that had a computer monitor on the handlebars, and the one exercising was running with someone through a beautiful land of hills. Instead of going for a run outside the house, you stay in your house and run with a computer! There was a time when people created things with their hands, but now they create things on a computer screen. How sad!

What is happening to this internet generation is the forming of one's character without the Godly guidelines needed to make a proper judgment of what is right and what is wrong. I see that we are producing a cheap, immoral, humanistic edition of humanity that we aren't going to like very much in the future. Goodness based, humanly kind, and politically polite has given way to flimsy, shoddy, superficially hard, and morally a sham. We are producing a generation of kids that have no social behavior, no human compassion, and no concern or care for another human being because on those internet monitors, we kill, mutilate, and destroy by the hundreds in our video games. Is there any wonder that mass shooting has become symbolic of this internet generation? Maybe, we need to take a page out of what happened when the Gospel came to Ephesus through the preaching of Paul: *"And this was known to all the Jews and Greeks also dwelling at Ephesus; and fear fell on them all, and the name of the Lord Jesus was magnified. And many that believed came, and confessed, and shewed their deeds. Many of them also which used curious arts brought their books together, and burned them before all men: and they counted the price of them, and found it fifty thousand pieces of silver. So mightily grew the word of God and prevailed."* (Acts 19:17-20) You don't suppose we need a computer game and cell phone bomb fire, do you?

I have come to believe the best way to describe this "internet generation" is to apply Paul's words to the Corinthian Church when he wrote: *"Now if any man build upon this foundation gold, silver, precious stones, wood, hay, stubble; every man's work shall be made manifest: for the day shall declare it, because it shall be revealed by fire; and the fire shall try every man's work of what sort it is."* (I Corinthians 3:12-13) The internet is a whole lot of wood, hay, and stubble with very little gold, silver, and precious stones. I am convinced the first thing that will be burned in the judgment will be the contents of the internet. Not only is the internet full of trash, garbage not even worthy for a landfill, but it is full of falsehoods and lies, misinformation, cheap and worthless in light of eternal truth. Cover stories and content and composition of so much knowledge based on human reasoning and logic has only continued to corrupt the human mind with useless information that keeps the mind earth-bound rather than heaven-minded: **"Set your affection on things above, not on things on the earth."** (Colossians 3:2) Today, mediocre is enough to make you a star on the internet; individuals getting hundreds if not thousands of hits a day to a run-of-the-mill philosophy or lifestyle; cheap and corrupting of another generation that aspire to be like their internet idol, and just as quick as this internet star has their fifteen minutes of fame another comes along because the poor material being delivered cannot stand the wear and tear of time. It's just wood, hay, and stubble.

Like the soil in Jesus famous parable, the internet generation has *". . . no root in himself . . ."* (Matthew 13:21) They don't seek permanent truth or any established knowledge that will last the test of time. Oh, there is such truth and knowledge, but it is not found on the internet, but in the Bible. Don't get me wrong. I have found some good Biblical truth on certain websites, but the sheer volume of information on the web dilutes and diminishes the effect of that eternal truth and knowledge. Instead of studying (II Timothy 2:15) for ourselves, the internet generation wants their truth and knowledge delivered on a screen in simple bits of information. What is happening to the world is happening to the Church and the Christian. I believe we have too many internet Christians, internet churches, fly-by-night, here today gone tomorrow, and what does that say about our faith? Remember the "fire test" is coming (I Corinthians 3:14-15) and so much of what seemed so important now will only be a pile of ashes then. I feel we ought to seek that "well done" (Matthew 25:21) from

God on that day, not how many hits we get on our "live stream" video. During the Covid crisis I, too, was asked to start sharing on the internet, and I did. I, too, got lured into looking at the numbers grow as more and more people viewed my postings. According to the internet calculator, I have reached more people in the last five months than I have reached in the last five decades, but what about the eternal results?

58.

A HOME RUN TO WIN THE GAME

AFTER FOUR MONTHS OF waiting because of the Covid crisis, I have finally buried my dear wife. In an interesting twist to that burial, I also buried my mother and my mother-in-law all on the same day. I bet few have done that! What came with those burials was a closure to one aspect of my life and the beginning of another. I am still trying to figure out what my final years will hold in store for me, but I do have the aspiration to hit a home run to win the game, to sink a basket to win the contest, and to score the final touchdown to win the match!

My desire is to make the last chapter of my life the best chapter of my life, and, despite the difficult innings up until the ninth inning, I hope that I can rally from my earlier losses and make a thrilling comeback and hit a home run to win the series. I still remember well two sporting events in my high school sports career in which I was the hero. Starting on the varsity baseball team in my freshman year, I was a four-letter baseball player, but the game I remember best was against our archenemies from MarsHill when I hit the only home run of my high school career and won the game. Then in my senior year I was the shooting guard for my basketball team, and on one of those nights I couldn't miss and taking the game into overtime I made the shot to win the game. I want that same excitement in my final minutes, in the last inning, and I want to hear the cheers of a race well run, a glorious finish, a wonderful finale to a life played to the final inning.

I take as my inspiration three heroes of the Bible who I believe hit a homer to win the game and sank the final hoop to stage a victorious comeback. The first was the Apostle Paul himself, a man who faced many a defeat (Read II Corinthians 11:23-27), but in the end wrote this: *"For I am now ready to be offered, and the time of my departure is at hand. I have fought a good fight, I have finished my course, I have kept the faith: henceforth there is laid up for me a crown of righteousness, which the Lord, the righteous judge, shall give me at that day: and not to me only, but unto all them also that love his appearing."* (II Timothy 4:6-8) Does this sound like the words of a defeated old man (Philemon 9)? No, it is the words of a victorious saint who just hit a home run in the bottom of the ninth inning to win the game. This bruised and battered veteran came to his final bat and hit the ball out of the park. How do I know? Because he speaks of a crown waiting for him, and crowns were not for losers but winners! This same batter told the Corinthian Church: *"Know ye not that they which run in a race run all, but one receiveth the prize?* ***So run, that ye may obtain.*** *And every man that striveth for the mastery is temperate in all things. Now they do it to obtain a corruptible crown; but we an incorruptible. I therefore so run, not as uncertainly; so fight I, not as one that beateth the air: but I keep under my body, and bring it into subjection: lest that by any means, when I have preached to others, I myself should be a castaway."* (I Corinthians 9:24-27) If my departure is at hand, I want to be able to say with confidence that I have played a good game, I have played by the rules, and I have finished the game as a winner, just like Paul.

The other Biblical character that has been an inspiration to me for most of my life ever since I heard his story from childhood is the man, Caleb. Maybe not as well-known as Paul, Caleb also finished well: *"And now, behold, the LORD hath kept me alive, as he said, these forty and five years, even since the LORD spake this word unto Moses, while the children of Israel wandered in the wilderness: and now, lo, I am this day fourscore and five years old. As yet I am as strong this day as I was in the day that Moses sent me: as my strength was then, even so is my strength now, for war, both to go out, and to come in. Now therefore give me this mountain, whereof the LORD spake in that day; for thou heardest in that day how the Anakims were there, and that the cities were great and fenced: if so be the LORD will be with me, then I shall be able to drive them out, as the LORD said."* (Joshua 14:10-12) Caleb should have retired at his age (85), but instead he still wanted to bat with the game on the line. How many Bible heroes started well but finished poorly (Gideon, David, Solomon to name a few), but not Caleb! Caleb did some of his best work in the final innings. Caleb might have been an old player, but he had no intention of simply fading away. He was willing to face Satan's fearsome closer (the giants), the closer who had defeated Israel forty years before (Numbers 13:33). But in the end, Caleb hit a home run to win the game. Oh, like Caleb I have played the whole game, and there are some who want me to step aside and let those more youthful pinch hit, but I believe that a younger man, even a man like Othniel (a future judge in Judges 3:8–11) needs a mentor like Caleb to develop, and as Vance Havner once wrote: **"Youth has never been and never will be qualified to take over alone!"** Like Caleb, I want to bat in the final inning and be an example to the younger players of what it means to play until the end. And that is why when all my pastor friends have retired I press on in the pastorate, the pulpit, and in the path the Lord started me nearly fifty years ago!

You have already probably figured out my last hero in this category of "a home run to win the game." Who better to illustrate this precept than Jesus Christ? In the greatest contest of all time Jesus became the hero when in the final inning called Calvary He took Satan's greatest pitch and hit the ball to heaven. Satan had tried to strike Jesus out on several occasions (remember the three pitches in the wilderness in Matthew 4:1–13), but Jesus wasn't surprised by Satan's curve balls and fastballs because Jesus was well prepared. The challenge to each of us is that we, too, do not need to be fooled by Satan's pitches as so many are for Paul tells us what Jesus knew: *"Lest Satan should get an advantage of us: for we are not ignorant of his devices."* (II Corinthians 2:11) Any batter does well when he knows what pitch is coming, and the same is true for us. Jesus, the greatest hitter of all time, never missed, a 1000% average against the Wicked One because He knew what was coming. And when it came to the last inning of Jesus' life, with two outs and two strikes, Jesus struck a blow for mankind unequalled when He gave up His life for all (I John 2:2). There were those and there are still those who believe that Jesus Christ struck out on Calvary, but we know just the opposite because in His death he hit the ball of redemption so hard that every sin was removed *"As far as the east is from the west, so far hath he removed our transgressions from us."* (Psalm 103:12) Now that is quite a home run! Though our final at bat will never be as dramatic or far reaching, I believe we still ought to strive to end well just as Paul, Caleb, and Jesus did.

I like these words from Vance Havner when he concluded the article that inspired this chapter in my 70th yearbook: **"This home run in the last inning does not always take the form of a public triumph. This rally in the ninth may be staged on a bed of infirmity, but in his spirit the old warrior may be scaling mountains. And to end one's course** with joy, keeping sweet and radiant, thrashing the giants of bitterness and churlishness that so often bedevil old age-that is a victory greater than taking Hebron. A good batting average to the end of the season is a mighty testimony to the grace of God that is well able to see us through." So, there you have it, my aspiration and my desire as I enter alone the ninth inning. I certainly don't know how long it will take to play and, maybe, just maybe, I will like others have to go into extra innings before the game is over. So, let it be, that whether the ninth or the fifteenth, I want to be still at bat waiting the last pitch, and my hope is that I will lay such a swing on that pitch that I will hear "well done!"

59.

HOW WILL THE LORD FIND YOU?

I AM PONDERING TODAY about the Lord's return. My desire is that He would come back in my 70th year so that I might experience a doctrine I have heard about all my life and believed in most of my life and preached the rest. That doctrine is the Rapture of the Church: *"For the Lord himself shall descend from heaven with a shout, with the voice of the archangel, and with the trump of God: and the dead in Christ shall rise first: then we which are alive and remain shall be caught up together with them in the clouds, to meet the Lord in the air: and so shall we ever be with the Lord."* (I Thessalonians 4:16–17) I am ready to die in the Lord, but I would love to be caught up with Scott and Coleen and meet the Lord in the air with them.

When the Lord does return, what shall He find? Jesus proposed this question: *"Nevertheless when the Son of man cometh, shall he find faith on the earth?"* (Luke 18:8) In this chapter I would like to suggest a number of things the Bible suggests we might be doing when our Lord and Saviour returns. **NUMBER ONE: SCOFFING.** *"Knowing this first, that there shall come in the last days **scoffers**, walking after their own lusts, And saying, Where is the promise of his coming? . . . "* (II Peter 3:3–4) We preachers use this as a sign of the times, but more often than not speak of the unbelievers and their scoffing as the scoffers in the world. This chapter isn't for the world, but the Church, and I have lived long enough to hear scoffing about the Lord's return, and, particularly, the Rapture of the Church. Once the advent of Christ was a mainstream doctrine preached and taught regularly, but now it is rarely mentioned. Oh, there have been periods when the return of Christ has been exalted, but in my seventy years I have watched as this doctrine has been put on the shelf.

The Church is partly at fault because of those in the past and present that try to predict the time of the Rapture, and, when it doesn't happen, more scoffers arise. Let us remember this: *"But of that day and hour knoweth no man, no, not the angels of heaven, but my Father only."* (Matthew 24:36) Dear Christian Brother and Sister, don't give up hope. Jesus mentioned more about His return than just about any other doctrine He taught!

NUMBER TWO: SURFEITING. *"And take heed to yourselves, lest at any time your hearts be overcharged with **surfeiting**, and drunkenness, and cares of this life, and so that day come upon you unawares."* (Luke 21:34) This is a word we don't use much anymore, but is certainly happening more and more. The word basically means "the act of excess in eating and drinking." Let us be honest with ourselves and what we see happening around us in this category. The world is doing it, but so is the Church. In both of Jesus' analogies about the days of Noah and the days of Lot being like the coming back of the Lord, this characteristic is seen (Luke 17:26-30). Jesus warned that if He delayed His return, this is what will happen: *"But and if that servant say in his heart, my lord delayeth his coming; and shall begin to beat the menservants and maidens, and to eat and drink, and to be drunken."* (Luke 12:45) More are found in the bars and restaurants than at the church today on Sunday!

NUMBER THREE: SLEEPING. *"Therefore let us not **sleep**, as do others; but let us watch and be sober. For they that **sleep sleep** in the night; and they that be drunken are drunken in the night."* (I Thessalonians 5:6-7) Again, note the context that Paul is exhorting believers not nonbelievers to stay awake. Paul also told the Romans: *"And that, knowing the time, that now it is high time to awake out of sleep: for now is our salvation nearer than when we believed. The night is far spent, the day is at hand: let us therefore cast off the works of darkness, and let us put on the armour of light. Let us walk honestly, as in the day; not in rioting and drunkenness, not in chambering and wantonness, not in strife and envying."* (Romans 13:11-13) I have been a pastor for nearly 50 years now, and I see the Church falling into a strange stupor. The Church seems to be tired, bewildered, and dizzy from the attack of Satan and the delay of the Lord's return. We have become exhausted in the last mile of the way, and we are sleepy!

NUMBER FOUR: SIGHING. *"For my life is spent with grief, and my years with **sighing**: my strength faileth because of mine iniquity, and my bones are consumed."* (Psalm 31:10) I like Vance Havner on this: "They [the Church] have listened to so much from platform and pulpit and radio [now television and internet], read so much from papers and magazines, been preached at and preached to, lectured and electioneered, cussed and discussed, gypped and cheated and lied to, and have bought gold bricks and white elephants, until they come to church with their fingers crossed, ready to take what they hear with a grain of salt, and the preacher has two strikes against him before he utters a word!" They sigh because they see no results and no good in all they have done and all they have given. They sigh over the times and the trials and the tests they face!

NUMBER FIVE: STUDYING. "*Study* to shew thyself approved unto God, a workman that needeth not to be ashamed, rightly dividing the word of truth." (II Timothy 2:15) And we have plenty of people studying the prophesies and predictions in the Bible, and most of them can give you remarkable explanations of why now is the time, but mixed among the good are the bad who are only using these terrible times to peddle their crackpot theories to deceive many and cast doubt in the minds of others. This is not the first age that the planets have aligned, and the signs have been seen, and with the passing of their time these students of the Word were proven to know more about the future than the Bible ever revealed. I am persuaded that I must live like He is coming today, but work like He will tarry another hundred years. That's my take on the Scriptures!

NUMBER SIX: SINGING. "Make a joyful noise unto the LORD, all ye lands. Serve the LORD with gladness: come before his presence with *singing*." (Psalm 100:1-2) Of course, there are numerous church hymns about the Second Coming of the Christ, but for many that is all they are doing, singing the words. Anybody can sing the national anthem during peace because many go through the motions at a baseball game, but their hearts aren't in it. It is another matter to sing the national anthem during a time of war. I was always impressed with Paul and Silas in the Philippi jail: *"And at midnight Paul and Silas prayed, and sang praises unto God: and the prisoners heard them."* (Acts 16:25) When Jesus comes, will He find us singing or just mouthing the words?

NUMBER SEVEN: SERVING. *"Wherefore we receiving a kingdom which cannot be moved, let us have grace, whereby we may* **serve** *God acceptably with reverence and godly fear."* (Hebrews 12:28) Again, I like Vance Havner on this: "Not merely occupied with His coming, but occupying till He comes (Revelation 2:25). I am afraid that there is a sort of theoretical interest in the Lord's return prevalent among the saints that somehow does not seem to be hitched up to practical service . . . The best evidence that the Lord's return has really gotten hold of us is when we occupy till He come, do business for God, buy up the opportunities because the days are evil!" There is an old church hymn that contains this line: "There is joy in serving Jesus as we travel on our way . . . " When He comes back, I believe Jesus would love to find His Church serving, serving one another (Galatians 5:13), serving faithfully where He has placed us (I Corinthians 4:2), and serving God in an acceptable manner. Peter says it best: "... *what manner of persons ought ye to be in all holy conversation and godliness.*" (II Peter 3:11) How will He find you?

60.

PERILOUS TIMES ARE HERE

I AM WRITING THIS seventieth year chapter from the quiet retreat of the Anchorage on Big Lake near Princeton in Downeast Maine. This is my 110th day here overall and my 30th trip to this cottage in the pines to fish, to read, and to write. It was exactly fifteen years ago that I last made a visit to this cabin owned by my brother-in-law's family. I brought my dear wife Coleen here to recover from a spring of three operations and a summer of seven chemo reatreatments that cured her breast cancer but left her vulnerable to other diseases. Why we never came back I don't know, but I am here again, this time alone. I am here to mourn and grieve Coleen's departure and get some perspective on what is next for me in the ministry--the rest of my 70th year and beyond.

Over the years (I first came here in 1987), I have found the fishing very good (One of the world's best landlock salmon fisheries is just 18 miles up the road, and I enjoy dry fly fishing for all kinds of fishing.), but for me, the peace and tranquillity is better adaptable to my kind of reading and writing, as I am doing tonight. I had a good morning fishing on the lake (seven smallmouth bass and three white perch out of the same hole), but my mind all day has been on this chapter, a chapter inspired by something I read in a book by Vance Havner entitled <u>It Is Time</u>. As I have already mentioned in previous chapters, this is the year of great loss for me (my mother, my wife, an uncle, two great church members, and I just found out yesterday a former friend, all have passed this year and it is only September) and, added to these separations, there has been the Covid-19 crisis that I have been dealing with since March. There appears to be no end in sight for the restrictions that has altered my ministry at nursing and boarding homes (it would be 15 months before I would get back to my first love), not to mention the Church. I have come to believe that the time I am living in is the time Paul described to Timothy as: "*This know also, that in the last days* <u>perilous times</u> *shall come!*" (II Timothy 3:1) As I have my Bible open to Paul's description of these "perilous times", I am at the same time observing the world, listening to the news, checking the internet, and watching the TV. Even though I shouldn't be shocked, I am surprised just how clearly Paul's characteristics of this age is found in his twenty phrases and words!

I am living in a world where men live for themselves, so selfish and self-centered that it is all about them (the "me" generation). It is as if the teaching of our Lord and Saviour and His followers has never been studied and I read: (1) ***"for men shall be lovers of their own selves"*** (II Timothy 3:2), but Jesus taught: *"But I say unto you, Love your enemies, bless them that curse you, do good to them that hate you, and pray for them which despitefully use you, and persecute you!"* (Matthew 5:44) I am living in a world as Vance Havner put it with people who <u>"live for what they can grab not what they can give</u>." Whatever happened to *"it is more blessed to give than to receive"* (Acts 20:35)? I read that the world that I live in will be (2) ***"covetous"*** (II Timothy 3:2), but I also read this instruction from the Christ: *"And he said unto them, Take heed, and beware of covetousness: for a man's life consisteth not in the abundance of the things which he possesseth."* (Luke 12:15) I am living in a world that brags and boasts about just about every accomplishment as if they and they alone are the author of such accomplishments. (What did Daniel say? *"And he changeth the times and the seasons: he removeth kings, and setteth up kings: he giveth wisdom unto the wise, and knowledge to them that know understanding: he revealeth the deep and secret things: he knoweth what is in the darkness, and the light dwelleth with him."* Daniel 2:21–22), and what did Moses say about getting wealth and health? *"And thou say in thine heart, my power and the might of mine hand hath gotten me this wealth. But thou shalt remember the LORD thy God: for it is he that giveth thee power to get wealth . . . "* (Deuteronomy 8:17–18). I read that the world I will live in will have (3) ***"boasters"*** (II Timothy 3:2). James tells us: *"But now ye rejoice in your boastings: all such rejoicing is evil."* (James 4:16) I am living in a world where the proud and arrogant are constantly extoling the greatness of our time with its advancement in medicine (but we can't find a cure for Covid or the common cold?) and technology and a myriad of other categories because I read that the world I will live in will be (4) ***"proud"*** (II Timothy

3:2). Solomon told the world three thousand years ago: *"Pride goeth before destruction, and an haughty spirit before a fall."* (Proverbs 16:18) I am living in a world that is at war with God, and the name of God is at best a swear word, and the things of God are the butt of nighttime talk show jokes. We hear the scorn any time and every time a concept about God is bought up because I read that the world I will live in will contain (5) **"blasphemers"** (II Timothy 3:2). According to Revelation 16:9 this sacrilege is only going to get worse in the last days and into the days of the Great Tribulation: *"And men were scorched with great heat, and blasphemed the name of God, which hath power over these plagues: and they repented not to give him glory."* I am living in a world where the younger generation has thrown off all parental authority in the home, all teacher authority in the classroom, and all police authority in the street because I read that the world I will live in is known by the characteristic of (6) **"disobedient to parents"** (II Timothy 3:2). Yet Paul writes: *"Children, obey your parents in the Lord: for this is right."* (Ephesians 6:1) I am living in a world that shows little gratitude and thankfulness, and that no wonder Paul described this age as (7) **"unthankful"** (II Timothy 3:2). Yet Paul tells us: *"In everything give thanks: for this is the will of God in Christ Jesus concerning you."* (I Thessalonians 5:18) I am living in a world that is so rotten socially and so wicked morally that Paul simply called this time (8) **"unholy"** (II Timothy 3:2). Peter counters with: *"Because it is written, be ye holy; for I am holy."* (I Peter 1:16) I live in a world where love no longer protects a baby in the womb, a wife in a marriage, and the child in the home. Paul was right about this age (9) **"without natural affection"** (II Timothy 3:3). I live in a world where marital vows and business contracts and national treaties are continually being broken, not worth the paper they are printed on, because who keeps their word anymore? Even as Paul described this age with the word (10) **"trucebreakers"** (II Timothy 3:3), Jesus taught: *"But let your communication be, yea, yea; nay, nay: for whatsoever is more than these cometh of evil."* (Matthew 5:37) I am living in a world of fake news, propagated lies, and publicized falsehood that are accepted as truth and trustworthy. That the best way to get the finger pointed away from you is to point the finger at someone else with a fabrication that will catch the six o-clock news and the front page of the major newspapers. Paul was right when he wrote that perilous times would include (11) **"false accusers"** (II Timothy 3:3). Paul tells us: *"But speaking the truth in love . . . "* (Ephesians 4:15). I am living in a world that is totally and completely out of control, without self-control. Who is any longer in control of their hands and feet and tongues? People do what they want and say what they want to say without the slightest thought of right or wrong. Paul was right, (12) ***"incontinent"*** (II Timothy 3:3). Paul's great fear was this: *"But I keep under my body, and bring it into subjection: lest that by any means, when I have preached to others, I myself should be a castaway."* (I Corinthians 9:27) I am living in a world that is angry, so angry they have become violent with such a cruelty and brutality that Paul called (13) ***"fierce"*** (II Timothy 3:3). I have come to believe what Jesus said about the end times: *"But as the days of Noe were, so shall also the coming of the Son of man be."* (Matthew 24:37) And though Jesus doesn't mention this characteristic, Moses does: *"The earth also was corrupt before God, and the earth was filled with violence."* (Genesis 6:11) Paul tells us just the opposite: *"If it be possible, as much as lieth in you, live peaceably with all men."* (Romans 12:18) I am living in a world that is day by day according to Paul producing people that are (14) ***"despisers of those that are good"*** (II Timothy 3:3). Why would people hate goodness? Yet we are seeing a world moment by moment turning to the dark rather than the light, from the good to the bad. Jesus taught: *"And this is the condemnation, that light is come into the world, and men loved darkness rather than light, because their deeds were evil. For every one that doeth evil hateth the light, neither cometh to the light, lest his deeds should be reproved. But he that doeth truth cometh to the light, that his deeds may be made manifest, that they are wrought in God."* (John 3:19–21) Peter told Cornelius that Jesus *" . . . went about doing good . . . "* (Acts 10:38) and look what they did to Him! Paul tells us: *"But glory, honour, and peace, to every man that worketh good . . . "* (Romans 2:10). I am living in a world where people are betraying their companies, their friends, and their country for money. Paul simply said that this would be an age of (15) ***"traitors"*** (II Timothy 3:4). The Bible is very clear that we are to be trustworthy, not traitors, no matter the relationship. Paul speaks of this truth this way: *"And such trust have we through Christ to God-ward."* (II Corinthians 3:4) I am living in a world that is so headstrong, reckless, and rash that it goes beyond imagination why people do what they do, yet Paul called them (16) ***"heady"*** (II Timothy 3:4). There is such a daring, brazenness about this age, a daring recklessness that is being praised and glorified as carefree and soul lifting, yet it smacks of thumbing one's nose at God and says I fear neither God nor man. Much like the judge of Jesus' parable: *"And he spake a parable unto them to this end, that men ought always to pray, and not to faint; saying, There was in a city a judge, which* *feared not God, neither regarded man."* (Luke 18:1–2) Men and women who have never understood the reason for fear have missed this proverb: *"The fear of the LORD is the beginning of knowledge: but fools despise wisdom and instruction."* (Proverbs 1:7) I am living in a world that has become so conceited and haughty that it is almost nauseating. Paul calls it (17) **"highminded"** (II Timothy 3:4). You know the type--my way or the highway, people who think they have the answers for everything. I think the word "mind" in highminded is the key to this characteristic. The world has gotten so smart, too smart, to need God. The world is revisiting Babel (Genesis 11:1–9) all over again. As mankind tries to exalt itself, we need to be reminded of this teaching by James: *". . . God resisteth the proud, but giveth grace unto the humble."* (James 4:6) I am living in a world where entertainment and pleasures are where it is at. Even amid the Covid-19 crisis the bars are full, the night clubs are crowded, and the sin-cities of our country are doing just fine. Even though we can't go to the baseball field, basketball arena, and the football stadiums, the cable companies and television stations are still filling our lives with plenty of pleasure. Paul was right, (18) **"lovers of pleasure more than lovers of God"** (II Timothy 3:4). Granted, there are more people watching me on Sunday morning on Facebook than at the Emmanuel Baptist Church sanctuary, but at the height of this crisis over the coronavirus we saw no demand for more prayer. Repentance isn't being proclaimed or the godly precept of how events like this can be turned around, offered, or applied: *"If my people, which are called by my name, shall humble themselves, and pray, and seek my face, and turn from their wicked ways; then will I hear from heaven, and will forgive their sin, and will heal their land."* (II Chronicles 7:14) I like Vance Havner on this: "Was there ever words that describe better this age? Would you not think that in such an hour, with the foundations crumbling, with humanity wallowing in blood and tears, churches would be crowded and men setting their houses in order and getting right with God? Far from it; revelry and not repentance is the spirit of the age. America is at the night club, not at the prayer meeting. Even the saints have caught the fever and Christianity has been made a frolic instead of a fight, a picnic instead of a pilgrimage. The only fire left in many a church is down in the kitchen, where a defeated handful pour hot chocolate and read the minutes of the last meeting in a cheap imitation of the clubs of this world!" So, what of the Church?

I have come to believe that the last two characteristics of this list of descriptive words and phrases are for the church. Without a doubt we are in the last age of the Church as well, and John doesn't paint a very pretty picture of it in the Revelation: *"And unto the angel of the church of the Laodiceans write; these things saith the Amen, the faithful and true witness, the beginning of the creation of God;* **I know thy works, that thou art neither cold nor hot: I would thou wert cold or hot.** *So then because thou art lukewarm, and neither cold nor hot, I will spue thee out of my mouth.* **Because thou sayest, I am rich, and increased with goods, and have need of nothing**; *and knowest not that thou art wretched, and miserable, and poor, and blind, and naked: I counsel thee to buy of me gold tried in the fire, that thou mayest be rich; and white raiment, that thou mayest be clothed, and that the shame of thy nakedness do not appear; and anoint thine eyes with eyesalve, that thou mayest see. As many as I love, I rebuke and chasten: be zealous therefore, and repent.* **Behold, I stand at the door, and knock**: *if any man hear my voice, and open the door, I will come in to him, and will sup with him, and he with me. To him that overcometh will I grant to sit with me in my throne, even as I also overcame, and am set down with my Father in his throne. He that hath an ear, let him hear what the Spirit saith unto the churches."* (Revelation 3:14–22) Paul describes it first as (19) **"having a form of godliness"** (II Timothy 3:5). The apostate church will have all the trappings of the True Church and will in some ways look better than the real Church. This church will say as Jesus predicted in Matthew 7:21–23: *"Not every one that saith unto me, Lord, Lord, shall enter into the kingdom of heaven; but he that doeth the will of my Father which is in heaven. Many will say to me in that day, Lord, Lord, have we not prophesied in thy name? and in thy name have cast out devils? and in thy name done many wonderful works? And then will I profess unto them, I never knew you: depart from me, ye that work iniquity."* Why? Because of Paul's last characteristic of the age (20) **"but denying the power thereof"** (II Timothy 3:5). What was and is and always will be the "power" of the Church: *"But ye shall receive* **power, after that the Holy Ghost** *is come upon you: and ye shall be witnesses unto me both in Jerusalem, and in all Judaea, and in Samaria, and unto the uttermost part of the earth."* (Acts 1:8) When that power leaves with the True Church (II Thessalonians 2:7), the apostate church (II Thessalonians 2:3 *"a falling away first"* is our word apostasy) will remain with the false prophet.

So, what are we to do with these last day, perilous times characteristics **"from such turn away"** (II Timothy 3:5)? If you are wondering what manner of people we ought to be in these last days (II Peter 3:11), all you must do is live the opposite of these traits.

61.

THE DANGERS OF ... ISMS

As I near the end of my 70th year, I still have a few more opinions and observations I would like to make to those who might read my ramblings and in particular some of the greatest dangers in these latter days. For me, they all fall under the category of . . . isms!

The world is rushing towards the open arms of the Anti-Christ; the nations are hurrying to the open plain of Megiddo and the mother-of-all-battles that will be called Armageddon; and the church is hastening the appearing of the False Prophet as apostasy deepens and darkens the very heart and soul of the Church. The Church has become an organization of . . . isms and it is these . . . isms that are corrupting and changing the Church today. Let me start with the one that will surprise you the most, *fundamentalism.*

If anybody would have asked me just a few years ago what . . . ism I belonged to, I would have said I was a fundamentalist. But I have come to believe this statement by Vance Havner: **"Unfortunately, the name 'fundamentalist,' if it does not cover a multitude of sins, certainly does cover a multitude of schisms!"** Is there an . . . ism that has more cliques than fundamentalism? For me, the tragedy is that the current fundamentalism is becoming more like the Pharisees of Jesus day, self-righteous, law abiding (legalist), separated from the world, godly, and doing good, yet they were the ones Jesus spoke out against most, and so must I. The fundamentalists are taking the high road today and forgetting some of the basic teaching of their Saviour. The once faithful, Bible-based faith preached the Gospel, believed in the old-time religion, and kept alive the visible, bodily return of Christ. But so many segments of fundamentalism have left these tenants and are loving this present world like Demas (II Timothy 4:10). They have decided that a godless president will bring back morality and christianity to the nation. They have given up on the Lord's return to change things and have decided that by legislation they can change the morality of mankind and the Kingdom. Other segments of fundamentalists have followed Diotrephes who loved the preeminence (II John 9), and now christianity is promoted by those who seek popularity. It is pretty sad when Christianity has to be recognized by Hollywood believers and Wall-Street saints. I have come to believe that we are not to follow any . . . ism, just Jesus. I no longer accept this label on me.

The second . . . ism might surprise you even more, **denominationalism.** I was a denominationalist for the first twenty years of my life. I was raised in a denominationalist convention church. Groups that started out with the right intent and desiring to do the right thing, over time slipped into man-run organizations with the original purposes being forgotten with the passing of their founder. It seems that each generation needs to put their own stamp on something, so change takes place and very rarely is the change for the good. Take for example the Salvation Army that once was an evangelistic movement that only sought the souls of men, and now it is a social organization seeking only to meet the needs of men. Did Christ ever intend for His Church to be divided into this denomination or that denomination? Yet, everyone that belongs to a denomination claims to be the True Church. I like what Paul asked: *"Is Christ divided?"* (I Corinthians 1:13) I gave up on denominationalism fifty years ago.

The third . . . ism also might surprise many of you, **Pentecostalism.** I wasn't going to add this to my list until just a few days ago. I was listening to a pastor friend speak on Pentecostalism during a live stream service from his church. I was home from my church because of kidney stones. In his entire 45-minute message he only extolled the virtues of Pentecostalism, and he is a Baptist. Granted, I agree that there are a variety of good Biblical attributes with the Pentecostals, but there are some clear heresies in many of their groups. The most striking one is the adding of the speaking of tongues as a sign of salvation, and then there is the emotionalism that promotes the flesh over the Spirit. What of those who believe that new revelations can be given by their modern prophet, not to mention their faith healers and the prosperity "gospel" gang. I am not saying that there are not genuine believers in the group, but, like with the Roman Catholic religion, there are too many trees that obscure a clear view to the Christ and His teachings. I reject this . . . ism.

The fourth . . . ism that is all through the church today, **modernism.** The modern church movement has no message because they have given up on the only message: *"For I delivered unto you first of all that which I also received, how that Christ died for our sins according to the scriptures; and that he was buried, and that he rose again the third day according to the scriptures."* (I Corinthians 15:3-4) They deny the only "Gospel" proclaimed in a supernatural book (which they reject) and a supernatural Christ (which they have reduced to a good man and a good teacher). It's belief about creation is rooted in evolution which denies God's hand on all that is and will ever be on this planet. They deny the depravity of man, that man is basically good and just evolving and will be better in the future. They reject the blood of Jesus as a "slaughter house theology" and just a doctrine of an unenlightened past. Modern christianity is all about man, not God.

The fifth . . . ism I would highlight to you, **formalism.** Paul defined it best by saying that in the last days: *"Having a form of godliness, but denying the power thereof: from such turn away."* (II Timothy 3:5) Outward religion versus inward religion. In this . . . ism their churches, cathedrals, and chapels are all show, rituals, and rites rehearsed again and again thinking their much speaking and singing and show will be heard and seen by God (Matthew 6:7) They call weakness what God calls wickedness; culture instead of Calvary; and, as Vance Havner puts it, **"it has tried to revise the Bible, streamline the Gospel, remodel heaven, explain away the Devil, and air-conditioned hell!"**

The sixth . . . ism I would underline for you, <u>secularism.</u> When society gets its hands on religion, watch out! This is a dull attempt to be religious without God; to make one feel redeemed with our regeneration. It has no hallelujah, no joy, and the soul never needs reviving. It never saves the soul but gratifies the body. It never convicts a sinner because it never speaks about sin. It never converts a druggy to a disciple because whatever is right in one's eyes is right (Judges 21:25). It never transforms a criminal into a Christian because there is no crime or criminal in the world of the secularist.

The seventh and last in this group of . . . isms that I will mention, **ecumenicalism.** I left this for last because I believe this is the most dangerous movement for the Church itself. This promotes the concept that if you have the name Christian, believe in anything about the Christ, and are organized into an institution you can call church, then a common denominator can be found to fellowship and organize into a massive movement. By the time all the elements are removed that are not acceptable to all within the organization, there is little left. Yet, the National Council of Churches and the World Council of Churches have functioned for years. Again, as Vance Havner puts it: **"It is form without force, a religion without redemption. It defies the Bible, denies the Blood and derides the Blessed hope, and the wrath of God abides on it."** Despite standing for nothing, they continue to stand and will until their ultimate leader, the False Prophet, appears and leads them into an alliance with the Anti-Christ and their rendezvous with Christ (Revelation 19:20).

62.

THE LAST OF THE PROVERBS

1- If Jesus is praying for me, and He is, why would or should I fear a thousand enemies?

2- Someone has already written a classic church hymn with the title of <u>Trust and Obey</u>; what we need today is someone to write <u>Love and Obey</u>!

3- It is Christ who sustains us when our physical strength is gone; it is Christ who preserves us when our will power runs out; and it is Christ who recharges us with energy when all our might is used up.

4- "One door and only one, and yet its sides are two: inside and outside, on which side are you?" A question from childhood that still needs to be answered in adulthood.

5- The problem today, as in Jesus' day, is there a lot of people following Christ as an intellectual exercise. They know about Him and His teachings. They are fascinated by His instructions and philosophies. They practice His concepts and precepts in their lives and living and lifestyle, yet they never see beyond that. They know of Him, but don't know Him. What a tragedy!

6- The law has always demanded our loyalty and faithfulness to it, but it never helped us keep it.

7- The incarnation of Christ brought the infinite God within reach of finite man.

8- The Eternal Fatherhood demands an Eternal Sonship.

9-By what measurement does God test our alignment? By what plumbline does God test our straightness? There is only one measuring stick in God's tool chest, Jesus Christ. Our lives are to be square and straight according to the measurement of our Saviour.

10-Christ had such a success with people because He knew that force was no substitute for gentleness.

11-Jesus is like the leaders of old who led from the front, not the back. When the charge is sounded, all we have to do is look ahead because we will always find our Leader leading the attack.

12-Jesus came so that man would be able to get proper directions to His Father's house.

13-There are some worthy of admiration, but only Jesus is worthy of adoration!

14-Either Christ will become your Corner Stone or your Grinding Stone. Your choice.

15-Omnipotent, omnipresent, omniscient, all we know about God and so much more.

16-Humanity that tries to live outside the perfection of Christ will become a monstrosity.

17-Almost all the images we have of Jesus are when He was grown up; we rarely envision Him growing up.

18-There was a day when the "womb" was the safest place on this planet, but since the onslaught of abortion it is now one of the most dangerous places in the world.

19-Silence is a powerful form of speech.

20-One day the Lord will return and gather us up into His Almighty Hands and then lift us up with His Everlasting Arms, place us safely onto His Eternal Shoulders, and carry us to His Eternal Home to live with Him forever.

21-Ours is a success-oriented age, not a Saviour-oriented age; a "youth" time, not a "yoke" time; a wealth-run world, not a Word-run world; and because of that we have failed to see the glory that can be found in following Jesus.

22-Let us so live that Christ will not only be pleased with what He sees and hears, but what He smells as well.

23- The burden of discipleship is much like the burden of wings on a bird. Wings and weight, but it is with those wings the bird is able to soar. So, too, with us!

24- The first church didn't have a pew, a pulpit, a program, a PA system, a pastor, or property, but it did have power.

25- With all the "comforters" mentioned in the Bible, I am amazed that so many Christians are still so miserable.

26- From our "high tower" we can gaze upon Beulah land.

27- By far, Jesus is the fairest of the fair!

28- We don't need an attorney, we need an advocate.

29- Human wit has an end; human will has an end; human wisdom has an end, so what is the answer? You will find it in "the end."

30- How do you pray to God--as a customer in need of a product or as a child in need of a Heavenly Father?

31- The best among us, the least among us, the worst among us are all among us.

32- Philip was looking for a snack for the people, but Jesus wanted to give them supper.

33- Hell: a prepared place for perverted people with a perimeter ever pushing outward, and permanent!

34- Mercy will follow us until grace can get us back on course.

35- Where mercy and grace are found, so is love found.

36- Mercy opened Abraham's ears, but grace opened his eyes.

37- It is not a sin to ask, but I do believe at certain times it is a sin not to ask.

38- We have lost sacred music because singing has become professional, and the audiences have become spectators instead of participants.

39- When does ministry become industry? When the heart is not in tune with the tongue (professional gospel singers).

40- As the daystar ushers in the light after the night so, too, Jesus brought in a new light as our Daystar.

41- Brusied but not beaten because Christ, though bruised Himself, will one day bruise the bruiser (Satan) for the last time.

42- All salvation requires is a simple "thank you."

43- Reconciliation is just a simple "cross" that bridges the ravine of sin that separates us from God.

44- In order to pray affectively for a good spiritual harvest, we must also keep on sowing and hoeing.

45- The heart will experience no "rainbows" if the eyes shed no tears.

46- When you can't go on, remember, Christ will carry you on.

47- It will bring no shame to you when you look around and find that Jesus is your cellmate.

48- Heaven's delights will far outweigh earth's difficulties.

49- Don't fear, Jesus is the contractor on your heavenly mansion, and the same details He used to make the universe and all that is within will be put into your future home.

50- It is easier for people to celebrate Christ's holidays (Christmas and Easter) than to keep His holy commandments.

51- Christ is coming. Are you packed? Remember, pack light!

52- A small deed done for Christ is no small thing.

53- Your poverty will never tax Christ's resources.

63.

IT IS TIME

LAST NIGHT IN ONE of my lonely moments I cried out to the Lord, "It is time!" What I was referring to was my time to go home. Sometimes in my loneliness in this my 70th year, I just want to go to heaven. Coleen left in April, mother left in June, and so many others left before that. Yet, I am still here so for me it is time, but I know my theology well enough to know, *"But of that day and hour knoweth no man, no, not the angels of heaven, but my Father only."* (Matthew 24:36) So I decided to refocus my attention to those times in the Bible when others made this proclamation: "It is time!"

*"****It is time*** *for thee, LORD, to work . . . "* (Psalm 119:126) The Psalmist found himself in a situation that I feel we are in today. With the signs of the times repeating itself over and over with every new news cycle, it is time for the Lord to work. Oh, I know the Lord is at work, but most of us who believe on and in Him are looking for a specific work, an end of the age work, and that being the blessed return of our Lord and Saviour Jesus Christ: *"Looking for that blessed hope, and the glorious appearing of the great God and our Saviour Jesus Christ."* (Titus 2:13) I believe the present world is in such a hopeless situation that unless the Lord intervenes there will be no hope. I like what Vance Havner said: **"The pendulum has swung about as far as it can in one direction. We face the Lord's return or ruin!"** Like John of old, after witnessing the revelation in the Revelation, he finished his prophetic book with a prayer, a prayer that is on my lips today: *"He which testifieth these things saith, Surely I come quickly. Amen.* **Even so, come, Lord Jesus.***"* (Revelation 22:20) It is time for Thee, Lord, to work: even so, come!

"*Sow to yourselves in righteousness, reap in mercy; break up your fallow ground: for **it is time** to seek the LORD . . .*" (Hosea 10:12) If we are in the later days (read II Timothy 3:1–5), and I believe we are, then this second admonition is for us. Seeking the Lord has always been the exhortation: "*Seek ye the LORD while he may be found, call ye upon him while he is near.*" (Isaiah 55:6) But as the end of the age draws near, it is more urgent than any time before. I was told when I was young that as one gets older time seems to speed up. I was young; now I am old, and I see what those that told me that meant. We all know time hasn't changed, but with time running out for this present age it is important one has settled things with the Lord. But there must first be a "breaking up of fallow ground." Being the sixth-generation son of farmers, I know that before any real planting can happen the field has to be plowed and disked and harrowed. You will get no harvest until the seed is planted in soft soil. Fallowed ground is unproductive, unfruitful, because it is undisturbed, undisrupted. Hard hearts, thorns and thistles in the mind, and weeds in the soul are not what God is looking for. But before the Good Lord can water, we must prepare, and we prepare by seeking the Lord. Jeremiah warns: "*. . . Break up your fallow ground, and sow not among thorns.*" (Jeremiah 4:3) It is time, isn't it?

"*And that, knowing the time, that now **it is high time** to awake out of sleep . . .* " (Romans 13:11) I like this. It is not just time, it is high time, more than urgency, a necessity! You talk about an age that is asleep at the wheel, it must be this age, and you talk about a Church age that is asleep, it has to be this one. Paul also warns: "*Therefore let us not sleep, as do others; but let us watch and be sober.*" (I Thessalonians 5:6) There are so many things today that are making the believer drowsy. We know why the devil wants the saint sleepy: "*Be sober, be vigilant; because your adversary the devil, as a roaring lion, walketh about, seeking whom he may devour.*" (I Peter 5:8) He seeks to devour your testimony and your witness, to make you ineffective in this age. The world wants you to be sleepy so that it can go on as it wishes without any interference by those that might expose their sins. They don't want to know that "*. . . the fashion of this world passeth away.*" (I Corinthians 7:31) If we don't stay awake, who will warn this old world?

"*But this I say, brethren, **the time is short** . . .*" (I Corinthians 7:29) What a solemn statement. I like the story of Thomas Chalmers who started life as a mathematician, but eventually yielded to the Lord's commissioning and became a preacher later in life. In his own testimony he tells of the change that happened to him when he remembered the two greatest mathematical truths about time--the shortness of time and the vastness of eternity. I have come to believe that the world needs to brush up on spiritual mathematics. The sands of time are running out in the hourglass of this age. There needs to be revealed the eternal seriousness and the everlasting urgency about this time in which we are living. I know there have been other preachers in other generations that have proclaimed this shortness of time and certainly the scoffers are out in full force. *"Knowing this first, that there shall come in the last days scoffers, walking after their own lusts, and saying, Where is the promise of his coming? For since the fathers fell asleep, all things continue as they were from the beginning of the creation."* (II Peter 3:4) Yet, like the days of Noah and the days of Lot (Luke 17:26-32), we go on as if we had all the time in the world. One can understand the world that is already spiritual asleep (Ephesians 2:1), but any believer and every saint ought to know: *"Whereas ye know not what shall be on the morrow. For what is your life? It is even a vapour, that appeareth for a little time, and then vanisheth away."* (James 4:14) The time has always been short, and this time is no exception to this rule!

*"For **the time is come** that judgment must begin at the house of God: and if it first begin at us, what shall the end be of them that obey not the gospel of God? And if the righteous scarcely be saved, where shall the ungodly and the sinner appear?"* (I Peter 4:17-18) For me, I have left the most sobering of our "it is time" verses for last. If you believe that we are living as a Church in the Laodicean Age (Revelation 3:14-22), then you know that with Christ on the outside knocking to get inside (Revelation 3:2) judgment must first start with us! **"It is time"** for the Christian to: *"Examine yourselves, whether ye be in the faith; prove your own selves. Know ye not your own selves, how that Jesus Christ is in you, except ye be reprobates?"* (II Corinthians 13:5) If we don't judge ourselves: *"For if we would judge ourselves, we should not be judged. But when we are judged, we are chastened of the Lord, that we should not be condemned with the world."* (I Corinthians 11:31-32) We expect the world to repent, but it is we who first needs repentance. In my study of the great revivals throughout Church history each happened when the Church repented and then they changed their times. If there is one great revival before the Lord returns, then it must first start in "the house of God!"

As my time draws to an end, and whether or not I go in the rapture or through a simple departing of my soul through death, I hope this time sensitive message will be heard far and wide. There are two judgments needed at this time, a corrective judgment for the Christian and a condemnatory judgment for the sinner. Peter spoke of just how close these are: "*. . . and if the righteous scarcely be saved . . .*" Part of the last days in the Church is the apostatizing of a segment of it (II Thessalonians 2:3 and I Timothy 4:1). I have been an observer of the Church for 60 years, and exactly what the Bible predicted has happened. **"It is time!"** Time for God to work; time for us to seek God by breaking up the fallowed ground; time for us to wake up because the time is short. It's judgment time!

64.

IF MY PEOPLE . . .

2020 IS GOING DOWN as the most negative year in my life; perhaps, my seventieth year will be the worst I could ever imagine. If the unexpected departure of my wife wasn't enough and the expected departure of my mother not enough, there has been this Covid Crisis that had disrupted my ministries and brought my beloved country to making choices that has brought on a legislative persecution from the governor of my State of Maine, and I believe with the election of my 14th President a national persecution on my constitutional religious rights! If there has ever been a time my land needs a revival, it is now, but instead of seeking God, my country is legislating God out of everything. My 70th year might not be my last year on this planet, and my threescore and ten might not be my last year as an American citizen (I do have another citizenship in heaven: *"Now therefore ye are no more strangers and foreigners, but fellowcitizens with the saints, and of the household of God."* Ephesians 2:19), but if the Lord shall tarry and I continue to live, I am praying for a revival, the only revival that will save this land!

What makes me hopeful is that God has brought revival to our land in similar times. One of the tragedies of today is that most are ignoring our real history to the rewriting and revising American history. I believe if you asked the average citizen who Jonathan Edwards or George Whitefield is, they wouldn't know. What of Roger Williams and Charles Finney? What of Wesley, Asbury, Dwight, or Cartwright, men who did more for America than all the politicians combined! Most today are looking to the government for their salvation, not the Church, and that is tragic because no politician will ever save us from ourselves. Only the Lord Jesus

Christ can do that through the men and women of His Church. Yet there remains in this year of grace a chance *"if my people . . . ."* I also feel the problem isn't with the average American, but the average Christian: *"if my people . . . ."* Those who name the name of Christ, the Christians of this land, are God's people, or they are supposed to be. But this all hangs on a simple two-letter word: "IF."

I was taught at an early age that revival was of God and here nearly seven decades later I still believe it, but we play a part "if . . . " The verse that has started most revivals, if not in practice in precept, is II Chronicles 7:14: *"If my people, which are called by my name, shall humble themselves, and pray, and seek my face, and turn from their wicked ways; then will I hear from heaven, and will forgive their sin, and will heal their land."* Everybody knows this verse, most can quote this verse, but how many are really willing to apply this verse? This might be my last time to share what I believe on this verse so for me these are the conditions the people of God must make if there is going to be any hope of revival of our land in these last days.

First, *"shall humble themselves."* Today so many believers are praying that God would humble them, but that isn't the challenge. Humble yourselves. *"Whosoever therefore **shall humble himself** as this little child, the same is greatest in the kingdom of heaven."* (Matthew 18:4) *"And whosoever shall exalt himself shall be abased; and he that **shall humble himself** shall be exalted."* (Matthew 23:12) *"**Humble yourselves** in the sight of the Lord, and he shall lift you up."* (James 4:10) *"**Humble yourselves** therefore under the mighty hand of God, that he may exalt you in due time."* (I Peter 5:6) Is that enough evidence for you? It must be God's people acknowledging their lowly estate, not an arrogant president. It must be God's people confessing their sins, not a president-elect.

Second, *"and pray."* Everybody agrees that praying is a wonderful virtue, both believers and non-believers, but few rarely pray except in a crisis. I have discovered in the worst health crisis in my life, fewer people come to the prayer meeting and praying is still only offered when people are at death's door. Prayer is hard work, time consuming, and difficult. *"And pray"* for me is Paul's version of prayer: *"Pray without ceasing"* (I Thessalonians 5:17); round the clock, continual prayer, but instead of organizing a prayer vigil we are organizing a virus screening. Jesus set the example through His personal example (Luke 6:12), His personal exhortation (Matthew 6:9–13), and personal instruction (Luke 18:1–8). If the

Son of God felt it necessary to pray all night at vital times in His earthly life, what should this say to us in this time of national crisis?

Third, *"and seek my face."* I have come to understand that what is being said here when it speaks of seeking God's face means to seek God's approval, God's favor, seeking to do those things that pleases God. We don't need to debate or question what this means because the Bible is full of suggestions on what pleases God. *"Furthermore then we beseech you, brethren, and exhort you by the Lord Jesus, that as ye have received of us how ye ought to walk and* **to please God***, so ye would abound more and more."* (I Thessalonians 4:1) The problem today is most people would rather do things that please the neighbor, or the wife, or the boss! *"Servants, obey in all things your masters according to the flesh; not with eyeservice, as menpleasers; but in singleness of heart, fearing God."* (Colossians 3:22) We have a choice: menpleasers or Godpleasers?

Fourth, *"and turn from their wicked ways."* This tenant of revival is certainly out of favor today in our nation. Instead of turning away, we are running towards in a sprint. Even the Church is being shamed into no speaking about specific sin, immoralities that are infecting our nation at such a rate that we soon will have to take the name of Sodom. We can pray all we want, but like Joshua of old when his army returned from Ai defeated, he found that until he took care of the sin in the camp there would be no victory. Until we take care of the sin in the Church and in the land, there will be no revival either. Remember, *"He that covereth his sins shall not prosper: but whoso confesseth and forsaketh them shall have mercy."* (Proverbs 28:13) You know it, and I know it, that sin is having its own way in our lives and in our land today, just like in the age of the judges: *"In those days there was no king in Israel: every man did that which was right in his own eyes."* (Judges 21:25) Isaiah said it best: *"All we like sheep have gone astray; we have turned every one to his own way . . ."* (Isaiah 53:6) Before revival there must be repentance and real repentance is not just turning from our sin, but also turning from having our own way and letting God have His way in our lives and the life of our land.

Only after we do those four things, then and only, "*. . .* **then will I hear from heaven, and will forgive their sin, and will heal their land.**" (II Chronicles 7:14) Only when we do certain things will God do certain things: "IF . . . THEN." This will not only be a blessing to the individual, but his land as well. When people repent and gain forgiveness, then those people around them will be blessed in so many ways. What of a change in a family when the alcoholic father gets saved and sober? What of the change in a company when the thieving employee gets saved and stops stealing? What of the nation when a president stops lying and gets saved and tells the truth? I have come to believe that the Almighty has given us the prescription for our national illness. There is a remedy for the sickness that is plaguing our land, but God's prescription is being drowned out by the political voices that claim man can fix himself. There is no substitute for this prescription.

65.

UNITY IN DIVERSITY

I MAY NOT BE the only one to see the irony in this simple fact, that after two thousand years the Church of the Living God is more diverse than it ever has been in its very long history. After countless thousands of pages of theology by the great scholars of the Church; after millions of sermons and spiritual speeches by the great preachers of the Church; after all the countless good works by the saints of the Church; and after century after century of trying to conform, after all this and more, we still find ourselves in the Body of Christ more different, more diverse, and more divided than ever before. You would think after these two millennials we would have figured out how to unite, join as one, yet, just the opposite has happened. What we have failed to learn and understand is the fundamental truth about **"the freedom in Christ,"** a freedom which, in the final product, must allow the individual, the assembly, the national church, the room to pursue his or her own understanding of God and His Christ in light of his or her own revelation and revealing of the truth of just what the Church was supposed to become.

There are those who would have us divorce ourselves from diversity, no matter how painful and unpleasant that would be. There are those who would have us have a solitary, single image of God, His Son, and the Church. To accept diversity, with all the possibilities for danger and deception and division, is to embrace a concept of Christ which is infinite in variety and virtues hard to comprehend. Diversity may be the only thing we have to truly guide our hearts and minds to the complexity and mystery of the Divinity of the Christ. But there is a caution I must mention here because we must have the first truths, and the most elemental truths, accepted and embraced, before we can begin that journey of diversity that will eventually lead us to the land where we can allow our brother in Christ to be different from us, to worship differently than we do, to sing differently than we sing, to like a different version of the Bible than we do, to like another style of spiritual music than we like, or to read a different translation of the Bible than we read! What about meeting on Saturday night instead of Sunday morning or having three Sunday services versus one. As a dear friend of mine, Mark Honey, once put it, **"We have no problem with the lily; we have a problem with how we are going to gild-the-lily!"**

Paul clearly taught this doctrine of diversity in I Corinthians 12:4–6: *"Now there are diversities of gifts, but the same Spirit. And there are differences of administrations, but the same Lord. And there are diversities of operations, but it is the same God which worketh all in all."* Paul would go on in this classic chapter on the spiritual gifts given to the Church to illustrate this concept with the object lesson of the parts of the human body: *"For the body is not one member, but many. If the foot shall say, because I am not the hand, I am not of the body; is it therefore not of the body? And if the ear shall say, because I am not the eye, I am not of the body; is it therefore not of the body? If the whole body were an eye, where were the hearing? If the whole were hearing, where were the smelling? But now hath God set the members every one of them in the body, as it hath pleased him. And if they were all one member, where were the body? But now are they many members, yet but one body. And the eye cannot say unto the hand, I have no need of thee: nor again the head to the feet, I have no need of you."* (I Corinthians 12:14–21) How has the Church missed this simple teaching because we all realize that our natural body is only functional because it is so diverse? Why can't we see that Jesus wants the same thing for His Body (Ephesians 1:20–23)

Do not Paul's writings teach us that Christ has created His Body like a human body, diverse in nature and that Jesus wants and has always wanted His Body to be diverse? If I have learned anything from my trips to India, it is the beauty in diversity. I have found over the years that my brothers and sisters in India do few things as we do in America. They serve a different Communion. They worship in a different kind of sanctuary. They read their Bible in a different language. They live differently; they talk differently; they act differently, yet, we believe in the same Christ, the same Cross, and belong to the same Church. Paul was right when he used the words *"diversities of operations"* in I Corinthians 12:6.

Why is it we think our God is too small that He can't reveal Himself in diverse manners, in different ways, and through different means?

"God, who at sundry times and in divers manners spake in time past unto the fathers by the prophets." (Hebrews 1:1) If God spoke, worked in "divers" means then, why can't we accept that He can do it now? I know I was trained to see division, not diversity, in the variety of Christian fellowships and denominations scattered across our land, if not in our state or community. I saw it all in the negative; I believe now I saw it all wrong. I would question how sad it was that the Body of Christ couldn't get along, worship together, and serve the Master the same way. Now I am seeing that this might not be the plan of man, but an act of God. I once saw depravity and diversity on the same line, at the same level, but now after years of consideration and contemplation I see these examples of diversity in a different light, in a different way.

As difficult as the problem of this doctrine may be to you, or me, the greatest problem of the diversity of the Body of Christ is the simple fact that we have never been able to find a balance when it comes to the matter of diversity. Balance, moderation, has been the one aspect that most Christian groups have never been able to handle for very long, and, yet the Apostle Paul's admonition to the Church at Philippi was, **"Let your moderation be known unto all men. The Lord is at hand."** (Philippians 4:5) Over the centuries the Church has been its own worst enemy. I believe, ultimately, the Church has never been at risk from outside forces. It has always been the internal forces that have threatened our survival. We have never managed to understand that Christ is quite capable of understanding all the various nuances embraced throughout the ages by His Church, and that He has given each of us that freedom to pursue Him with whatever understanding we have at the time, whether we are a white man trying to understand why we must follow Roman Catholic dictates, or a brown man trying to understand why we should follow an English point of view! Yes, the fundamentals of the faith must be embraced. There is no dispute about that, but after that, there is personal freedom and, yes, risk involved when we decide on our own how the other matters connected to the Church are to evolve. Paul was also right when he wrote: *"For now we see through a glass, darkly; but then face to face: now I know in part; but then shall I know even as also I am known."* (I Corinthians 13:12) We all have the moral right to disagree with our brother over music and sports on Sunday and the County Fair, but to say you are right and he is wrong or he is right and you are wrong is an attack against diversity.

We have the right to define what makes us peculiar, and, yes, we have the right to gather with those of similar persuasions, but not to disown those who choose to do it differently or be different in their approach to spiritual matters. That is what diversity is all about.

I have discovered over the years through travel to different areas of this country and different countries on this planet that the church does practice certain things differently. Throughout the ages the Church has changed, depending on the region of the world and the culture of the area in which the Church has been planted. There have been a few mystic times in Church history when diversity of practice has been allowed and a "unity of diversity" has happened. John called those times "the Philadelphia era" (Revelation 3:7–13). Philadelphia means "brotherly love." I have read of those amazing times, and what times they were, times when nothing could cause division because diversity was accepted for the greater good of the Gospel. Those periods of time have been characterized by evangelistic passion and revival fire. Saving of souls and the building of the Church were the priority, and differences in music style and worship methods and diverse denominationalism couldn't stop the advance of the Gospel across a country or around the world no matter how events unfolded.

So many today, and I, too, was one of them, sought only to condemn that which wasn't just as I did it. I saw only "the devil" in diversity, and then it was that my eyes were opened to this doctrine of diversity, and I realized that the devil loves to "divide and conquer." Jesus preached unity and nowhere can I find Him condemning diversity. Did He not create diversity, both in the natural world and the animal world? Even the human race is a diverse lot, and the brown face is as much loved as the red face or even the white face. It is my desire in the coming years to see the beauty that can be found in diversity. I saw it in India for the first time this year, and I am determined to see it and seek it in Ellsworth because, when it comes to doctrine, I will not be diverted from the "faith of my fathers," but, when it comes to issues that Paul called ". . . doubtful disputations . . ." (Romans 14:1), "unity in diversity," at best, will be my guiding precept!

I have reviewed my thoughts on this topic for this my 70th year and my 30th year at the Emmanuel Baptist of Ellsworth, Maine, and would like to add these thoughts to close. My own emotional and spiritual journey has led me to this present article in a manner designed to provoke public debate and personal discussion. I think that faith, no matter the peculiar embrace, needs to be shaken up from time to time, and the only way to do this is to take an individual beyond and outside his or her "comfort zone." I learned in my travel to India and back that the so called "comfort zone" is not where you can find the most comfort in your faith. I can honestly say that I was more comfortable in Kerala than I would be in Kansas, in a strange land among strange people living in a strange culture, than I have been in America over the last half of my life. India brought me out of my intellectual rut, out of a spiritual sleep, and the "same ole, same ole" to a new reality of the wonders of Biblical diversity.

It is not a matter of destroying one's faith or as a direct challenge to the mindset of most Baptists, but as a matter of freedom and as a matter of understanding that the realm of faith is far deeper and broader than we Americans could ever imagine. I found in India a group of brothers and sisters in Christ that were living and sharing their faith in a bolder manner and a more open way than I had ever experienced before. They gave me a new boldness and a new freedom I had never enjoyed before in my faith. Ours is not the whole world, and ours is not the whole Church. There are certain critical doctrines which must be accepted as fact, and I found a kindred spirit in those doctrines in India in which the theology of the Christ is well defended there, but beyond this we must recognize the freedom the Bible gives to practice other aspects of the faith as each individual sees fit. As Paul put it: *"One man esteemeth one day above another: another esteemeth every day alike. Let every man be fully persuaded in his own mind. He that regardeth the day, regardeth it unto the Lord; and he that regardeth not the day, to the Lord he doth not regard it. He that eateth, eateth to the Lord, for he giveth God thanks; and he that eateth not, to the Lord he eateth not, and giveth God thanks. For none of us liveth to himself, and no man dieth to himself. For whether we live, we live unto the Lord; and whether we die, we die unto the Lord: whether we live therefore, or die, we are the Lord's."* (Romans 14:5–8) This is the lesson of Church history, and this is the lesson of the Biblical record, and this is the example of those who have in their own lands and cultures made this truth of Christianity work for them and Christ's Church.

Each of us has been given a measure of freedom in this theology of diversity because the simple fact that we never need to worry about partisanship. Christ is the Head of His Church, not me, or even the Pope. Church membership will answer to Him, not me, or the Archbishop of Canterbury. When will we clearly hear these words by Paul: *"Who art thou that judgest another man's servant? To his own master he standeth or falleth . . . But why dost thou judge thy brother? Or why dost thou set at nought thy brother? For we shall all stand before the judgment seat of Christ . . . So then every one of us shall give account of himself to God."* (Romans 14:4, 10, 12) It is not my job to destroy, correct, or justify the credibility of another Christian or his choice of a local assembly. I can stand on what I believe, embrace my own personal beliefs and values, and go on with my form of Christianity, knowing that I do not necessarily need to have measured the mind and movement of God in the manner taught by my denomination. Evangelicals, no more or no less than any other Christian group, are guilty of putting God in a box, their box, with boundaries set by their own prejudices. We have the answer down pat, and we can give chapter and verse why we are right. God has become a creature of our own imagination, and we cannot think anything more arrogant and vainer than this. It is the sin of pride, and we would do well to ponder the matter in the light of what the Bible says.

I am walking a very delicate and narrow line I know, and I would be the first to tell you that I remain confused on many of the issues that are connected to this doctrine of diversity. I do not have all the answers for sure, nor do I have the former vanity which leads me to embrace a religious framework which has everything figured out, with every appropriate box on every item checked off. Church history is a record of diversity in all arenas, and a diverse people who tried to understand their newfound faith in a matter which would help them live in their world, in their culture, and in their lands. They met with some success and a whole lot of failures and missed opportunities just like us, but they did do something we can all be thankful for and that is they passed this faith on and on, generation after generation, until it came to us. Despite their brief successes and their well recorded failures, God seemed to have continued His Church despite them to another generation in which He has showed the same level of grace and mercy, patiently working through these twenty centuries to the building of His Church: *"And the Lord added to the church daily such as should be saved."* (Acts 2:47) It is still a mystery to me, and the only part that I have figured out is this. We do ourselves a great injustice when we define the activities of God through the framework of only one segment of His saints. It should not be unusual that a diverse God would produce a diverse Church which one day will include: *". . . every kindred, and tongue, and people, and nation . . . After this I beheld, and, lo, a great multitude, which no man could number, of all nations, and kindreds, and people, and tongues . . . "* (Revelation 5:9, 7:9) If you can't stand diversity in the Church on earth, what are you going to do when you get to heaven?

66.

A FALLING AWAY FIRST, A DEPARTING FROM THE FAITH

THE TREND STARTED EARLY in my seventy years, and by the time I had come to Emmanuel (1991) I recognized its dangerous precedence and disappointing characteristics. It has been, for me, the most overlooked "sign of the times." Jesus' disciples wanted to know *". . . and what shall be the sign of thy coming, and of the end of the world?"* (Matthew 24:3) Over the years the students of the Word, like myself, have compiled through Jesus' teachings, Paul's teachings, Peter's teaching, and the teachings of the Old Testament authors lists of these indications, these descriptions, these signs of the "end of time."

- The Sign of Deceivers (Matthew 24:4) *"take heed that no man deceive you."*
- The Sign of Duplication (Matthew 24:5) *"For many shall come in My name."*
- The Sign of Disagreements (Matthew 24:6) *"wars and rumors of wars."*
- The Sign of Dearth (Matthew 24:7) *"and there shall be famines."*
- The Sign of Diseases (Matthew 24:7) *"and there shall be pestilence."*
- The Sign of Disturbances (Matthew 24:7) *"and there shall be earthquakes."*
- The Sign of Dislike (Matthew 24:9,10) *"ye shall be hated of all nations."*
- The Sign of Disguises (Matthew 24:11) *"many false prophets."*

The Sign of Depravity (Matthew 24:12) *"iniquity shall abound."*

The Sign of Decreasing Love (Matthew 24:12) *"love of many shall wax cold."*

The Sign of Deception (Matthew 24:24) *"if it be possible . . . the very elect."*

The Sign of Dromomania (Daniel 12:4) *"many shall run to and fro."*

The Sign of Discovery (Daniel 12:4) *"knowledge shall be increased."*

The Signs of the Days of Noah (Matthew 24:37–41) *"eating and drinking . . . "*

The Sign of Dual Wives (Genesis 4:19) *"Lamech took unto him two wives."*

The Sign of Deviltry (Genesis 6:2,4,11–13) *"earth was filled with violence."*

The Signs of the Days of Lot (Luke 17:28–32) *"they sold and they planted . . . "*

The Sign of Debauchery (Genesis 19:4–7) *"that we may know them."*

The Sign of Detestation (Ezekiel 16:48–50) *". . . and committed abomination."*

The Sign of Difficulty (II Timothy 3:1–7) *"perilous times shall come . . . "*

The Sign of Disrespect (II Timothy 3:2) *"blasphemers."*

The Sign of Disobedience (II Timothy 3:2) *"disobedient to parents."*

The Sign of Despisers (II Timothy 3:3) *"despisers of those that are good."*

The Sign of Debasement (II Timothy 3:3) *"without natural affection."*

The Sign of Disloyalty (II Timothy 3:4) *"traitors."*

The Sign of Delectation (II Timothy 4:4) *"lovers of pleasure."*

The Sign of Denying (II Timothy 3:5) *"denying the power thereof."*

The Sign of Defiance (II Timothy 3:6) *"they which creep into houses."*

The Sign of Divers Lusts (II Timothy 3:6) *"led away with divers lusts."*

The Sign of Doubting (II Timothy 3:7) *"ever learning, and never able to . . . "*

The Sign of Disbelievers (II Peter 3:3–7,9) *"scoffers . . . and saying, where . . . "*

The Sign of Darkness (I Thessalonians 5:1–9) "as a thief in the night."

The Sign of Demonic Activity (I Timothy 4:1–3) *"doctrines of devils."*

The Sign of Departures (I Timothy 4:1) *"some shall depart from the faith."*

Paul wrote of this end of time disaster in the Church in another epistle with these words: *"Let no man deceive you by any means: for that day [the end of days] shall not come, except there come 'a falling away first . . . '"* (II Thessalonians 2:3)

While I was away on my fifth short terms mission trip (2016) to India, an interesting development happened in the United Church of Canada. It seems that one of their women ministers was fired from her parish, and she was suing to get her job back. Why was she fired? She was fired because she is now an atheist! The United Church of Canada had abandoned many of the churches' doctrines and theology years ago, but it appears that there is a line drawn when a minister stops believing there is a God. Such is the state of the Church today as many of its members are seeking something else, going on spiritual odysseys and religious quests to find enlightenment after rejecting the central tenets of Christianity, a faith they once believed, a church they once attended, and a Saviour they once emulated. The people I have known that would "depart" (*"fall away"*) over my nearly 50 years in the pastorate didn't go to the extreme as the lady minister in Canada, but they did leave the fellowship and sought no new fellowship elsewhere.

As I have been watching and listening to all the major Biblical signs being fulfilled leading up to the Lord's return, I have been hurt by the last one most. Wars and rumors of wars prevail, earthquakes in divers place abound, the flight of children starving in Africa still haunts me when I see the pictures, but when people who have been a part of the Church of God for years just up and leave, never to return, it hurts a pastor's heart. There is little heartache for a brother or sister in Christ that departs for Heaven (II Timothy 4:6), but a brother or sister that departs for a motorcycle club, a county club, or a night club is another matter. I still believe that *"Blessed are the dead which die in the Lord from henceforth . . . "* (Revelation 14:13), but there is no blessing to this pastor when they *". . . forsake me, having loved this present world."* (II Timothy 4:10) And whether it is your own son or a son in the Lord, it is an extremely bitter pill to swallow!

What has been especially hard for me has been the young people that have "departed from the faith" on my watch. Staying as long as I have in the pastorate, I have watched nearly two generations "fall away" in my nearly five decades, strong and numerous generations with few rarely attending church anymore. Granted, there are the exceptions to this prophetic rule, but my pastor heart is saddened by the majority that has become an example of God's end time prediction. I still pray for them. And if that generation wasn't bad enough, I inherited a group of young married couples that slowly, gradually, one by one moved away from attending, participating, or sharing in the work of the Lord. I still pray for them. Time would fail me to list the individuals both younger and older that have decided that Christianity and Christ no longer fit into their weekly plans, let alone their daily plans. It would be one thing if these individuals and couples were unknown to me or our time serving the Lord was short, but for most of these names we fellowshipped and served together for years. So, if my churches have faced such a "departure," such a "falling away," what of the rest in the Body of Christ worldwide?

67.

THE NEON GODS

Perhaps Simon and Garfunkel said it best in their classic hit <u>Sounds of Silence</u> when they wrote this line that for me best describes what was happening in the world around me during my seventy years: "**. . . and the people bowed and prayed, to the neon gods they made.**" I never thought my country was a land of idols, but as I reflect on the dramatic religious changes over the last seventy years that have turned the Church upside down, I now see that it all has to do with these "neon gods."

I do not profess to understand or know what Simon and Garfunkel intended when they wrote that song in the early 1960s, but I have come to an understanding that there is no better phrase that defines the therapeutic (note, not theological) religion that has emerged and now dominates America. The "gods" of happiness, feel-good, god-within, prosperity, pleasure, and self-esteem now illuminate the religious landscape just as the great neon city (Las Vegas) brightens the desert in Nevada. Its show and entertainment services in most churches now include light shows, big screen televisions, and the technology that puts Las Vegas' showstoppers to shame. The music is Broadway at its best, the overheads and displays are Hollywood perfect, and the pastor is as charismatic, tailor-made, and CEOish as any Madison Avenue executive. The advantages of this therapeutic religion include **tolerance** (everybody is good and certainly everybody will make heaven despite what the Bible teaches), **freedom** (freedom to have it your way without God's interference), and **personal choice** (nobody can tell you what you can do or should do, including God). America has returned to the days of the Hebrew judges when: "*. . . every man did that which was right in his own eyes.*" (Judges 21:25) But despite the promises of the neon gods, they have yet to deliver us from all the ills of society and the wrongs of humanity they were supposed to have eradicated by now.

The statistics have revealed only a growing despair and depression among most in all this "doing it your way." Americans (including the Christian ones) are less happy in their marriages, their jobs, and with their country. When will the powers that be take notice that the declining rates of churchgoing and the belief in God has been accompanied by declining rates of just about everything in our society. People are not closer, they are further apart; neighbors don't help their neighbors more but less; volunteerism is on such a decline that most libraries, fire departments can't find enough volunteers to keep the needed hours up; and families of one parent or same sex parents have literally destroyed the purpose of family. We now have a modern appliance for just about every task, advance technology that has freed up countless hours, but people no longer have time for church, time for God, or time to help a neighbor because in this internet world video-games, social networking, and Netflix has isolated us to our own private world void of real human contact, and in our own rooms, living rooms and bedrooms, we can bow to our neon god without anybody knowing who our god is. We are getting so bold in our worship of the god-within that we are now taking a selfie of it while the speedometer in our automobile is registering a hundred miles an hour!

We have lost all sense of a spiritual balance, a godly perspective, or a goodly proportion. Don't get me wrong, Netflix can fill up some lonely moments for a shut-in; the Internet has knowledge at your fingertips that can help in a crisis; and social media can help you keep in touch with loved ones on the other side of the country, or the world, but with all these gadgets there is still the need for a face to face conversation, a hug, a kiss, a pat on the back (the crisis of the Covid). I do not have trouble expressing my opinion on a topic, to take a picture of a favorite person, or sharing an intimate moment with a friend, but I don't understand why people today want the billions in this world to hear my conversation, see my picture, or join in with my intimate moment. Young girls are losing their privacy to total strangers. Young boys are losing their respect to someone they don't even know. People are losing their money to a machine and their time to a system that doesn't care whether it takes your virginity, your integrity, or your ideology. Could I share an interesting set of statistics I discovered in a 2010 Policy Review: "The United States has witnessed a 100-fold increase in the number of professional caregivers since 1950 [remember, I was born in 1951]. We have 77,000 clinical psychologists [remember these are 2010 statistics], 192,000 clinical social workers, 105,000 mental health workers, 50,000 marriage and family therapists, 17,000 nurse psychotherapists, 30,000 life coaches, and hundreds of thousands of non-clinical social workers and substance abuse counselors as well. [And don't forget all the grief counselors.] Most of the professionals spend their days helping people cope with **everyday life**, not true mental illness." If our neon gods are so good, why do we need all this help?

In my lifetime we have trained a generation or two that the only way you can cope with life is with a happy pill, illicit drugs, alcohol, a day off, or another neon god. We have become so obsessed with being "happy," we don't care what the cost is. I am not happy with my first wife so I seek another; I am not happy with my job so I will seek another. Even America has become so unhappy with the current crop of politicians, we are now going to choose a president from two people that nobody likes. Instead of delight, we are falling deeper and deeper into despair, depression, and despondency. This situation in the religious communities of America has orientated our spiritual instinct towards a higher thought of self, and our inner spirit is now our guiding force. Therapeutic religion raises expectations that can never be achieved because without the Creator being involved, we are lost. Self-regard will not stem the tide of troubles that comes to an individual or a nation in which God is placed on the sidelines during the game, placed outside the courtroom when a law is being debated, or placed outside a life that must cope with life. We live in a world that thinks life is easy, manageable, practical, and predictable. It never has been, and those that promote therapeutic religion are just doing what Paul predicted would happen in the last days when neon gods are in charge: *"For the time will come when they will not endure sound doctrine* [theology]*: but after their own lust shall heap to themselves teachers, having itching ears; and they shall turn away their ears from the truth, and shall be turned unto fables."* (II Timothy 4:3-4) This is the day I am living in and, whether in the world or the church, the teachers of neon gods are as thick as fleas on the back of your dog!

The result of such a lifetime is a nation filled with gurus and therapists that now fill the role once filled by friends and family and the local pastor; where professional caregivers minister, not the minister, and like seraphim's and cherubim's around the throne, the needs of the person, taught from childhood, to look inside themselves for God, or to an image on a monitor or screen, a neon god. Therapeutic religion offers contentment, but in all cases it only delivers a sort of isolationism that is at times comfortable, but in the end leaves us all alone in the universe with no one to care; alone with the god inside with no hope. What a joy, while all this was happening, I was pastoring people who believed in the True and Living God, and the glow was not manmade.

68.

CONSUMERISM AND CHRISTIANITY

ONE OF THE DRASTIC changes that has taken place in Christianity over my time in the church is the control consumerism has on the Church. I can't tell you the year Madison Avenue or Wall Street realized that there was money to be made off Christians and Christianity, but that year has come and gone and consumerism in the Church is now numbered in the billions of dollars. The mixing of religious faith and consumerism is now an accepted part of Christian television ministries, Christian radio ministries, and I understand now there are churches that accept credit cards during the taking of the weekly offering. (VISA and MASTERCARD now gets a piece of God's tithe!)

Prosperity preachers also profit from the consumer that wants more stuff, even if it is religious stuff. When I came to Emmanuel, the best Christian bookstore in the region was Lamb's. There were a few others, including a small one in Ellsworth run by a member (Millie Burns) of our church. Eventually, online shopping and the bigger stories drove the little ministries out. I know a little bit of what I speak seeing that in my last two churches I have been involved in the Christian bookstore ministry. My church before Emmanuel (Washington Street Baptist of Eastport, Maine) had its own Christian bookstore run by a wonderful couple in the church, Fred and Helen Boone. It was non-profit, a way to expose the community to good Christian literature, and an open door to evangelize the residents and the tourists that came to the small island off the coast of Maine. It, too, closed its doors because of little interest and the inability to keep up with the bigger and more progressive ministries. "You can get that cheaper online or at Lamb's," they said.

I no longer haunt the Christian Bookstore (now closed) in Bangor because 90% of what is in the store comes under consumerism or commercialization (in my opinion), mostly Christian stuff, trinkets, bobbles, and bangles, and for most of the spiritual stuff, fluff. Oh, you can find Bibles in any translation; again, most of them are fluff. You can find the latest best-sellers, more fluff. Instead of the stuff being subservient to the Spirit, the Spirit is now subservient to the latest fad. American consumerism has replaced theology and doctrine, worship and the Word, singing and sermon! The average American Christian is looking for a deal, a bargain at church, and, if not at church, then at the thousands of Christian websites hawking everything from Jesus tie-shirts to Jesus-first mugs. Were the things of Christ to be sold like soap? One of the very first instructions Jesus ever gave to His disciple was this command: "*. . . . freely ye have received, freely give.*" (Matthew 10:8) I still hear those who claim that the Gospel is free, and the rest is fair game. I know this seems to be harsh, even heretical, to the modern preacher who claims the profits from their consumerism preaching is spreading the Gospel around the world, feeding the poor, and providing clean drinking water to the masses. I get the impression that they are smiling at me with a tolerant grin suggesting I haven't got an open enough mind to understand what true Christianity really is. When did Christianity become a business and the Christian a businessman or woman?

This is one of the prices Christianity and Churchianity has paid for generations of preachers and Bible teachers who have failed to proclaim Scriptural theology. Nobody knows what is in the Bible any longer, and for what the average Christian really believes can be seen in the numbers that now rely on their Christian stuff for their spirituality versus the Scriptures. There has been no systematic approach to theology for decades in this country, and no application of this theology to developments like consumerism and commercialization of the Faith. I would dare to suggest that the ever-prevalent flirtation with legalism has only made matters worse in the Church. We have given generations of individuals free license to think about Christianity as they want it or see it. The self-sacrifice and free-of-stuff teaching of Christ doesn't fit in the mind of the consumer-crazed society that America has become. Why did Jesus tell the rich young ruler to get rid of his entire storehouse of stuff? (Matthew 19:21) Jesus knew his stuff would be a distraction in this discipleship, as it has been to so many Christians today. What was it that kept this young man from following Christ: "*. . . for he had great possessions* [lots of stuff]." (Matthew 19:22) The man was a consumer and consumerism was his god.

So, what happened? How did I miss this? Why am I only now clearly seeing the consumerism that crept in unawares? When did we go from a congregation that fed itself, studied for itself, and meditated and pondered for itself? When did most parishioners become spoon-fed congregations? When was critical thinking and spiritual discernment replaced with "spiritual maturity in five minutes a day?" When were debate, discussion, and discourse replaced with "40-days to know God?" We have come to a place where we are developing our theology through Christian greeting cards and daily devotionals on postcards. We need to go on a spiritual diet from all this stuff, and I am not talking about the kind of diet where we gorge ourselves at Burger King and buy a diet soda to keep the calorie count down. And instead of confronting the issue of immature Christians, we resolve the problem by leaving it unresolved and pushing more spiritual stuff at the immature. Paul was right when he warned: *"Of whom we have many things to say and hard to be uttered, seeing ye are dull of hearing. For when for the time ye ought to be teachers, ye have need that one teaches you again which be the first principles of the oracles of God..."* (Hebrews 2:11–12) One of the very first oracles of Christ was the fact that property and possession are not to be an important part of our lives. The early Church understood this teaching as they were constantly selling what they had for the betterment of the believers (Acts 2:45). Note again, one of the very first practices.

The Church has gotten so wrapped up in consumerism, it will be hard for it to be weaned off the money once you get a taste of what you can do. Who can you impress with your fancy malls within the church? (I know that my readers might find this hard to believe, but I have visited one of the biggest churches in Dallas, Texas, and in the middle of their huge complex is a strip mall with store after store selling the latest Christian consumer goods!) I will admit that I, too, have over the years gone along with the gospel singer who has wanted to sell his CDs after his concert in the church, or the evangelist that has wanted to sell his books after special meetings. I am still haunted by the lady that once attended Emmanuel but left after a selling took place in the church. She (now home in glory) called me on Monday to tell me that she would no longer be attending the services of Emmanuel. I asked why and she simply told me that I was allowing the house of God to become "a house of merchandise!" (John 2:16) What happened at the Temple (Matthew 2:14) is now happening in the church, and we don't see it! It starts so simply, with a good reason and an admirable cause, but has led to consumerism replacing ceremony, commercialization replacing commandments, and possessions replacing prayer. If we were honest with ourselves, we can clearly see that "stuff" has replaced sections of our spirituality that we once craved and coveted above all things. Stuff is now keeping us from Sunday school, worship services in the summer, and Prayer Meeting!

69.

WHEN DID ACADEMICS REPLACE FAITH?

I RECEIVED A SIMPLE eighth-grade (no kindergarten in my early childhood development) education from a simple four-room country school. I then went on to a small-town high school and by the end of my four years the graduation class numbered only 56. My education then took me to a small Bible school in South Carolina, and in 1973 I graduated with no aspirations for a higher education, just God educated. Today things have changed to the point that education has become a career for some, and they never do anything but get smarter. Paul wrote of this age to Timothy: *"Ever learning, and never able to come to the knowledge of the truth."* (II Timothy 3:7) It has amazed me at the end of my seventy years just how brilliant my generation of scholars have become. They have after two thousand years discovered the real truth about Jesus Christ and Mary Magdalene concealed for centuries but brought to light by those who have unraveled the mystery of The Da Vinci Code; that the fundamental, traditional teachings of the Church are falsehood, fabrications, and foolish because of the new truths being revealed by Harvard scholars, Yale intellectuals, and Princeton academics. These experts in Greek and ancient texts and archeology can be believed because they are smarter than Paul and Peter and John. You can be a horses rear-end today, but, if you have the degrees and pedigrees behind your name, you can preach hogwash and get away with it. I like to remind people that Balaam's donkey could speak (Numbers 22:28), but he was still an ass! It is time the Christian Church starts *"trying the spirits"* (I John 4:1)!

What they are saying today about the relationship Jesus and Mary Magdalene had pales in comparison to what they are proclaiming about the resurrection of Christ. Why I have become so hostile against men like the imaginary Robert Langdon, the brilliant Harvard scholar, the conspiracy hero of The Da Vinci Code, is the claims of the author that the multitude of witnesses in the New Testament are all lying and in a conspiracy to lead the world into a false hope of a resurrected Saviour. During a trip to India I was confronted with another explanation about Jesus' resurrection that is still alive and well. It appears that Jesus didn't die but was found alive by those that took him off the cross. Instead of staying around to be killed by the Sanhedrin again, he left the country for India where he lived out his life and finally died of old age and was buried in a grave in Northern India. According to those that believe this fable, his grave is still there today. So, all those recorded appearances never really happened, just a figment of Peter's and John's imagination to give some credence to their new faith and a conspiracy by men like Paul and Barnabas to entice people to believe in a risen Messiah. How this new generation of so-called religious scholars love to play loosey-goosey with the history of the early Church. Revisionists in the prominent, prestigious religious schools are trying to whitewash the facts with fables, and the sad thing is many are flocking to this new standard of Biblical interpretation just as Paul warned would happen: *"For the time will come when they will not endure sound doctrine; but after their own lusts shall they heap to themselves teachers, having itching ears; and they shall turn away their ears from the truth, and shall be turned unto fables."* (II Timothy 4:3–4)

The real problem today is that the true evangelicals are allowing these accommodationists to get away with their weird theories, conspiracy theories, and secret revelations. We are bowing to these men and women because they speak a higher vocabulary, recite from memory the ancient text, and appear superior in knowledge and intellect. I have watched the new discovery shows for years, and most fail to invoke "faith" in any of their explanations. It is all about the archeological facts and the new discoveries like the Gnostic gospel, which is not new, just rediscovered. Deconstructing the historical Jesus has led to the deconstruction of the historical doctrines and the historical Church. I like what Adam Gopnik wrote about the new theory advanced in The Da Vinci Code: "If this book is right, Jesus is reduced from the Cosmic Overlord to the founder of a minor line of Merovingian despots. Better far to leave the question open, to posit a hidden truth so astonishing that it makes orthodoxy seem thin and pathetic by comparison, without ever answering the question of what that hidden truth might mean." Do I know all the facts? Do I understand all the connections? Do I have all the answers to the countless questions about Jesus and the first Church? The answer is no, but I believe the orthodox, historical account because by faith it makes more sense than the new theories that have come out during my seventy years (Hebrews 11:1)!

We have arrived at a period in our Church's history that we might call "cafeteria" Christianity. As with any cafeteria there is a variety of items on the long counter. You pick your tray up and start down the line deciding as you go what you will choose and what you will reject. This is what has happened in the Church of the 21st century. So many alternatives have been suggested that we must choose. Different theories of how and why and who Jesus really was. Then you get into the various interpretations of Jesus' teachings, and down through the years the Church scholars have placed their names (or those behind them have placed their names) to a variety of ways of seeing the Faith. Christianity was never supposed to be a cafeteria line. Paul condemned the church at Corinth because they had divided into four camps (I Corinthians 1:12–13). His question, "Is Christ divided?" Well, if that was true in the first century, what of today, Bakkers, Swaggarts, Swindols, Jeremiahs, we have our four today and more. Our Faith has been polarized and politicized to the place that cafeteria is a good explanation of what has happened. The scholars and their surrogates have filled the air waves with alternative forms of Christianity, and Heinz no longer has a monopoly on 57 varieties. Add to this the explosion of written material and the mass media which now includes publishing companies that must, in order to keep their sell rate high, come out with a new version of the Bible every few years (consumerism). Shopping in America is so complicated because now you have fifty bars of soap to choose from (remember when there were three?) and twenty fast food places to eat (remember when there were two?). Variety doesn't make things easier, but more difficult, and what is true with our economy is true with our Christianity. I remember when there were only a few versions of the Bible, a few good Bible teachers, a few good publishing companies, and they all held true to the traditional, orthodox Christianity of my grandfather. Faith was not complicated in Perham (my hometown) because there was only one church (Baptist), one Bible (KJV), and one standard of Faith. There was only one thing on the menu, and you ate it or rejected it, but there were no alternatives. Buffet was never intended to be a part of the Christian's experience, and cafeteria was never intended to be a part of the Church, but we have gotten too smart for our own good. We have analyzed and explored our faith to death instead of simply accepting it by faith. The problem today is the Bible is written the way I want it written, Jesus is the one I have invented myself, and the Church is patterned and shaped around my time, my schedule, and my wants. So, I ask why has academics replaced faith? Simply, it is because we have gotten smarter than God, but Paul says we have become fools (Romans 1:22).

70.

THE FINAL MAJOR CROSSROAD

LIFE IS JUST A series of crossroads. The word doesn't appear in the Old King James Bible, but a similar word does: *"Neither shouldest thou have stood in the **crossway**, to cut off those of his that did escape; neither shouldest thou have delivered up those of his that did remain in the day of distress."* (Obadiah 14) Old Webster defined my topic for this last 70th year thought as "often regarded metaphorically as the point where one must choose between two different courses of actions!" If life is a series of crossroads, then the Bible is the best instruction book to deal with crossroad situations and circumstances because it is filled with illustrations of people at the crossroad of their lives, like me.

I have come to believe that the best crossroad verses in the Bible are Proverbs 3:5,6: **"Trust in the LORD with all thine heart; and lean not unto thine own understanding. In all thy ways acknowledge him, and he shall direct thy paths [at the crossroads of your life]."** Think with me through the pages of Holy Writ and see what happens at the crossroad. I think of the first major crossroad in history when Adam and Eve woke one morning and strolled down past *"the tree of the knowledge of good and evil"* (Genesis 3). In my opinion they shouldn't have been near that tree, but that day on that path they came to a crossroad when they were confronted with two totally opposite ways to go. I believe God had set them on a course where there would have been no crossroads, but they chose another path. They still could have gotten back on the right road if they would have chosen wisely, but they didn't, as we know. Instead of listening to the Almighty (*"though shalt not eat of it"*), they listened to Satan (*"if you eat of it you shall be like god"*) and took the road well-traveled, a broad way that led to death: *"And the LORD God commanded the man, saying, Of every tree of the garden thou mayest freely eat: but of the tree of the knowledge of good and evil, thou shalt not eat of it: for in the day that thou eatest thereof thou shalt surely die."* (Genesis 2:16-17) And they would eventually die because at the crossroad of their lives at Eden they chose the wrong path and set up the choice each and every one of us must make when we come to this crossroad (Read Paul on this in Romans 5:12-21). Jesus described the choices and ways best when he said: *"Enter ye in at the strait gate: for wide is the gate, and broad is the way, that leadeth to destruction, and many there be which go in thereat: because strait is the gate, and narrow is the way, which leadeth unto life, and few there be that find it."* (Matthew 7:13-14) Which road did you take when you came to this crossroad in life?

Another man by the name of Abram also came to a major crossroad, and the decision he made changed the course of history. Abram was the son of a man named Terah who left Ur of the Chaldees (Genesis 11:26-32) and settled in Haran, but God gave Abram an instruction to leave Haran for an unknown land that God would show him. Often crossroads are as simple as that, stay or go? Paul describes best what Abram chose: *"By faith Abraham, when he was called to go out into a place which he should after receive for an inheritance, obeyed; and he went out, not knowing whither he went."* (Hebrews 11:8) Crossroads will challenge your faith and will determine who you place your faith in. Abram's choice at the Crossroad at Haran was illogical and not rational or even wise according to modern standards. Abram wasn't even told where he was going, just to trust God. Could you do that? Yet, this act of faith is at the very heart of the definition of godly faith: ***"Now faith is the substance of things hoped for, the evidence of things not seen."*** (Hebrews 11:1) Is this not the very substance of our original two verses, Proverbs 3:5-6?

If we continue through the book of Genesis, we will discover that Isaac come to a crossroad, the Crossroad at Gerar during a day of famine. Instead of following his father's example and journeying on to Egypt, he stayed in Canaan and sowed *"and there was a famine in the land . . . "* (Genesis 26:1) and he *"received in the same year an hundredfold."* (Genesis 26:12) There are rewards for trusting the Lord, staying on course, and not taking those other roads well-travelled by others because they were trusting in logic, reason, and worldly wisdom. And what of Jacob at Bethel (Genesis 28) when he saw the ladder to heaven, and he was asked to make a choice and he chose God, the God of his father and the

God of his grandfather. Didn't God bring him back home and wasn't he blessed and protected throughout his journey? Yes, and all because at the Crossroad at Bethel he chose to trust God and go God's way for him and to follow the path the Almighty had laid out for him. And then there was Joseph and the multitude of crossroads that highlighted and underlined his life, from the day he left home to check on his brothers for his father (Genesis 37).

Sometimes others make the decision for us at a crossroad of our life. Joseph wouldn't have in a thousand years made the decision to take the Egyptian crossroad on his own. He would have rather returned to his father, but it would be over twenty years before he would see his beloved father again. Yet, we learn that it was all of God's leading and Joseph's yielding that played a great part in the story. He would later tell his brothers: *"Now therefore be not grieved, nor angry with yourselves, that ye sold me hither: for God did send me before you to preserve life. For these two years hath the famine been in the land: and yet there are five years, in the which there shall neither be earing nor harvest. And God sent me before you to preserve you a posterity in the earth, and to save your lives by a great deliverance. So now it was not you that sent me hither, but God: and he hath made me a father to Pharaoh, and lord of all his house, and a ruler throughout all the land of Egypt."* (Genesis 45:5-8) But once in Egypt, Joseph had to make his own decisions at some vital crossroads in his life, including the crossroad in Potiphar's house when Mrs. Potiphar tried to rape him and he had to make a choice to stay or run.

How many young people haven't come to this crossroad in their lives? A crossroad of whether you are going to yield to a temptation or going to take God's route and a way of escape. I believe Joseph's theology saved him that day and in following God's way saved his entire family and most of the world. Remember, *"There is none greater in this house than I; neither hath he kept back any thing from me but thee, because thou art his wife: how then can I do this great wickedness, and sin against God?"* (Genesis 39:9) When we come to a crossroad that has sin on one sign and flee on the other sign, the Biblical admonition is to take the road less travelled: *"Flee also youthful lusts: but follow righteousness, faith, charity, peace, with them that call on the Lord out of a pure heart."* (II Timothy 2:22) Joseph did and though it landed him in jail, jail was the path to the prime minister's job and reunion with his dad. Sometimes people at a crossroad feel that there is no other route, no other way, yet there always is if one will look for it. Paul's pen promises: *"There hath no temptation taken you but such as is common to man: but God is faithful, who will not suffer you to be tempted above that ye are able; but will with the temptation also make a way to escape, that ye may be able to bear it."* (I Corinthians 10:13) Every crossroad of temptation has an alternate route. Look for it!

Moses came to the Crossroad at Horeb (Exodus 3:1) thinking his life was established and that no more crossroads would come his way. Raised as the Prince of Egypt, Moses came to a crossroad at 40 (Acts 7:23), but instead of waiting on the Lord's time, he, like a lot of us, simply took the road he thought was right. He was going to deliver the Israelites by killing the Egyptians one at a time. Now, how did that work out for him, or you? Who of us hasn't tried that, maybe not killing, but dealing with our crossroad situations in our own way? Solomon writes: *"There is a way which seemeth right unto a man, but the end thereof are the ways of death."* (Proverbs 14:12) Adam and Eve thought they were doing right. Moses thought he was doing right, and it almost cost him his life at the hands of Pharaoh (Exodus 2:15). So, by the time Moses sees the bushing bush that wasn't being consumed, he thought he had crossed all his crossroads. He was eighty, just a shepherd, the glory days were behind him, yet God led him to another major crossroad and had to persuade Moses to take the road back to Egypt. Will he do the same for me at seventy?

Have you stood in the middle of a crossroad and debated God? Questioned the Lord's leading? I have, and most have! Like Moses, we throw into God's face every excuse in the book of why not us, why not this way, yet there stands an unalterable precept that can be resisted, but can never be overcome: **"For the gifts and calling of God are without repentance."** (Romans 11:29) Moses knew of it in Egypt when he was forty: *"For he supposed his brethren would have understood how that God by his hand would deliver them: but they understood not."* (Acts 7:25) Moses wasn't wrong in knowing what God wanted, he was wrong in knowing God's timing. Now it was God's time, and Moses was resisting the time. But Moses was God's man for the job just like Jonah was God's man for the job. Despite taking the wrong road at the Crossroad of Joppa (Jonah 1:3), God eventually got his prophet back and gave him a second chance (Jonah 3:1) to make the right choice. Moses and Jonah should tell us something about what God does with His saints when they make a wrong choice at the crossroad. You will be back at the junction!

Crossroads are not only for individuals, but groups as well--families, churches, communities, and nations. One of the greatest tragedies in history took place at the Crossroad at Kadesh (Number 13). Can groups make the right choices for themselves and others: *"By faith they passed through the Red sea as by dry land: which the Egyptians assaying to do were drowned. By faith the walls of Jericho fell down, after they were compassed about seven days."* (Hebrews 11:29-20) Both are examples of group faith. What is tragic about verse 29 is the same group that by faith walked through the Red Sea on dry land was the same group that refused by faith to walk into the Promised Land just two years after they left Egypt. Instead, all died in a terrible wilderness wandering that took thirty-eight years! It would be the children (verse 30) of these people that would make the Jordan crossing and conquer the Promised Land starting with Jericho. Is your family facing a crossroad situation? Is your church in a crossroad circumstance? I feel our nation is standing in the middle of a crossroad, but is leaning the wrong way. The sad truth about these crossroads is that the majority does rule and, like with Joshua and Caleb who did want to go up and conquer, they were left to wander with the rest and waste 40 years of their lives when they could have gone in. Some crossroads you can't choose what your family decides to counter-choose. When my son decided to go a different route than what he was taught, the next twenty years he drugged his mother and me through many situations and circumstances we never wanted to be involved in, but because he was our son and we loved him unconditionally, we had to endure his wandering, too.

Another one of the tragedies of crossroads is that you can make all the right choices, crossroad by crossroad, only to fail at the last crossroad of your life. I have for a long time been concerned about finishing well. Many people start out well, Solomon for example, yet, in the end he had forsaken his father's God and was worshipping a panoply of gods (I Kings 11:1-8). Uzziah was one of the greatest kings of Judah, yet he ended life a leper because of a wrong path he took at the crossroad of the Temple (II Chronicles 26). Demas started out so well following Paul even to prison, but we all know of the last verse about him in II Timothy 4:10. Time would fail me to write about Judas, Aaron, Moses, and even the man after God's own heart, David. I find more stories in the Bible of people who started well but ended poorly than stories in the Bible of people who started poorly, but ended well. But for me, the most tragic of all these stories is found in I Kings 13. I have been haunted with this story since I first read it with understanding and recognized the tragedy described in the unnamed prophet from Judah that was commissioned to go to the new country of Israel (after the split during the reign of Rehoboam) and condemn the alterative worship system set up by Jeroboam. I hope you would read and reread, if necessary, to get the full magnitude of this crossroad story.

The story tells us that this man was *"a man of God."* (I Kings 13:1) Do you know how rare that designation is in the Bible? This prophet performed miracles (I Kings 13:4) and spoke "Thus saith the Lord" (I Kings 13:3). You would think that a man of his caliber would be able to resist anything, but in the critical moment this man of God made a wrong choice because of bad information and would never again see his homeland. The Lord's instruction to this prophet was very clear: get in, deliver My message, and get out. He was not to stay for lunch, even drink water in the land (I Kings 13:8), and at first, he resisted the temptation to stay from Jeroboam. After he finished his commission, the prophet heads for home, but in what I see as the last mile of the way, decides to rest a bit under an oak tree (I Kings 13:14), his first mistake. In delaying his return home, he set himself up for a crossroad decision that he should never have had to make. In that land was a false prophet who, hearing of the exploits of this man of God, finds him under the oak tree and invites him for supper, to which the prophet refuses, but in a lie (I Kings 13:18) he convinces this man of God that God had spoken to him and told him to change the prophets orders, that he, indeed, was to stay for supper. Surely, the man of God knew that God doesn't change orders (Romans 11:29), but he bit on the forbidden fruit, and it cost him his life (I Kings 13:24). Death often is found on a road God never intends for us to walk.

Surely, by now you see the point that I am trying to make that crossroads in our lives will come regularly. They will not all be the same because some will be just another lane or staying on the lane you are in. Others will give you a couple of choices as you come to the end of the road you are on, so which way now, right or left. Then there is the most complicated crossroads of all and that being a four-way intersection that gives you the option to keep going straight or take the right road or the left road. Remember, these are roads you have never been on, paths you have never trod, lanes that are a mystery to where they lead, so what do you do? Do you trust in your own judgment, what feels right, or do you put your trust into the One that has travelled this way before, a guide! I learned very early that in the maze that is life you need a guide. By my nature I have very poor directional skills. I get lost easily, and I learned in the first few times I got lost that I despise being lost. I love knowing where I am going. Very early on I trusted and put in charge my Lord

Jesus Christ of all my crossroads! So, that is why as I cross the seventieth-year crossroad I am going to trust Him for this final major crossroad of my life, a life alone (widower) with Him and him alone. He brought me to this crossroad with the departure of my wife, and I crossed over into widowhood with Him.

Fourscore

POSTLUDE

> PSALM 90:9,10 "... *we spend our years as a tale that is told. The days of our years are threescore years and ten; and if by reason of strength they be fourscore years, yet is their strength labour and sorrow; for it is soon cut off, and we fly away.*"

SO, THERE YOU HAVE it, a collection of my aging thoughts and old observations after seventy years of life, the bulk of them in the Lord's work in the pastorate. Today I finish my 70th year (March 6, 2021) and begin my next quest for "fourscore," eighty years. Whether I finish this decade or not is up to the Good Lord, but I will continue on this pilgrimage fully confident in the plain "old fashioned" philosophy I have just highlighted and underlined in this book until I either crossover to heaven's golden shore in a **"departure"** we call death, (II Timothy 4:6-8 *For I am now ready to be offered, and the time of my departure is at hand. I have fought a good fight, I have finished my course, I have kept the faith: henceforth there is laid up for me a crown of righteousness, which the Lord, the righteous judge, shall give me at that day: and not to me only, but unto all them also that love his appearing.*) or I will depart in an event we like to call **"the rapture"** of the Church. (I Thessalonians 4:16-17: *For the Lord himself shall descend from heaven with a shout, with the voice of the archangel, and with the trump of God: and the dead in Christ shall rise first: then we which are alive and remain shall be caught up together with them in the clouds, to meet the Lord in the air: and so shall we ever be with the Lord.*)

I am not living with my head in the sand about the time ahead of me. They will not be the golden years as the world calls them because the

Christian's golden years will only come when we walk the golden streets of God's heaven. I have come to believe and understand what the Psalmist meant when he said that after "threescore and ten" the road to "fourscore" would be full of *"labour and sorrow."* I haven't lived that life yet, but I have lived the years with others to "fourscore." Grandparents (three of four lived into this decade and beyond) and parents (both my parents lived into their 90s), countless parishioners, and during a half-century ministry with the elderly, the senior citizen, and the nursing home and the boarding home resident, and how many, many, many more? Granted, some seem to get through better than others, but all have started to **labor** with a weakening body and some **sorrow** with a failing mind. Labor and sorrow will come in many forms such as the death of a spouse, or a child, or a friend or two, and numerous other sorrows and labors that will bring sadness and suffering and sickness during those years leading up to "fourscore," to a time that you will be known as an "octogenarian." There are some I have met who have desired the title and the time, while most I have ministered to during that time wish the Good Lord would have taken them long before "fourscore."

I like what Vance Havner (a preacher who reached his fourscore at 86) wrote in his "Fourscore" book: **"But eighty is an enviable mark and all the more so if we can reach it foursquare as well as fourscore! The dictionary says foursquare can mean 'unyielding, firm.' Eighty can find us stubborn and churlish on one hand or the other pleasantly agreeable to anything with a grandfatherly tolerance of the status quo. Either position is a mistake. To be firm in principle and sweet in spirit is a rare attainment whether eighty or otherwise."** As for me, I wish, if I make it, to be like my favorite Old Testament character. This is Caleb in his own words at the grand age of 85: *"And now, behold, the LORD hath kept me alive, as he said, these forty and five years, even since the LORD spake this word unto Moses, while the children of Israel wandered in the wilderness: and now, lo, I am this day **fourscore** and five years old. As yet I am as strong this day as I was in the day that Moses sent me: as my strength was then, even so is my strength now, for war, both to go out, and to come in. Now therefore give me this mountain, whereof the LORD spake in that day...."* (Joshua 14:10–12).

Caleb was a saint that had quite the remarkable life, born into slavery in the brick pits, who for 40 years suffered the reproach of Egypt. Delivered by Moses in the great Exodus, Caleb spent the next 40 years of his life in the wilderness wandering, a trip he never wanted to take.

Remember, Caleb and Joshua wanted to go into the land after just a two-year trip to the borderland of Canaan, but the people believed the other spies. Then for five years Caleb helped his fellow Israelites conquer their land, but now it was his turn. Instead of seeking retirement, he claimed a mountain, fortified and containing giants! Finally, this "octogenarian" claimed God's promises and presence and conquered his mountain (Hebron). If God wills it, I would desire fourscore and a "mountain," but only if, like Caleb, I will be still preaching and teaching the Word of God and still "foursquare" and executing this commission for me in old age: *"Now also when I am old and grayheaded, O God, forsake me not; until I have shewed thy strength unto this generation, and thy power to every one that is to come."* (Psalm 71:18)

I would also love to end my life in my 80s (I will never desire the 90s because in my experience few enter with any kind of health, and even fewer exit that decade with any kind of life) as the little known Biblical character Barzillai: *"And Barzillai the Gileadite came down from Rogelim, and went over Jordan with the king, to conduct him over Jordan* [this takes place during the Absalom Rebellion]. *Now Barzillai was a very aged man,* **even fourscore years old**: *and he had provided the king of sustenance while he lay at Mahanaim; for he was a very great man. And the king said unto Barzillai, Come thou over with me, and I will feed thee with me in Jerusalem. And Barzillai said unto the king, how long have I to live, that I should go up with the king unto Jerusalem? I am* **this day fourscore years old**: *and can I discern between good and evil? Can thy servant taste what I eat or what I drink? Can I hear any more the voice of singing men and singing women? Wherefore then should thy servant be yet a burden unto my lord the king? Thy servant will go a little way over Jordan with the king: and why should the king recompense it me with such a reward? Let thy servant, I pray thee, turn back again, that I may die in mine own city, and be buried by the grave of my father and of my mother . . . And all the people went over Jordan. And when the king was come over, the king kissed Barzillai, and blessed him; and he returned unto his own place."* (II Samuel 19:31–39) This is what I seek during my fourscore years, to serve my King, the Lord Jesus Christ, in whatever capacity I am still able, and if my King shall tarry, I, too, want to be buried next to my father and mother and my wife and my son (a plot I already have with a stone already prepared so those who come behind me will know of my final earthly dwelling place). I like Barzillai don't want to be burdensome to anyone. I simply want to live out the rest of my days confident that I did my best for Jesus right to the end and accomplished my commission for Him.

Finally, I want to be like Anna: *"And there was one Anna . . . And she was a widow of about **fourscore and four years**, which departed not from the temple, but served God with fastings and prayers night and day . . . . and spake of him to all them that looked for redemption in Jerusalem."* (Luke 2:36–38) I, too, want to end my days in the House of the Lord (the church) serving, praying, and proclaiming His coming to all who will listen.

And it is my final prayer that any who, like me, makes threescore and ten will, like me, desire only the days left to be ones of service for their King of Kings and Lord of Lords. If I am allowed to live through the next decade and have the ability to share with you my thoughts, I will write another book, but until then I cross into another decade fully prepared to go it alone with Christ and Christ alone. Amen and Amen!

Barry Blackstone
March 6, 2021

www.ingramcontent.com/pod-product-compliance
Lightning Source LLC
Chambersburg PA
CBHW071230230426
43668CB00011B/1371